CAMBRIDGE LIBRARY COLLECTION

Books of enduring scholarly value

Linguistics

From the earliest surviving glossaries and translations to nineteenth-century academic philology and the growth of linguistics during the twentieth century, language has been the subject both of scholarly investigation and of practical handbooks produced for the upwardly mobile, as well as for travellers, traders, soldiers, missionaries and explorers. This collection will reissue a wide range of texts pertaining to language, including the work of Latin grammarians, groundbreaking early publications in Indo-European studies, accounts of indigenous languages, many of them now extinct, and texts by pioneering figures such as Jacob Grimm, Wilhelm von Humboldt and Ferdinand de Saussure.

Australian Aborigines

James Dawson first published Australian Aborigines in 1881, after deciding that his careful description of the tribes, languages, customs, and characteristics of the indigenous peoples of the western district of Victoria was too bulky for its originally intended publication in a newspaper. Essentially a field-inspired anthropological account of the dwindling Aboriginal population, written before the emergence of anthropology as a formal discipline, Dawson's book draws on his daughter's ability to speak the local languages and attempts a balanced description of a culture he considered ill-used and under-appreciated by white settlers. Minute details about clothing, tools, settlement and beliefs combine to depict a complex society that possessed highly ritualised customs deserving of respect. Dawson also included an extensive vocabulary of words in three indigenous languages that he hoped would facilitate further cross-cultural understanding. His work provides valuable source material for modern researchers in anthropology and linguistics.

T0371440

Cambridge University Press has long been a pioneer in the reissuing of out-of-print titles from its own backlist, producing digital reprints of books that are still sought after by scholars and students but could not be reprinted economically using traditional technology. The Cambridge Library Collection extends this activity to a wider range of books which are still of importance to researchers and professionals, either for the source material they contain, or as landmarks in the history of their academic discipline.

Drawing from the world-renowned collections in the Cambridge University Library, and guided by the advice of experts in each subject area, Cambridge University Press is using state-of-the-art scanning machines in its own Printing House to capture the content of each book selected for inclusion. The files are processed to give a consistently clear, crisp image, and the books finished to the high quality standard for which the Press is recognised around the world. The latest print-on-demand technology ensures that the books will remain available indefinitely, and that orders for single or multiple copies can quickly be supplied.

The Cambridge Library Collection will bring back to life books of enduring scholarly value (including out-of-copyright works originally issued by other publishers) across a wide range of disciplines in the humanities and social sciences and in science and technology.

Australian Aborigines

*The Languages and Customs of Several Tribes
of Aborigines in the Western District of
Victoria, Australia*

JAMES DAWSON

CAMBRIDGE
UNIVERSITY PRESS

CAMBRIDGE UNIVERSITY PRESS

Cambridge, New York, Melbourne, Madrid, Cape Town, Singapore,
São Paolo, Delhi, Dubai, Tokyo

Published in the United States of America by Cambridge University Press, New York

www.cambridge.org
Information on this title: www.cambridge.org/9781108006552

© in this compilation Cambridge University Press 2009

This edition first published 1881
This digitally printed version 2009

ISBN 978-1-108-00655-2 Paperback

KAAWIRN KUUNAWARN

(HISSING SWAN),

Chief of the Kirra Wuurong,

(BLOOD TIP TRIBE).

AUSTRALIAN ABORIGINES

THE LANGUAGES AND CUSTOMS OF SEVERAL TRIBES OF ABORIGINES
IN THE WESTERN DISTRICT OF VICTORIA, AUSTRALIA

BY

JAMES DAWSON

GEORGE ROBERTSON
MELBOURNE, SYDNEY, AND ADELAIDE
MDCCCLXXXI

PREFACE.

A NUMBER of years ago there appeared in the columns of the *Australasian* newspaper a short account of the language of one of the native tribes of the Western District of Victoria, written by my daughter, whose long residence in the Port Fairy district, and intimate acquaintance from infancy with the aboriginal inhabitants of that part of the colony, and with their dialects, induced her to publish that sketch. Some time afterwards our attention was directed to the formation of a vocabulary of dialects spoken by aboriginal natives of Australia, and a request was made that she 'would assist in collecting and illustrating all connected with their history, habits, customs, and languages.' In undertaking so interesting a work, our intention was to publish the additional information in the columns of the *Australasian;* but, finding it to be too voluminous for that journal, it was resolved to present it to the public in its present shape.

Great care has been taken in this work not to state anything on the word of a white person; and, in obtaining information from the aborigines, suggestive or leading questions have been avoided as much as possible. The natives, in their anxiety to please, are apt to coincide with the questioner, and thus assist him in arriving at wrong conclusions; hence it is of the utmost importance to be able to converse freely with them in their own language. This inspires them with confidence, and prompts them to state facts, and to discard ideas and beliefs obtained from the white people, which in many instances have led to misrepresentations. All the information contained in this book has been obtained from the united testimony of several very intelligent aborigines, and every word was approved of by them before being written down. While co-operating in this arduous task, which they thoroughly comprehended, our sable friends showed the utmost anxiety to impart information, and the most scrupulous honesty in conveying a correct version of their own language, as well as of the languages of the neighbouring tribes; and so proud and jealous were they of the honour, that, by agreement among themselves, each was allotted a fair proportion of questions to answer and of words to translate; and if levity was shown by any individual present who could not always resist a pun on the word in question, the sedate old chief, Kaawirn Kuunawarn, at once reproved the wag, and restored order and attention to the business on hand.

During this tedious process, occupying several years in its accomplishment, I found my previous good opinion of the natives fell far short of their merits. Their general information and knowledge of several distinct dialects—in some instances four, besides fair English—gratified as well as surprised me, and naturally suggested a comparison between them and the lower classes of white men. Indeed, it is very questionable if even those who belong to what is called the middle class, notwithstanding their advantages of education, know as much of their own laws, of natural history, and of the nomenclature of the heavenly bodies, as the aborigines do of their laws and of natural objects.

In recording my admiration of the general character of the aborigines, no attempt is made to palliate what may appear to us to be objectionable customs common to savages in nearly every part of the globe; but it may be truly said of them, that, with the exception of the low estimate they naturally place on life, their moral character and modesty—all things considered—compare favourably with those of the most highly cultivated communities of Europe. People seeing only the miserable remnants to be met with about the white man's grog-shop may be inclined to doubt this; but if these doubters were to be brought into close communication with the aborigines away from the means of intoxication, and were to listen to their guileless conversation, their humour and wit, and their expressions of honour and affection for one another, those who are disposed to look upon them as scarcely human would be compelled to admit that in general intelligence, common sense, integrity, and the absence of anything repulsive in their conduct, they are at least equal, if not superior, to the general run of white men. It must be borne in mind, also, that many of their present vices were introduced by the white man, whose contact with them has increased their degradation, and will no doubt ultimately lead to their extinction.

And even, in censuring customs and practices which we may regard as repugnant to our notions and usages, we should bear in mind that these may appear right and virtuous from the stand-point of the aborigines, and that they have received the sanction of use and wont for many ages. If our habits, manners, and morals were investigated and commented upon by an intelligent black, what would be his verdict on them ? What would he think of the 'sin of great cities,' of baby-farming, of our gambling hells, of our 'marriage market,' of the universal practice of adulteration, of the frightful revelations made by Mr. Plimsoll's committee with respect to rotten ships freighted and insured on purpose to founder, of the white slavery in all great cities, and of the thousand and one evils incidental to our highly artificial civilization ? Living, as we do, in a conservatory constructed of such remarkably fragile materials, we should hesitate before picking up the smallest pebble wherewith to lapidate the despised blackfellow.

To several friends who have assisted me in various ways in the publication of this book my thanks are due : to Professor Strong, of the Melbourne University ; to James Smith, Esq., Melbourne ; to Mr. Goodall, Superintendent of the Aboriginal Station, Framlingham ; and especially to the Rev. F. R. M. Wilson, formerly of Camperdown, now of Kew.

To my sable friends who have kindly given us their aid I express my gratitude for their patience and their anxiety to communicate information ; especially to the very intelligent chiefess Yaruun Parpur Tarneen, whose knowledge greatly exceeded expectation ; as also to Wombeet Tuulawarn, her husband, who assisted her. In return for their friendship and confidence, I trust that this little contribution to the history of an ill-used and interesting people, fast passing away, may lead to a better estimate of their character, and to a more kindly treatment at the hands of their 'Christian brethren' than the aborigines have hitherto received. If so, this volume will attain its chief object, and will confer intense gratification on their sincere friend,

JAMES DAWSON.

INTRODUCTORY NOTE.

As it has been found almost impossible to represent the correct sounds of the Australasian languages by adhering to the rules of English orthography, these rules have been necessarily laid aside, together with the signs of accentuation. Double consonants are used to express emphasis, and double vowels to express prolongation of the sound. People who are unacquainted with the difficulty of communicating in writing the pronunciation and sound of foreign words may cavil at the employment of so many double letters, but this mode has been adopted, after very careful consideration, as the most suitable for the purpose.

The following examples will fully illustrate what is meant. The English word 'car' would be 'kaar,' 'can' would be 'kann,' 'rain' would be 'ræææn,' 'rainy' would be 'ræænæ,' 'meat' would be 'meet,' 'met' would be 'mett,' 'life' would be 'liif,' 'live' would be 'livv,' 'tome' would be 'toom,' 'tom' would be 'tomm,' 'boot' would be 'buut,' 'cut' would be 'kutt,' 'one' would be 'wunn,' 'magpie' would be 'magpii,' 'pussy cat' would be 'puusæ katt.' The k and g which appear before consonants in the syllables of many aboriginal words represent sounds barely perceptible, yet indispensible to right pronunciation. The nasal sound of 'gn' or 'ng' often occurs at the beginning of syllables in the aboriginal languages. As it is found at the beginning of, and only occurs in words like poignant and poignard, derived from a foreign source, it is somewhat difficult for English people to pronounce it. Some sounds which lie beyond the scope of the English alphabet are represented by the letters which come nearest to them, so as to give an approximately correct idea of what is intended to be conveyed.

CONTENTS.

		PAGE
CHAPTER	I.—Tribes : their names, boundaries, languages, and dialects ...	1
CHAPTER	II.—Population.	3
CHAPTER	III.—Chiefs : their power, dignity, and succession	5
CHAPTER	IV.—Property : of the family, laws of, inheritance	7
CHAPTER	V.—Clothing : men's, women's, at night, adoption of European clothing, rugs—how made	8
CHAPTER	VI.—Habitations : permanent, temporary	10
CHAPTER	VII.—Cleanliness : superstition relative to, the muurong pole, parasites	12
CHAPTER	VIII.—Domestic Furniture : baskets for carrying and for cooking, wooden bowl, bark bucket, water bags, water troughs, mortars, means of producing fire	14
CHAPTER	IX.—Cooking and Food : ovens, roasting, animals eaten, shell-fish, roots and vegetables, grubs, gum, manna, drinking water, fruits, division of the spoils of hunting, story of the Selfish Fellow	17
CHAPTER	X.—Tools : stone axe, stone chisel, scrapers, rasp, mortar and pestle, bone chisel and bodkin, knives	24
CHAPTER	XI.—Laws of Marriage : tribal, class, origin of classes, other relations, polygamy, rank, re-marriage of widows, consent of chiefs, strictness of laws, betrothal, mothers-in-law, "turn-tongue," initiation into manhood, marriage-dress and ceremonies, first two months, divorce, selection of wives, gifts of wives, dissolution of marriage, spells, treatment of wives	26
CHAPTER	XII.—Children : birth, nursing, clothing, killing the weak, language, strange law relative to language ...	38
CHAPTER	XIII.—Names of Persons : naming of children, changing names, the effect of death on names, lists of names ...	41
CHAPTER	XIV.—Superstitions and Diseases : supernatural beings, celestial, infernal and terrestrial, ghosts, wraiths, shades, haunted cave, witches, dreams, superstitions relative to animals, etc.; fires, spells, sorcerers, "White Lady," doctors, common remedies, supernatural remedies, and artifices, sorcery stones, sunstroke, moon-stroke, pulmonary complaints, epidemics, other diseases	49

PAGE

CHAPTER XV.—DEATH AND BURIAL : putting old people to death, suicide, burial, cremation, wakes, death and funeral of a chief, relics, spirits appearing, mourning, eating of human flesh 62

CHAPTER XVI.—AVENGING OF DEATH : finding out the spell-thrower, modes of destroying him, pææt pææts, executioner's club, revenge a sacred duty 68

CHAPTER XVII.—GREAT MEETINGS : summons, preliminaries, message-stick, test-message, messengers, how distinguished, Weeratt Kuuyuut hears of Buckley, public executioner, Pundeet Puulatong, accusations, satisfaction for private wrongs, public wrongs, wild blacks, quarrels between tribes, tournament, trading, necessity to attend meetings, drives of game 72

CHAPTER XVIII.—AMUSEMENTS : music, songs, korroboræ, gala dress, ornamental cicatrices, nose ornaments, dancing, clowns, stalking the emu, wrestling, football, spear-throwing, toy-boomerang, wuæ whuuitch ... 80

CHAPTER XIX.—WEAPONS : spear, spear-thrower, light shield, liangle and heavy shield, clubs and boomerangs 87

CHAPTER XX.—ANIMALS : dingo, kangaroo, opossum, wombat, native bear, emu, extinct large bird, turkey bustard, gigantic crane, water fowl, eagles, fish, eel-fishing, crayfish, etc.; snakes, stories of boas 89

CHAPTER XXI.—METEOROLOGY, ASTRONOMY, ETC. : signs of weather, rain-making, astronomical knowledge, list of heavenly bodies, earthquakes, volcanoes 98

CHAPTER XXII.—NATIVE MOUNDS : their origin, sometimes used for burial 103

CHAPTER XXIII.—ANECDOTES : the first white man, the first ship, the first bullock, the first formation of water-holes, the tortoise and the snake, the blue heron, the native companion and the emu, the bunyip, the ghost, the meteor, Buckley's widow 105

CONVEYANCE, BY PRINCIPAL CHIEFS TO JOHN BATMAN, OF 100,000 ACRES OF LAND, BETWEEN GEELONG AND QUEENSCLIFF ... 112

VOCABULARIES.—WORDS ; ANIMALS ; RELATIONSHIPS ; NAMES OF PLACES ; GRAMMAR AND SENTENCES ; NUMERALS, cardinal and ordinal i

NOTES TO CHAPTERS XI., XII., XIII., AND XIV., by J. D. ci

NOTE—REPORTS OF GOVERNMENT INSPECTORS OF ABORIGINAL SCHOOLS ... ciii

YARRUUN PARPUR TARNEEN

(VICTORIOUS),

Chiefess of the Morporr Tribe.

AUSTRALIAN ABORIGINES.

CHAPTER I.

TRIBES.

THE country belonging to a tribe is generally distinguished by the name or language of that tribe. The names of tribes are taken from some local object, or from some peculiarity in the country where they live, or in their pronunciation; and when an individual is referred to, 'Kuurndit'—meaning 'member of'—is affixed to the tribal name, in the same way as the syllable 'er' is added to London, 'Londoner,' or 'ite' to Melbourne, 'Melbournite.' Thus the Mount Rouse tribe is called 'Kolor,' after the aboriginal name of the mountain; and a member of the tribe is called 'Kolor kuurndit.' The language of the Kolor tribe is called ' Chaap wuurong,' meaning 'soft' or 'broad lip,' in contradistinction to other dialects of harder pronunciation. The Kolor tribe and its language occupy the country commencing near Mount Napier, thence to Germantown, Dunkeld, Wickliffe, Lake Boloke, down the Salt Creek to Hexham, to Caramut, and to starting point.

The Kuurn kopan noot tribe is known by the name of its language, 'Kuurn kopan noot,' meaning 'small lip,' or 'short pronunciation,' with 'Kuurndit' affixed for an individual of the tribe, who is called 'Kuurn kopan noot kuurndit.' Its territory, commencing in the middle of the Tarrone swamp, 'Yaluuk,' extends to Dunmore House dam, Upper Moyne Falls, Buunbatt, Goodwood main cattle camp, Marramok swamp, and round by South Green Hills station to starting point.

The Hopkins tribe is called after its language, 'Pirt kopan noot,' and a member of the tribe 'Pirt pirt wuurong kuurndit;' and its language, which is very slightly different from the ' Chaap wuurong,' is called 'Pirt kopan noot,' meaning 'jump lip.' Its country is bounded by Wickliffe, Lake Boloke, Salt Creek, Hopkins Hill, Ararat, and Mount William.

The Spring Creek tribe is called 'Mopor,' and a member of it 'Mopor kuurndit.' Its language is called 'Kii wuurong,' meaning 'Oh, dear! lip.' Its country, commencing at the swamp Marramok on Minjah station, extends to Woolsthorpe, to Ballangeich, up Muston's Creek to Burrwidgee, through the centre of Mirræwuæ swamp to Goodwood House, thence to Buunbatt, and to starting point.

The Port Fairy tribe is called 'Peek whuurong,' and a member of it 'Peek whurrong kuurndit.' Its language, 'Peek whurrong,' 'kelp lip,' is taken from the broad-leafed seaweed so very abundant on the sea shore. Its territory lies along the sea coast, from the mouth of the Hopkins River to nearly half-way between Port Fairy and Portland, thence to Dunmore dam, Tarrone swamp, Kirkstall, Koroit, Woodford, Allansford, Framlingham, and down the Hopkins River to the sea.

The Mount Shadwell tribe and its language are called 'Kirræ wuurong,' 'blood lip,' with Kuurndit affixed for a member of the tribe. Its territory commences at the Hopkins Hill sheepwash on the Hopkins River, and extends to Mount Fyans, Mount Elephant, Cloven Hills, Minninguurt, Mount Noorat, Keilambete Lake, Framlingham aboriginal station, and up the east side of the Hopkins River to starting point.

The Camperdown language is called 'Warn talliin,' 'rough language.' The Colac language is 'Kolak gnat,' 'belonging to sand,' and is hard in pronunciation. The Cape Otway language is 'Katubanuut,' 'King Parrot language.' The country between Cape Otway and the Hopkins River is called 'Yarro wætch,' 'Forest country,' and the language 'Wirngill gnatt tallinanong,' 'Bear language.'

At the annual great meetings of the associated tribes, where sometimes twenty tribes assembled, there were usually four languages spoken, so distinct from one another that the young people speaking one of them could not understand a word of the other three; and even the middle-aged people had difficulty in ascertaining what was said. These were the Chaap wuurong, Kuurn kopan noot, Wiitya whuurong, and Kolac gnat. The other tongues spoken at the meeting might be termed dialects of these four languages.

The aborigines have a very ready way of distinguishing the ten dialects enumerated above, by the various terms which are employed by each to denote the pronoun 'you,' as Gnuutok, Gnuundook, Winna, Gnæ, Gnii, &c. The differences of language are also marked by peculiarities of pronunciation, especially by the way in which the end of a sentence is intoned. Natives of Great Britain will remember similar differences between the various counties or towns of their fatherland, which will serve to illustrate the differences of aboriginal pronunciation.

CHAPTER II.

POPULATION.

In attempting to ascertain the numbers of individuals in the different tribes, it has been found almost impossible to make the aborigines comprehend or compute very large numbers, or even to obtain, from the very few now alive, an approximate estimate of the aggregate strength of the tribes of the Western district previous to the occupation of the country by the white man. It has been found necessary to ascertain from some of the most intelligent middle-aged persons among them, first, the number of friendly tribes which met annually in midsummer for hunting, feasting, and amusements,—occasions of all others the most likely to draw together the largest gatherings,—and then the average strength of each tribe.

These great meetings were held at Mirræwuæ, a large marsh celebrated for emus and other kinds of game, not many miles to the west of Caramut. This place was selected on account of its being a central position for the meetings of the tribes occupying the districts now known as the Wannon, Hamilton, Dunkeld, Mount William, Mount Rouse, Mount Napier, Lake Condah, Dunmore, Tarrone, Kangatong, Spring Creek, Framlingham, Lake Boloke, Skipton, Flat-topped Hill, Mount Shadwell, Darlington, Mount Noorat, Camperdown, Wardy Yallock, and Mount Elephant. None of the sea coast tribes attended the meetings at Mirræwuæ, as they were afraid of treachery and of an attack on the part of the others. According to the testimony of the intelligent old chief Weeratt Kuyuut, and his equally intelligent daughter Yarruum Parpurr Tarrneen, and her husband, Wombeet Tuulawarn, when two of these tribes fought a pitched battle, each mustered at least thirty men; and for every able-bodied warrior present (and no one durst absent himself on such an occasion under the penalty of death) there would be at least three members absent, as the old men, women, children and invalids were kept at home; thus making an average of one hundred and twenty in each tribe; and, as the twenty-one tribes enumerated were generally present, there must occasionally have been the large gathering of two thousand five hundred and twenty aborigines.

In the estimation of some of the earliest settlers, this calculation of the average strength of each tribe is too low ; but, as they could not tell how many tribes or portions of tribes were seen by them at one time, the statements of the natives who attended these great meetings, and of those who remember the accounts given of them by their parents, are the most reliable.

On questioning old Weeratt Kuyuut—who was privileged as a messenger to travel among the tribes between the rivers Leigh and Glenelg—about the population of the Great Plains, which have Mount Elephant as a centre, he said the natives were like flocks of sheep and beyond counting.

At this date, July, 1880, there are only seven aborigines who speak the Chaap wuurong language, three who speak the Kuurn kopan noot language, and four who speak the Peek whuurong language.

CHAPTER III.

CHIEFS.

EVERY tribe has its chief, who is looked upon in the light of a father, and whose authority is supreme. He consults with the best men of the tribe, but when he announces his decision, they dare not contradict or disobey him.

Great respect is paid to the chiefs and their wives and families. They can command the services of everyone belonging to their tribe. As many as six young bachelors are obliged to wait on a chief, and eight young unmarried women on his wife; and, as the children are of superior rank to the common people, they also have a number of attendants to wait on them. No one can address a chief or chiefess without being first spoken to, and then only by their titles as such, and not by personal names, or disrespectfully. Food and water, when brought to the camp, must be offered to them first, and reeds provided for each in the family to drink with; while the common people drink in the usual way. Should they fancy any article of dress, opossum rug, or weapon, it must be given without a murmur.

If a chief leaves home for a short time he is always accompanied by a friend, and on his return is met by two men, who conduct him to his wuurn. At his approach every one rises to receive him, and remains silent till he speaks; they then inquire where he has been, and converse with him freely. When a tribe is moving from one part of the country to another, the chief, accompanied by a friend, precedes it, and obtains permission from the next chief to pass, before his followers cross the boundary. When approaching a friendly camp, the chief walks at the head of his tribe. If he is too old and infirm to take the lead, his nearest male relative or best friend does so. On his arrival with his family at the friendly camp, a comfortable wuurn is immediately erected, and food, firewood, and attendance are provided during his visit. When he goes out to hunt, he and his friends are accompanied by several men to carry their game and protect them from enemies. A strange chief approaching a camp is met at a short distance by the chief, and invited to come and sit down; a fire is made for him, and then he is asked where he has come from, and what is his business.

The succession to the chiefdom is by inheritance. When a chief dies the chiefs of the neighbouring tribes, accompanied by their attendants, assist at the funeral obsequies; and they appoint the best male friend of the deceased to take charge of the tribe until the first great meeting after the expiry of one year, when the succession must be determined by the votes of the assembled chiefs alone. The eldest son is appointed, unless there is some good reason for setting him aside. If there are no sons, the deceased chief's eldest brother is entitled to succeed him, and the inheritance runs in the line of his family. Failing him, the inheritance devolves upon the other brothers and their families in succession.

If the heir is weakly in body, or mentally unfitted to maintain the position of chief,—which requires to be filled by a man of ability and bravery,—and if he has a brother who is more eligible in the opinion of the tribe, or who aspires to the dignity, the elder brother must either yield or fight the younger brother in single combat, at the first great meeting, for the supremacy.

There is an impression among the aborigines that the second son of a chief is generally superior to his elder brother; and, if proved to be so in fight, the latter gives up his claim as a matter of custom, and the tribe accepts the conqueror as its head.

Should the heir be a boy, his nearest male relative is appointed regent till he is initiated into manhood. If there is no heir, the chiefs of the neighbouring tribes elect a successor from the deceased chief's tribe; but if their votes are divided between two candidates, the matter must be decided by these in single combat, which sometimes leads to the whole tribe quarrelling and fighting. As the tribe, however, cannot be divided, the result of the combat is accepted, and all are again friends.

CHAPTER IV.

PROPERTY.

THE territory belonging to a tribe is divided among its members. Each family has the exclusive right by inheritance to a part of the tribal lands, which is named after its owner; and his family and every child born on it must be named after something on the property. When the boundaries with neighbours meet at lakes or swamps celebrated for game, well-defined portions of these are marked out and any poaching or trespassing is severely punished. No individual of any neighbouring tribe or family can hunt or walk over the property of another without permission from the head of the family owning the land. A stranger found trespassing can legally be put to death.

When the father of a family dies, his landed property is divided equally among his widow and his children of both sexes. Should a child of another family have been born on the estate, it is looked upon as one of the family, and it has an equal right with them to a share of the land, if it has attained the age of six months at the death of the proprietor. This adopted child is called a 'woork', and calls the owner of the property by the same name. Should a family die out without leaving 'flesh relatives' of any degree, the chief divides the land among the contiguous families after the lapse of one year from the death of the last survivor. During that period the name of the property, being the same as the name of its last owner, is never mentioned, but is called 'Yaamp yaamp' in the Chaap wuurong and the other two languages. If, however, there are several claimants, with equal rights to the territory, the chief at once gives each an equal share, irrespective of sex or age. To those who are under age he appoints guardians to look after their property during their minority.

CHAPTER V.

CLOTHING.

THE aborigines are very fond of anointing their bodies and their hair with the fat of animals, and toasting themselves before the fire till their skin absorbs it. In order to protect their bodies from the cold, they mix red clay with the oily fat of emus,—which is considered the best,—or with that of water fowls, opossums, grubs, or toasted eel skins, and rub themselves all over with the mixture. Owing to this custom very little clothing is necessary.

During all seasons of the year both sexes walk about very scantily clothed. In warm weather the men wear no covering during the day time except a short apron, not unlike the sporran of the Scotch Highlanders, formed of strips of opossum skins with the fur on, hanging from a skin belt in two bunches, one in front and the other behind. In winter they add a large kangaroo skin, fur side inwards, which hangs over the shoulders and down the back like a mantle or short cloak. This skin is fastened round the neck by the hind legs, and is fixed with a pin made of the small bone of the hind leg of a kangaroo, ground to a fine point. Sometimes a small rug made of a dozen skins of the opossum or young kangaroo is worn in the same way.

Women use the opossum rug at all times, by day as a covering for the back and shoulders, and in cold nights as a blanket. When they are obliged to go out of doors in wet weather, a kangaroo skin is substituted for the rug. A girdle or short kilt of the neck feathers of the emu, tied in little bunches to a skin cord, is fastened round the loins. A band of plaited bark surrounds the head, and pointed pins, made of wood or of the small bones of the hind foot of the kangaroo, are stuck upright at each side of the brow, to keep up the hair, which is divided in front and laid over them.

Beds are made of dry grass laid on the ground; and in summer the body is covered with a thin grass mat, or a sprinkling of loose dry grass, but in cold weather a wallaby or opossum rug is used in addition. In rare instances the rug is made of skins of the ring-tailed opossum.

A departure from this primitive mode of covering, and the adoption of the white man's costume, have weakened the constitution of the aborigines, and rendered them very liable to colds and pulmonary diseases, more particularly as—though they overload themselves with European clothes during the daytime —they seldom sleep under their rugs, excepting in the cold season of the year.

Fur rugs were very scarce and valuable before the white man destroyed the wild dogs, the natural enemies of the opossum and kangaroo, as it took a year to collect opossum skins sufficient to make one. The ring-tailed opossums were more plentiful than the common kind, but the skins were less esteemed. Rugs were also made of the skins of the wallaby and of the brush kangaroo, which are likewise inferior to the common opossum. A good rug is made of from fifty to seventy skins, which are stripped off the opossum, pegged out square or oblong on a sheet of bark, and dried before the fire, then trimmed with a reed knife, and sewn together with the tail sinews of the kangaroo, which are always pulled out of the tail, and carefully dried and saved for thread. Previous to sewing the skins together, diagonal lines, about half-an-inch apart, are scratched across the flesh side of each with sharpened mussel shells. This is done to make them soft and pliable. The only addition to this kind of ornamentation is occasionally the figure of an emu in the centre skin of the rug. It may be stated that, although many of the opossum rugs of the aborigines are now ornamented with a variety of designs, some of which are coloured, nothing but the simple pattern previously described, with the occasional figure of an emu, was used before the arrival of the white man. The figures of human beings, animals, and things, now drawn by the natives, and represented in works on the aborigines of the colony of Victoria as original, were unknown to the tribes treated of, and are considered by them as of recent introduction by Europeans.

CHAPTER VI.

HABITATIONS.

Habitations—*wuurns*—are of various kinds, and are constructed to suit the seasons. The principal one is the permanent family dwelling, which is made of strong limbs of trees stuck up in dome-shape, high enough to allow a tall man to stand upright underneath them. Small limbs fill up the intermediate spaces, and these are covered with sheets of bark, thatch, sods, and earth till the roof and sides are proof against wind and rain. The doorway is low, and generally faces the morning sun or a sheltering rock. The family wuurn is sufficiently large to accommodate a dozen or more persons; and when the family is grown up the wuurn is partitioned off into apartments, each facing the fire in the centre, One of these is appropriated to the parents and children, one to the young unmarried women and widows, and one to the bachelors and widowers. While travelling or occupying temporary habitations, each of these parties must erect separate wuurns. When several families live together, each builds its wuurn facing one central fire. This fire is not much used for cooking, which is generally done outside. Thus in what appears to be one dwelling, fifty or more persons can be accommodated, when, to use the words of the aborigines, they are 'like bees in a hive.'

These comfortable and healthy habitations are occupied by the owners of the land in the neighbourhood, and are situated on dry spots on the bank of a lake, stream, or healthy swamp, but never near a malarious morass, nor under large trees, which might fall or be struck down by lightning. When it is necessary to abandon them for a season in search of variety of food, or for visiting neighbouring families and tribes, the doorway is closed with sheets of bark or bushes, and, for the information of visitors, a crooked stick is placed above it pointing in the direction which the family intends to go. They then depart, with the remark, 'Muurtee bunna meen,'—'close the door and pull away.'

Temporary habitations are also dome-shaped, and are made of limbs, bark of gum trees, and grass, scarcely rain-proof, and are smaller, opener, and more carelessly erected than the permanent residences. They are only used in summer or for shelter while travelling, and have a large open side, with the fire in front. In fine warm weather, a few green bushes, placed in a half circle to windward of the fire, suffice for a temporary dwelling.

The men share the labour of making the permanent dwelling, but the women are compelled to erect the smaller ones. Small weapons and personal property are taken inside the habitations; but as it would be inconvenient to have long spears there, they are stuck on end at each side of the doorway, to be at hand and ready for an attack.

In some parts of the country where it is easier to get stones than wood and bark for dwellings, the walls are built of flat stones, and roofed with limbs and thatch. A stony point of land on the south side of a lake near Camperdown is called ' karm karm,' which means ' building of stones,' but no marks or remains are now to be seen indicating the former existence of a building there.

These permanent residences being proof against all kinds of weather, from excessive heat in summer to frost in winter, suit the constitutions of the aborigines very much better than the wooden cottages used at the Government aboriginal stations. In cold weather a fire is kept burning day and night in the centre of the floor; and, the habitations being easily heated, a very small one suffices. To keep up a moderate, steady temperature, the ends only of the sticks meet in the centre of the fire, and, as they burn slowly away, are pushed inwards. Any other method would be a waste of fuel, and would raise too much heat.

In the event of the habitation being burned down by a bush fire, or accidentally—which often occurs in the absence of the inhabitants—the *debris* are levelled, and a new wuurn erected on the same spot, which is always preferred ; but, in other circumstances hereafter described under the head of native mounds, the spot is abandoned for ever as a place of residence.

CHAPTER VII.

CLEANLINESS.

It is worthy of remark that nothing offensive is ever to be seen near the habitations of the aborigines, or in the neighbourhood of their camps; and although their sanitary laws are apparently attributable to superstition and prejudice, the principles of these laws must have been suggested by experience of the dangers attendant on uncleanness in a warm climate, and more deeply impressed on their minds by faith in supernatural action and sorcery. It is believed that if enemies get possession of anything that has belonged to a person, they can by its means make him ill; hence every uncleanness belonging to adults and half-grown children is buried at a distance from their dwellings. For this purpose they use the muurong pole (yam stick), about six or seven feet long, with which every family is provided. With the sharpened end they remove a circular piece of turf, and dig a hole in the ground, which is immediately used and filled in with earth, and the sod so carefully replaced that no disturbance of the surface can be observed. Children under four or five years of age, not having strength to comply with this wholesome practice, are not required to do so; and their excreta are deposited in one spot, and covered with a sheet of bark, and when dry they are burned. It may be as well to say here, that, besides this sanitary use of the muurang pole, it is indispensable in excavating graves and in digging up roots, and is a powerful weapon of warfare in the hands of the women, who alone use it for fighting.

In every respect the aborigines are as cleanly in their persons and habits as natural circumstances admit; and, although the universal custom of anointing their bodies with oily fat may be repulsive to highly-civilized communities, it is an excellent substitute for cleansing with water, and must have arisen, not only from the comfort it affords to the skin in various ways, but also from the difficulty of obtaining water in most parts of the country, even to satisfy thirst. Neither are they troubled with parasites to such an extent as their habits might lead one to suppose. They say they never saw the common flea till it was introduced by the white man, and the accuracy of this assertion seems to be vouched for by the fact that they have no name for it. Nor did they ever see the white louse until they came in contact with the white man, previous to which the native louse was black ; but, foretokening the destiny of the aborigines, the latter insect has disappeared, and the white louse is now the only kind amongst them. So rare, however, is even this kind, that in no instance has the writer seen one on a native.

CHAPTER VIII.

DOMESTIC FURNITURE.

EVERY woman carries on her back, outside her rug, a basket made of a tough kind of rush, occasionally ornamented with stitches of various kinds. They also carry in the same way a bag formed of the tough inner bark of the acacia tree. Failing to procure this bark, which is the best for the purpose, they use the inner bark of the messmate or of the stringy-bark tree. This is spun into cord and knitted with the fingers into the required shape. The capacity of these articles is from two to three gallons each, and in them are carried food, sticks and tinder for producing fire, gum for cement, shells, tools, charms, &c.

The women also make a rougher kind of basket out of the common rush, which is used for cooking food in the ovens.

Domestic utensils are limited in number; and, as the art of boiling food is not understood, the natives have no pottery or materials capable of resisting fire. Their cookery is consequently confined chiefly to roasting on embers or baking in holes in the ground; but as they consume great quantities of gum and manna dissolved together in hot water, a wooden vessel for that purpose is formed of the excrescence of a tree, which is hollowed out sufficiently large to contain a gallon or two of water. This vessel is placed near enough to the fire to dissolve the contents, but not to burn the wood. It is called 'yuuruum,' and must be valuable, from the difficulty of procuring a suitable knob of wood, and from the great labour of digging it hollow with a chisel made of the thigh bone of a kangaroo.

Another vessel, named 'popæær yuu,' is used for carrying water, and is formed of a sheet of fresh acacia bark, about twenty inches long by twelve broad, bent double and sewed up at each side with kangaroo tail sinews, and the seams made water-tight with an excellent cement, composed of wattle gum and wood ashes, mixed in hot water. After the bucket is made it is hung up to dry, and the contraction of the inner bark causes the vessel to assume a circular shape, which it retains ever after. It is carried by means of a band of twisted wattle bark fixed across its mouth.

A small water-bag, called 'paanuung,' is formed of the pouch of the kangaroo, which, when fresh, is stuffed with withered grass till it is dry. A strip of skin is fixed across its mouth for a handle.

For carrying water to a distance a bag called 'kowapp' is used. It is made of the skin of a male brush or wallaby kangaroo, cut off at the neck and stripped downwards from the body and legs, and made water-tight by ligatures. The neck forms the mouth of the bag. This vessel is carried on the shoulders by the forelegs.

For keeping a supply of water in dry weather, a vessel called 'torrong'—'boat'—is made of a sheet of bark stripped from the bend of a gum tree, about four or five feet long, one foot deep, and one wide, in the shape of a canoe. To prevent dogs drinking from it, it is supported several feet from the ground on forked posts sunk in the earth. A wooden torrong is often used in the same way, and is formed from a bend of a gum tree, hollowed out large enough to hold from five to six gallons. As the water which they use is frequently ill-tasted, they put some cones of the banksia into the torrong, in order to give a pleasant flavour to its contents.

The millstone or mortar, so indispensable to the aborigines of the interior for grinding the nardoo seed, is known, but rarely met with among the natives of the sea coast, because they have not the nardoo, and have very little of any other kind of seed to grind. They depend for food almost entirely on animals and roots, which are more abundant than in the interior, where the seed of the nardoo occasionally forms the chief sustenance of the aborigines.

There are two kinds of millstones, both formed of slabs of grey marble or grey slate, of an oval shape, eighteen inches long by twelve inches broad. One kind is hollowed out, like a shallow basin, to a depth of two inches; the seed is put into it, and ground with a flat stone of the same material as the mortar. The other kind is about the same size, but, instead of being basin-shaped, it is flat, and has two parallel hollows, each one foot long, five inches broad, and one inch deep, in which the seed is placed and reduced to flour by two flat stones, held one in each hand, and rubbed backwards and forwards.

While travelling, the natives always carry burning pieces of the dry thick bark of the eucalyptus tree, to light their fires with, and to show the paths at night; but, as these might be extinguished while they are far from any fire, implements for producing combustion are indispensable. These consist of the thigh bone of a kangaroo, ground to a long fine point, and a piece of the dry cane of the grass tree, about eighteen inches long. One end of the cane is bored out, and is stuffed with tinder, made by teasing out the dry bark of the messmate tree. The operator sits down and grasps the bone, point upwards, with his feet; he then places the hollow end of the cane, containing the bark, on the point of the bone, and, with both hands, presses downwards, and twirls the upright cane with great rapidity till the friction produces fire. Or, in the absence of the kangaroo bone, a piece of dry grass tree cane, having in its upper side a hole bored to the pith, is held flat on the ground with the feet, and the sharp point of a piece of soft wood is pressed into the hole, and twirled vertically between the palms of the hands till combustion takes place. Some dry stringy-bark fibre having been placed round the hole, the fire is communicated to it by blowing. The writer has seen flame produced by this method in two minutes.

CHAPTER IX.

COOKING AND FOOD.

OVENS are made outside the dwellings by digging holes in the ground, plastering them with mud, and keeping a fire in them till quite hot, then withdrawing the embers and lining the holes with wet grass. The flesh, fish, or roots are put into baskets, which are placed in the oven and covered with more wet grass, gravel, hot stones, and earth, and kept covered till they are cooked. This is done in the evening; and, when cooking is in common—which is generally the case when many families live together—each family comes next morning and removes its basket of food for breakfast.

Ovens on a greater scale, for cooking large animals, are formed and heated in the same way, with the addition of stones at the bottom of the oven; and emus, wombats, turkeys, or forest kangaroos—sometimes unskinned and entire, and sometimes cut into pieces—are placed in them, and covered with leafy branches, wet grass, a sheet of bark, and embers on the top.

Ordinary cooking, such as roasting opossums, small birds, and eels, is generally done on the embers of the domestic fire. When opossums are killed expressly for food, and not for the skin, the fur is plucked or singed off while the animal is still warm; the entrails are pulled out through an opening in the skin, stripped of their contents, and eaten raw, and their place stuffed with herbs; the body is then toasted and turned slowly before the fire without breaking the skin, and, if not immediately required for food, is set aside to cool. Opossum thus prepared will keep and may be carried about much better than if uncooked. In this way the natives make provision for travelling through country where food is scarce. They are very fond of opossum when the animal is in ordinary condition, but dislike it when fat. Kangaroo tails are cooked unskinned, first singeing and scraping off the hair, and then toasting them before the fire till thoroughly done. By this method none of the juices of the meat escape; and what would otherwise be dry food is made savoury and nutritious. As the sinews, however, which are very strong, would render the meat tough, they are all pulled out previous to toasting, and are stretched and dried, and are kept for sewing rugs and lashing the handles of stone hatchets and butt pieces of spears. Skulls and bones are split up, and the brains and marrow roasted. The brains are considered a great delicacy, and keep for a long time after being cooked. Eels are seldom eaten quite fresh; and, to impart a high flavour to them, they are buried in the ground until slightly tainted, and then roasted.

The aborigines exercise a wise economy in killing animals. It is considered illegal and a waste of food to take the life of any edible creature for pleasure alone, a snake or an eagle excepted. Articles of food are abundant, and of great variety; for everything not actually poisonous or connected with superstitious beliefs is considered wholesome. The natives never touch putrid flesh, however, except that of the whale, which the Peek whuurong natives bury till quite rotten. They are aware of the danger of inoculation by dead animal matter, and will not eat any animal unless they know how it has lost its life. The kangaroo and the emu they will eat if they have reason to believe that they have been killed by wild dogs, but they will not touch any food which has been partaken of by a stranger. They have no objection to eat tainted flesh or fish. If it is too far gone it is thoroughly roasted to dispel the unpleasant flavour. Fish that have been exposed to the rays of the moon are rejected as poisonous. Maggoty meat is rejected; and to prevent the flies from blowing the meat, it is hung in the smoke of the domestic fire.

Of quadrupeds, they eat the several kinds of kangaroo, the wombat—which is excellent eating—the bear, wild dog, porcupine ant-eater, opossum, flying squirrel, bandicoot, dasyure, platypus, water rat, and many smaller animals. Before the occupation of the great plains by cattle and sheep, there were numerous black and brown quadrupeds, called the yaakar, about the size of the rabbit, and with open pouches like the dasyures. They were herbivorous, and burrowed in mounds, living in communities in the open plains, where they had their nests. They had four or five young ones at a time; and, from what the natives say about the numbers that they dug up, they must have furnished a plentiful supply of food at all times. As these animals are now extinct in the Western District, although the remains of their burrows are still to be seen, it is supposed that they were the jerboa or bilboa, which are still very plentiful and troublesome in the interior of Australia.

The aborigines eat eagles and birds of prey, the emu, turkey bustard, gigantic crane, herons, and swan; geese and ducks in great variety, cormorants, ibis, curlew, coot, water-hen, lapwings, cockatoos, parrots, pigeons, crows, quails, snipes, and a great many kinds of sea fowls. The pelican and its eggs are considered too fishy to eat.

The tortoise and its eggs are much sought after. Snakes are considered good food, but are not eaten if they have bitten themselves, as the natives believe that the poison, when taken into the stomach, is as deadly as when injected into the blood by a bite. Lizards and frogs of all sorts are cooked and eaten.

Of fish, the eel is the favourite; but, besides it, there are many varieties of fish in the lakes and rivers, which are eaten by the natives. One in particular, called the tuupuurn, is reckoned a very great delicacy. It is caught plentifully, with the aid of long baskets, in the mouths of rivers during its passage to and from the sea, of which migration the natives are well aware.

Vast quantities of mollusca must have been consumed from very remote periods by the natives occupying the country adjoining the sea coast; for opposite every reef of rocks affording shelter to shell fish, immense beds of shells of various sorts are to be seen in the sand-hills, in layers intermixed with pieces of charred wood, ashes, and stones having the marks of fire on them. In some places where the action of the wind and spray has caused the hummocks to slip down into the sea, the layers of shells are exposed to a great depth; and, as they could not have been placed in their present positions by natural means along with pieces of burnt trap-rock, charred wood, and ashes, there is no doubt that they are of similar origin with the aboriginal deposits found on the east coast of Scotland and sea shores of Denmark and Holland, called 'middens' by the Scotch and 'moedens' by the Dutch. These immense mounds of shells being met with only near the sea, and nowhere in the interior, leads to the conclusion that the aborigines who fed on the mollusca and fish, never left the shore during the fishing season; and that, if they came from the interior, they never carried away any shell-fish with them, otherwise sea shells would be found in abundance at their old camping places in the bush, at a distance from the sea. An ancient deposit of marine shells, having every appearance of an aboriginal midden, was some years ago exposed on the east bank of the Yarra-Yarra River, near the Falls Bridge. At this spot a reef of rocks—which has been since partially removed—kept back the tide, and preserved the water sufficiently fresh for domestic purposes. This, no doubt, enabled the natives to camp there for fishing purposes; and hence the large deposit of shells at this spot.

Of roots and vegetables they have plenty. The muurang, which somewhat resembles a small parsnip, with a flower like a buttercup, grows chiefly on the open plains. It is much esteemed on account of its sweetness, and is dug up by the women with the muurang pole. The roots are washed and put into a rush basket made on purpose, and placed in the oven in the evening to be ready for next morning's breakfast. When several families live near each other and cook their roots together, sometimes the baskets form a pile three feet high. The cooking of the muurang entails a considerable amount of labour on the women, inasmuch as the baskets are made by them; and as these often get burnt, they rarely serve more than twice. The muurang root, when cooked, is called yuwatch. It is often eaten uncooked. The bulbous root, muuyuup, of the common orchis, hinnæhinnitch, and of another named yarrayarupp, are eaten either raw or cooked. The weeakk, resembling a small carrot, is cooked in hot ashes without a basket. The bulb of the clematis, 'taaruuk,' is dug up in winter, cooked in baskets, and kneaded on a small sheet of bark into dough, and eaten under the name of murpit. The root of the native convolvulus, also called taaruuk, is cooked in the same way, and forms the principal vegetable food in winter, when the muurang is out of season. A tuber, called puewan, about the size of a walnut, and resembling the earthnut of Europe, is dug up, and eaten roasted. It has no stalk or leaf to mark its locality, and is discovered from the shallow holes scraped by the bandicoots in search of it, and from a scarcity of herbage in the neighbourhood. A variety of the sedge—the flag of the cooper—has a root of pleasant flavour, resembling celery, which is eaten uncooked as a salad. So also are the salsuginous plant, the mesembryanthemum, or pig's face, and the sow thistle. The latter is eaten to produce sleep. A kind of bread is made of the root of the common fern, roasted in hot ashes, and beaten into paste with a stone.

Mushrooms, and several kinds of fungi, are eaten raw; and a large underground fungus, about the size of an ordinary turnip, called native bread by white people, is eaten uncooked, and is very good.

Large numbers of pupæ, found in the ground at the foot of gum trees, are dug up in winter, and baked in hot ashes. They are the transitional forms of large green processional caterpillars, which crawl in lines on the stems of trees in search of a place to rest during their change into the pupa state. Of this transformation, and of their ultimately becoming moths, the aborigines are well aware. In addition to these there are many delicacies, chiefly collected by the women and children, and cooked in hot ashes, such as grubs, small fish, frogs, lizards, birds' eggs, lizard and tortoise eggs. The grubs are about the size of the little finger, and are cut out of trees and dead timber, and are eaten alive, while the work of chopping is going on, with as much pleasure as a white man eats a living oyster; but with this difference, that caution is necessary to avoid their powerful mandibles, ever ready to bite the lips or tongue. Roasted on embers, they are delicate and nutty in flavour, varying in quality according to the kind of tree into which they bore, and on which they feed. Those found in the trunks of the common wattle are considered the finest and sweetest. Every hunter carries a small hooked wand, to push into the holes of the wood, and draw them out. With an axe and an old grub-eaten tree, an excellent meal is soon procured; and when the women and children hear the sound of chopping, they hasten to partake of the food, which they enjoy above all others. The large fat grubs, to be found in quantities on the banks of marshes, drowned out of their holes, in times of floods, are gathered and cooked in hot ashes by the women and children.

The gum of the acacia, or common wattle tree, is largely consumed as food, as well as for cement; and each man has an exclusive right to a certain number of trees for the use of himself and family. As soon as the summer heat is over, notches are cut in the bark to allow the gum to exude. It is then gathered in large lumps, and stored for use.

A sweet substance, called buumbuul (manna), resembling small pieces of loaf sugar, with a fine delicate flavour, which exudes and drops from the leaves and small branches of some kinds of gum trees, is gathered and eaten by the children, or mixed in a wooden vessel with acacia gum dissolved in hot water, as a drink. Another kind of manna, also called buumbuul, is deposited in considerable quantities by the large dark-coloured cicadæ on the stems of white gum trees near the River Hopkins. The natives ascend the trees, and scrape off as much as a bucketful of waxen cells filled with a liquid resembling honey, which they mix with gum dissolved in cold water, and use as a drink. They say that, in consequence of the great increase of opossums, caused by the destruction of the wild dog, they never get any buumbuul now, as the opossums eat it all. Another sweet liquid is obtained by mischievous boys from young parrakeets after they are fed by the old birds with honey dew, gathered from the blossom of the trees. When a nest is discovered in the hole of a gum tree, it is constantly visited, and the young birds pulled out, and held by their feet till they disgorge their food into the mouth of their unwelcome visitant.

In summer, when the surface of the ground is parched, and the marshes dried up, the natives carry a long reed perforated from end to end, which they push down the holes made by crabs in swamps, and suck up the water. When obliged to drink from muddy pools full of animalculæ, they put a full-blown cone of the banksia tree into their mouths, and drink through it, which gives a fine flavour to the water, and excludes impurities. The name of the cone, when used for this purpose, is tatteen mirng neung weeriitch. gnat—'drink eye banksia tree belonging to.'

The southern portions of Australia are remarkably deficient in native fruits, and the only kind deserving the name is a berry which the aborigines of the locality call 'nurt,' resembling a red-cheeked cherry without the pip, which grows abundantly on a creeper amongst the sand on the hummocks near the mouth of the River Glenelg. It is very much sought after, and, when ripe, is gathered in great quantities by the natives, who come from long distances to feast on it', and reside in the locality while it lasts. In collecting the berries they pull up the plants, which run along the surface of the sand in great lengths, and carry them on their backs to their camps to pick off the fruit at their leisure. On the first settlement of the district by sheepowners these berries were gathered by the white people, and they made excellent jam and tarts.

There are strict rules regulating the distribution of food. When a hunter brings game to the camp he gives up all claim to it, and must stand aside and allow the best portions to be given away, and content himself with the worst. If he has a brother present, the brother is treated in the same way, and helps the killer of the game to eat the poor pieces, which are thrown to them, such as the forequarters and ribs of the kangaroos, opossums, and small quadrupeds, and the backbones of birds. The narrator of this custom mentioned that when he was very young he used to grumble because his father gave away all the best pieces of birds and quadrupeds, and the finest eels, but he was told that it was a rule and must be observed. This custom is called yuurka baawhaar, meaning 'exchange;' and, to show the strict observance of it, and the punishment for its infringement, they tell a story of a mean fellow named Wirtpa Mit, signifying 'selfish,' who lived on kangaroos, which were very scarce in those days. When he killed one he ate it all himself, and would not give away a morsel. This conduct so displeased his friends that they resolved to punish him, but as it was difficult to do so without infringing the laws of the tribe, they dug a deep pit and covered it over with branches and grass. When the trap was ready, they drove some kangaroos in its direction, and advised Wirtpa Mit to follow them. He fell into the trap, and they covered over the top of the pit, leaving only a small hole to give him air and sunshine. There they kept him without food till he was nearly dead. He begged of them to make the opening larger, and when they acceded to his request he made his escape, but was so weak from starvation that they afterwards killed him and put him into the hole and filled it up. To this day this place is named after him, and the story is told to the young people as a warning not to be 'selfish.'

CHAPTER X.

TOOLS.

THE natives have few tools; the principal one is the stone axe, which resembles the stone celts found in Europe. This useful and indispensable implement is of various sizes. It is made chiefly of green stone, shaped like a wedge, and ground at one end to a sharp edge. At the other end it is grasped in the bend of a doubled piece of split sapling, bound with kangaroo sinews, to form a handle, which is cemented to it with a composition of gum and shell lime. This cement is made by gathering fresh wattle gum, pulling it into small pieces, masticating it with the teeth, and then placing it between two sheets of green bark, which are put into a shallow hole in the ground, and covered up with hot ashes till the gum is dissolved. It is then taken out, and worked and pulled with the hands till it has become quite stringy, when it is mixed with lime made of burnt mussel shells, pounded in a hollow stone—which is always kept for the purpose—and kneaded into a tough paste. This cement is indispensable to the natives in making their tools, spears, and water buckets. The stone axe is so valuable and scarce that it is generally the property of the chief of the tribe. He lends it, however, for a consideration, to the best climbers, who use it to cut steps in the bark of trees, to enable them to climb in search of bears, opossums, birds, and nests, and also to cut wood and to strip bark for their dwellings. For the latter purpose the butt end of the handle of the axe is made wedge-shaped, to push under the sheets of bark and prize them off the trees.

Another stone tool, like a chisel without a handle, is used in forming weapons and wooden vessels. With splinters of flint and volcanic glass the surface of wooden articles is scraped and smoothed, and every man carries a piece of hard, porous lava, as a rasp, to grind the points of spears and poles. These stone implements, although well known to the middle-aged aborigines of the present day, are, in consequence of the introduction of iron, not now in use or to be met with, excepting about old aboriginal camping places.

The writer lately found, in a ploughed field, two stones, which he showed to one of the oldest and most intelligent men of the Colac tribe. One of them is an oval, silicious stone, very hard, about six inches long, five inches broad, and three inches thick, waterworn, and slightly hollowed on one side, as if used for pounding some hard substance upon, and rounded on the other side, with a funnel-shaped hole in the centre two inches in diameter at the mouth and one inch deep, and having a much smaller hole of the same form on each side of the larger one and joining it. The other stone, which was found lying alongside, is of the same material, of cylindrical shape, six inches long by three inches in diameter, with one end pointed so as to fit into the centre hole of the flat stone. The natives to whom these were shown said they had never seen anything like them before, and did not know their use. It is evident, however, that they were an aboriginal mortar and pestle for grinding shells for cement. The writer has them still in his possession.

A tool is made of the large bone of the hind leg of the forest kangaroo, sharpened to a chisel point. With this tool is cut the hole for the hand through the heavy shield, Malkar. A bodkin, or awl, is formed from the small bone of the hind leg of the forest kangaroo, ground to a fine point, and is used for sewing rugs. A finely-tapered sharp pin is made of the small leg bone of the brush kangaroo or opossum, and is essential for extracting thorns and splinters of wood from the hands and feet. Ti-tree pins are used for pegging out the skins of the forest kangaroo.

Knives are of various kinds and material, according to the purposes they are to serve. For skinning animals, marking rugs, and cutting the human skin to produce ornamental wens on the chest, back, and arms, knives are made of splinters of flint, or of sharpened mussel shells. The sea mussel shell found on the coast at Warrnambool is preferred, but freshwater mussel shells are also used. For skinning the ring-tailed opossum, and for dividing meat, the leaf of the grass-tree is used, and also the long front teeth of the bandicoot, with the jaw attached as a handle. The shells of the freshwater mussel and of the sea snail serve for spoons. Every person carries one. In making necklaces of the quills of the porcupine ant-eater, the holes at the roots of the quills are burned through with a wooden pin made red-hot in the fire.

CHAPTER XI.

LAWS OF MARRIAGE.

THE laws of marriage among the aborigines are remarkably well devised; and exhibit a method and ingenuity which could not have been looked for among a people who were so long considered the lowest of the human race.

The object of these laws is to prevent marriages between those of 'one flesh'—'Tow'wil yerr.'

As has been shown in the first chapter, the aborigines are divided into tribes. Every person is considered to belong to his father's tribe, and cannot marry into it. Besides this division, there is another which is made solely for the purpose of preventing marriages with *maternal* relatives. The aborigines are everywhere divided into classes; and everyone is considered to belong to his mother's class, and cannot marry into it in any tribe, as all of the same class are considered brothers and sisters.

There are five classes in all the tribes of the Western District, and these take their names from certain animals—the long-billed cockatoo, kuurokeetch; the pelican, kartpœrapp; the banksian cockatoo, kappatch; the boa snake, kirtuuk; and the quail, kuunamit.

According to their classes the aborigines are distinguished, as—

Kuurokeetch, male; kuurokaheear, female.
Kartpœrapp, male; kartpœrapp heear, female.
Kappatch, male; kappaheear, female.
Kirtuuk, male; kirtuuk heear, female.
Kuunamit, male; kuunamit heear, female.

Kuurokeetch and kartpœrapp, however, are so related, that they are looked upon as sister classes, and no marriage between them is permitted. It is the same between kappatch and kirtuuk; but as kuunamit is not so related, it can marry into any class but its own. Thus a kuurokeetch may marry a kappaheear, a kirtuuk heear, or a kuunamit heear, but cannot marry a kuurokaheear or a kartpœrapp heear. A kappatch may marry a kuurokaheear, a kartpœrapp heear, or a kuunamit heear, but cannot marry a kappaheear or a kirtuuk heear. A kuunamit may marry a kuurokaheear, a kartpœrapp heear, a kappaheear, or a kirtuuk heear, but cannot marry a kuunamit heear.

The traditions of the aborigines say that the first progenitor of the tribes treated of in this volume, the kuukuur minjer, or first great great grandfather, was by descent a kuurokeetch, long-billed cockatoo, but whence he came no one knows. He had for a wife a kappaheear, banksian cockatoo. She is called the kuurappa mœl, meaning first great great grandmother. This original pair had sons and daughters, who, of course, belonged to the class of their mother. The sons were kappatch, and the daughters kappaheear. As the laws of consanguinity forbade marriages between these, it was necessary to introduce wambepan tuuram, 'fresh flesh,' which could be obtained only by marriage with strangers. The sons got wives from a distance. Their sons, again, had to do the same; and thus the pelican, snake, and quail classes were introduced, which, together with those of their first parents, form the five maternal classes which exist all through the Western District.

The laws of the aborigines also forbid a man marrying into his mother's tribe or his grandmother's tribe, or into an adjoining tribe, or one that speaks his own dialect. A man is allowed to marry his brother's widow, or his own deceased wife's sister, or a woman of her tribe; but he is not permitted to do so if he has divorced or killed his wife. He may not marry his deceased wife's daughter by a former husband.

A common man may not have more than one wife at a time. Chiefs, however, may have as many wives as they think proper. The sons of chiefs may marry two wives.

Chiefs, and their sons and daughters, are married only into the families of other chiefs. If a chief persists in marrying a commoner, his children by that marriage are not disinherited; but such marriages are highly disapproved of. The natives say that if chiefs were permitted to marry commoners, it would lead to endless quarrels and jealousies.

When a married man dies, his brother is bound to marry the widow if she has a family, as it is his duty to protect her and rear his brother's children. If there is no brother, the chief sends the widow to her own tribe, with whom she must remain till her period of mourning is ended. Those of her children who are under age are sent with her, and remain with their mother's tribe till they come of age, when they return to their father's tribe, to which they belong. After the period of mourning for her deceased husband expires, the relatives of the widow, with the sanction of the chief, make arrangements for her re-marriage, and she must marry the man chosen for her. If the widow has no near relatives, the arrangements are made by the chief of her tribe. Her own inclinations are not consulted in the matter.

No marriage or betrothal is permitted without the approval of the chiefs of each party, who first ascertain that no 'flesh' relationship exists, and even then their permission must be rewarded by presents.

So strictly are the laws of marriage carried out, that, should any signs of affection and courtship be observed between those of 'one flesh,' the brothers, or male relatives of the woman beat her severely; the man is brought before the chief, and accused of an intention to fall into the same flesh, and is severely reprimanded by the tribe. If he persists, and runs away with the object of his affections, they beat and 'cut his head all over;' and if the woman was a consenting party she is half killed. If she dies in consequence of her punishment, her death is avenged by the man's receiving an additional beating from her relatives. No other vengeance is taken, as her punishment is legal. A child born under such conditions is taken from the parents, and handed over to the care of its grandmother, who is compelled to rear it, as no one else will adopt it.

It says much for the morality of the aborigines and their laws that illegitimacy is rare, and is looked upon with such abhorrence that the mother is always severely beaten by her relatives, and sometimes put to death and burned. Her child is occasionally killed and burned with her. The father of the child is also punished with the greatest severity, and occasionally killed. Should he survive the chastisement inflicted upon him, he is always shunned by the woman's relatives, and any efforts to conciliate them with gifts are spurned, and his presents are put in the fire and burned.

Since the advent of the Europeans among them, the aborigines have occasionally disregarded their admirable marriage laws, and to this disregard they attribute the greater weakness and unhealthiness of their children.

As a preventive of illegal marriages, parents betroth their children when just able to walk. The proposal to betroth is made by the father of the girl. If the boy's father approves, he gives the girl a present of an opossum rug, and shows her attention, and gives her 'nice things to eat' when he sees her at great meetings. The father of the girl takes her occasionally to see her intended husband, but he is not permitted to return the visit.

The girl's mother and her aunts may neither look at him nor speak to him from the time of their betrothal till his death. Should he come to the camp where they are living, he must lodge at a friend's wuurn, as he is not allowed to go within fifty yards of their habitation; and should he meet them on a path they immediately leave it, clap their hands, cover up their heads with their rugs, walk in a stooping position, and speak in whispers till he has gone past. When he meets them away from their camp they do not converse with him, and when he and they speak in each other's presence they use a lingo, called wiltkill ang iitch in the chaap wuurong dialect, and gnee wee banott in the kuurn kopan noot and peek whuurong dialects, meaning 'turn tongue.' This is not used with the intention of concealment of their meaning, for it is understood by all. The intended mother-in-law, though she may not speak to the boy, may express her approval of what he says by clapping her hands. He never mentions her name at any time, and when he speaks about her to anyone, he calls her gnulluun guurk in the chaap wuurong dialect, and gnulluun yerr in the kuurn kopan noot and peek whuurong dialects. She, in speaking about him, calls him gnalluun jœk in the chaap wuurong dialect, and gnalluun in the kuurn kopan noot and peek whuurong dialects.

Examples of turn tongue in chaap wuurong dialect :—

Where are you going just now ?
>> Winjalat·kuurna new ?
> *Turn tongue.*—Winja gniinkirna ?

It will be very warm by-and-bye.
>> Wulpiya gnuureen.
> *Turn tongue.*—Gnullewa gnuureen.

Examples in kuurn kopan noot dialect :—

Where are you going just now ?
>> Wuunda gnin kitneean ?
> *Turn tongue.*—Wuun gni gnin gninkeewan ?

It will be very warm by-and-bye.
>> Baawan kulluun.
> *Turn tongue.*—Gnullewa gnatnœn tirambuul.

A wild blackfellow is coming to kill you.
>> Wattatan kuut gno yuul yuul.
> *Turn tongue.*—Kulleet burtakuut yung a gnak kuuno nong.

In nearly all the aboriginal tribes of Australia young men are not allowed to marry until they have been formally initiated into manhood. In some tribes this initiation requires them to be subjected to ordeals and ceremonies more or less repulsive. In other tribes the trials are so severe that they often not only ruin the health, but cause the death of many delicate young men. Indeed, it is possible that they are designed to get rid of the weakly, who would be of no use either in hunting or in war, and would be only an encumbrance to the tribe. The customs, however, of those tribes which are treated of in this volume are quite free from this repulsiveness and severity.

A youth is not considered to be a man until he has undergone this probation, which is called katneetch in the chaap wuurong dialect, katnitt in the kuurn kopan noot dialect, and tapmet in the peek whuurong dialect. During the progress of this probation he is called kutneet, which is really 'hobbledehoy.' No person related to him by blood can interfere or assist in the proceedings. Should the boy have brothers-in-law, they come and take him into a wuurn, dress and ornament him, and remove him to their own country, where he remains for twelve moons. Should he not have brothers-in-law, strangers from a distant tribe come and take him to their country, where he is received with welcome by his new friends. After two moons he is allowed to visit his own tribe, but not without several men to take care of him and bring him back. If, during his sojourn, he becomes ill, he is sent home to his own tribe, for, were he to die, they would avenge his death. During the term of probation his wants are liberally supplied, and he is not permitted to do anything for himself. When he wishes to go anywhere, he must be carried by the men who brought him from his own country. The women also of the tribe must wait upon him with every mark of respect, and should any disobey his orders he has a right to spear them. He is not allowed to speak the language of the tribe, but he learns to understand it when spoken. At the end of twelve moons his relatives call and take him to attend the first great meeting of the tribes. Before leaving, they pull out all the hairs of his beard, and make him drink water mixed with mud; which completes his initiation into manhood. The knocking out of the upper front teeth, which is practised by some other tribes on such occasions, is unknown in the Western District.

He is then introduced to the young woman who is to be his wife. They may look at one another, but are not allowed to converse. When the young man's beard has grown again, and the young woman has attained a marriageable age, she is sent away from her tribe, and placed under the care of the young man's mother, or his nearest female relative, who keeps her until they are married, but not in the same wuurn with her intended husband. She is constantly attended by one of his female relatives, but is not permitted to speak their tribal language. She is expected, however, to learn it sufficiently to understand it. A day is fixed for the marriage, and invitations are sent to the relatives and friends of both parties.

As such ceremonies are always accompanied with feasting and amusements, great preparations are made, and all kinds of food collected, such, for example, as emus' and swans' eggs, opossums, kangaroos, and wild fowl. An emu which is killed while hatching is considered a great treat, as then both bird and eggs can be eaten; and if the eggs have young ones in them so much the greater will be the delicacy. These things are cooked at a considerable distance from the camp, and brought to it at mid-day by the friends of the bridegroom. At this stage of the proceedings they are partaken of only by the friends of the bride. At sunset, the friends and relations of the bridegroom and bride, numbering possibly two hundred, sit on opposite sides, within a large circle formed of the leafy boughs of trees, with a fire in the centre. The bride is introduced by her bridemaid, and seated in front of her friends. The bridal attire is very simple. Her hair is braided, and bound with a plaited bark brow band, coloured red. In front of the brow band is stuck a bunch of red feathers, from the neck of the long-billed cockatoo. White streaks are painted over and under her eyes, with red lines below. The usual kilt of emu feathers is worn round the loins, and she is covered from the shoulders downwards with an opossum rug.

The bridegroom also is painted with a white streak over and under the eyes, and red lines beneath them. He wears a brow band the same as that of the bride, but it is ornamented in front with a white feather from a swan's wing, the web of which is torn down, so as to flutter in the wind. He wears the usual apron, and a rug of the ring-tail opossum, thrown over the shoulders like a mantle. This is fastened in front with a bone pin, and reaches to the knees. He is attended by two or three young bachelors, who are painted and ornamented for the occasion. They lead him from the wuurn of a friend to his bride, who receives him with downcast eyes and in silence. He then declares that he accepts the woman for his wife. Feasting then begins. When everyone is satisfied, a chief calls out, "Let us have a dance before the children go to bed." The karweann is then commenced, and kept up till midnight.

The bridegroom is conducted by his bridemen to a new wuurn, erected for him by his friends; and his wife is taken to it by her bridemaids. For several days afterwards hunting, feasting, and amusements, with dancing and pantomime at night, are kept up till all friends depart for their homes with the usual ' wo, wo'—' good-bye, good-bye.'

The newly-married pair are well fed and attended to by their relatives. The bridemaid, who must be the nearest adult unmarried relative of the bridegroom, is obliged to sleep with the bride on one side of the fire for two moons, and attend her day and night. The bridegroom sleeps for the same period on the opposite side of the fire with the brideman, who is always a bachelor friend, and must attend him day and night. The newly-married couple are not allowed to speak to or look at each other. The bride is, during this period, called a tiirok meetnya—' not look round.' She keeps her head and face covered with her opossum rug while her husband is present. He also keeps his face turned away from her, much to the amusement of the young people, who peep into their wuurn and laugh at them. If they need to speak to one another they must speak through their friends.

On the termination of this period, the bridemaid, or some other adult female relative of the bridegroom, takes the bride to see her own relatives for a week or two. The husband remains at home. When she returns, the attendance of the brideman and bridemaid is dispensed with. Ever afterwards the bridemaid, and other female friends, may sleep under the same roof with the married people, but on the opposite side of the fire.

After they have been married some months, they are visited by the parents of the bride. The bride's father can enter their wuurn, and converse with them as formerly; but the mother lives with her husband in a separate residence specially erected for them, and sees her daughter there. This visit is returned by the bridegroom and bride, for whose accommodation a wuurn is erected by the bride's friends. The mother-in-law can never speak to her daughter's husband, or enter his wuurn. If she meets him, she must cover up her head with her rug, walk in a stooping position, and speak in whispers while he is near. To such a length is this remarkable law carried, that it is not departed from even while one of them is dying. After death, however, the living looks upon the dead. The aborigines, who show great willingness to give explanations of their laws and habits to those persons they respect, cannot give any reason for this very extraordinary custom, which is said to be observed all over Australia, and in several island groups in the Pacific Ocean.

A chief who has been married under the law of betrothal, is not permitted to marry another woman for a long time; and should he do so without obtaining the consent of his wife, there would be constant quarrelling, as the first wife is always superior in authority to the others, and is naturally jealous of a rival.

A man can divorce his wife for serious misconduct, and can even put her to death; but in every case the charge against her must first be laid before the chiefs of his own and his wife's tribes, and their consent to her punishment obtained. If the wife has children, however, she cannot be divorced. Should a betrothed woman be found after marriage to have been unfaithful, her husband must divorce her. Her relations then remove her and her child to her own tribe, and compel the father of the child to marry her, unless he be a relative. In that case she must remain unmarried. If a husband is unfaithful, his wife cannot divorce him. She may make a complaint to the chief, who can punish the man by sending him away from his tribe for two or three moons; and the guilty woman is very severely punished by her relatives.

The courtship of those who have not been betrothed to each other when young is regulated by very strict laws. Korroboræs, and great meetings of the tribes, are the chief opportunities for selecting wives; as there the young people of various and distant tribes have an opportunity of seeing one another. A married man or a widower can speak to a married woman or to a widow, but they are not allowed to go beyond the boundaries of the camp together at any time, unless they are accompanied by another married person. Unmarried adults of both sexes are kept strictly apart from those of another tribe, and are always under the eyes of their parents or guardians. The young women are not permitted to leave the neighbourhood of their wuurns at any time, unless accompanied by a near relative. As there can be thus no personal communication between marriageable persons outside of the limits of consanguinity, a mutual friend, called a gnapunda, 'match maker,' is employed to carry messages, but this can only be done with the approval of the parents or guardians of both parties.

When a man falls in love with a young woman, he does not always consult her wishes, or procure her consent to marriage, but makes his proposal to the father through her uncle or cousin. If the father approve, he informs the suitor that he may marry his daughter; and to this decision she must submit, whether she admires the man or not. From the time when the proposal is accepted till they are married they are not permitted to speak to each other. Should she express reluctance to the match—which is often the case—the friends of the suitor accompany him to her father's wuurn, with his hands tied together with a rope made of the twisted inner bark of the blackwood tree. He is then introduced to her, and the rope is removed by his friends; and, after sitting beside her till sunset, he conducts her to his wuurn, which has been enlarged for her accommodation. The woman generally reconciles herself to the match, and remains quietly among her new friends. But, if she is dissatisfied, and runs away, the husband, failing to entice her to return home, considers he has a right to kill her. If he does so, however, her father, brothers, or uncles, in retaliation, can kill any of his relatives. The exercise of this right would thus lead to a quarrel between the families and their respective tribes.

If a young orphan woman elopes with a man of another tribe against the wishes of her relatives, notice is sent to him that she must be brought back, or she will be taken by force. Should the warning be unattended to, his wuurn is visited at daybreak by four or five of the woman's male friends, armed with spears and marwhangs, but not with boomerangs; they seize and stupefy her with blows, and carry her off. If the man or his friends resist, the contest frequently ends in the death of some of them, and, it may be, of the woman herself. If no warning has been given of an intention to take her away, the man knows that she may be suddenly removed, and given to another. Sometimes he will kill her rather than allow her to be given to another man; but he does this with the certainty of retaliation on himself, or on his aunt or female cousin. Should the woman escape a second time from her relatives, and return to the man, she is then considered his lawful wife, and cannot be taken from him.

Besides the custom of selecting wives at the great meetings and korroboræs, any two young men of different tribes and classes, having each a sister or cousin, may agree, with the consent of their chiefs, to exchange the young women and marry them. This is done without any previous courtship, or consent on the part of the women, even although they may be perfect strangers to the men, and they must submit.

The rule is that a father alone can give away his daughter. If the father is dead the son can dispose of the daughter, with the consent of the uncle. Should the woman have no male relative, the chief has the power of bestowing her on anyone he thinks proper; but his consent is reluctantly sought, as it attracts his attention to his power over her, and frequently results in his taking the young woman himself.

If a chief is a man of ability, exhibiting bravery in battle or skill in hunting, he is often presented with wives from other chiefs, who have generally some whom they wish to part with. These women are given without their consent, and the man must take them as a mark of friendship. It would seem, however, that these gifts are not always appreciated, for Puulorn Puul, who communicated this information, at the same time moodily muttered aside, in his own language, 'Dear knows, there are plenty of them, when a husband has to put up with half-a-dozen.' In cases where they are aged and infirm, the transfer is made against the inclination of both parties.

A young man, who belongs to the chief's family, very reluctantly seeks the consent of the head of the family to his marriage, for it frequently ends in the old chief taking the young woman himself. To such an extent is this tyrannical system of polygamy carried on by the old chiefs, that many young men are compelled to remain bachelors, the native word for which means 'to look out,' while an old warrior may have five or six of the finest young women of other tribes for his wives.

Exchange of wives is permitted only after the death of their parents, and, of course, with the consent of the chiefs; but is not allowed if either of the women has children. When such an exchange is effected, both couples occupy different compartments in the same wuurn, and assist each other amicably in household duties.

A husband and wife without children can agree to dissolve their marriage. In such a case the woman must return to her tribe, and can marry again.

When a woman is treated with cruelty by her husband, she may put herself under the protection of another man, with the intention of becoming his wife. If he take upon him the duty of protecting her, he must challenge her husband and defeat him in single combat in presence of the chiefs and friends of both parties. Having done so, their marriage is recognized as legal; but ever afterwards the first husband calls her a wannagnum heear, 'cast-off wife,' and she calls him wannagnum, 'cast-off husband.' If a husband knows that his wife is in love with another man, and if he has no objection to part with her, he takes her basket to the man's wuurn, and leaves it. But as no marriage, or exchange of wives can take place without the consent of the chief, the wife remains with her husband till the first great meeting, when the bargain is confirmed. This amicable separation does not create any ill feeling between the parties, as the woman is always kind to her first husband without causing any jealousy on the part of the second. Such transactions, although lawful, may not be approved of by the woman's relatives, and she is liable to be speared by her brother.

A single woman or widow belonging to a chief's family, can, with his consent, marry another chief, or his son, by simply sitting down in his wuurn beside his wife, who cannot prevent the match. But the first wife is always the mistress.

A young chief who cannot get a wife, and falls in love with one belonging to a chief who has more than two, can, with her consent, challenge the husband to single combat, and, if he defeats him, he makes her his legal wife; but the defeated husband never afterwards speaks to her.

A man falling in love with a young woman who will not consent to marry him, tries to get a lock of her hair, and, should he obtain it, he covers it with fat and red clay, and carries it about with him for one year. The knowledge of this so depresses the woman that she pines away. Should she die, her relatives and friends attribute her death to his having cast a spell over her, and they punish the man severely, and keep up enmity against him for a long time. In consequence of this superstition, the natives always burn their superfluous hair in a fire outside their dwellings; never in the domestic fire, as the remains of it would get among their food.

When a wife treats her husband with such persistent disrespect or unkindness as to make him wish to get quit of her, he casts a spell over her in the following manner. While she is asleep he cuts off a lock of her hair, and ties it to the bone hook of his 'spear thrower,' and covers it with a coating of gum. Early next morning he goes to a neighbouring tribe, and stays with them. At the first great meeting of the tribes he gives the 'spear thrower' to a friend, who sticks it upright before the camp fire every night, and when it falls over he considers that a sign that his wife is dead. But until he is assured by a messenger that such is the case, he will not return to his tribe. In the meantime, as the wife has not been legally separated from her husband, she cannot marry; and as she is constantly subjected to the sneers and taunts of her friends, she ultimately visits her husband, apologizes for her conduct, and brings him home. As an earnest of reconciliation and mutual confidence the spear thrower is broken and thrown into a water-hole.

After marriage, the women are compelled to do all the hard work of erecting habitations, collecting fuel and water, carrying burdens, procuring roots and delicacies of various kinds, making baskets for cooking roots and other purposes, preparing food, and attending to the children. The only work the men do, in time of peace, is to hunt for opossums and large animals of various kinds, and to make rugs and weapons. But, notwithstanding this drudgery, and the apparent hard usage to which the women are subjected, there is no want of affection amongst the members of a family.

CHAPTER XII.

CHILDREN.

A WOMAN near her confinement is called a 'moægorm,' and must stay at home, in her husband's wuurn, as much as possible. When she has occasion to quit the wuurn, any person who meets her must leave the path, and keep away from her.

During her confinement her husband lives elsewhere; the neighbouring wuurns are temporarily deserted; and everyone is sent away from the vicinity except two married women, who stay with her. Should she not have a mother to attend on her, a professional woman, 'gneein'—two of whom are generally attached to each tribe—is sent for, and compelled to nurse her and the baby till she is able to attend to it, and to resume the performance of her domestic duties. In return for these services the nurse is kindly treated and well fed, and generally presented with an opossum rug. The sick woman is not assisted in any way, and everything is left to nature. She is allowed very little solid food for some time, and only tepid water to drink; and, if necessary, is kept warm with hot stones. The women rarely die in childbirth.

When newly born an infant is not black, and the dark colour appears first on the brow, and spreads gradually over the body. The child is not bandaged in any way, but laid before the fire on soft, dry grass, and afterwards wrapped in an opossum rug. It receives no nourishment of any kind for twenty-four hours, and no medicine. If the child seem to be still-born, the nurse repeats the names of all her acquaintances in her own and neighbouring tribes; and, if it show signs of life on her mentioning one of them, it gets the name of that person, who afterwards takes a kindly interest in it, makes it presents, and shows it attention at the great meetings. In two or three days the husband comes to see his wife and child, and the neighbours again occupy their usual residences. If the infant is a boy, the nearest relative is the father; if it is a girl, the nearest relative is the mother.

Married women voluntarily assist each other in rearing their babies when the mothers are unable to do so, or are in bad health. Should this not be done voluntarily, the chief can make it compulsory.

Until a child is able to walk its mother seldom carries it in her arms, but keeps it on her back under the opossum rug. The rug is worn round the shoulders with the fur side inwards, and is fixed with a wooden pin in front. As every woman carries on her back, outside her rug, a bag suspended from her shoulders by a belt of kangaroo skin, a pouch is thus formed for her baby in a fold of the rug above the bag; and to give the bag solidity, and thus prevent the child from slipping down, stones are sometimes carried in it, in addition to the articles which it usually contains. When the mother wishes to remove the child, she reaches over her shoulder, and pulls it out by the arms. She replaces it in the same way.

To assist the child in cutting its teeth there is fastened to its wrist by a strip of skin a kangaroo front tooth, which is used as a 'coral,' to rub its gums with. As soon as it has teeth to masticate its food, it is fed on anything partaken of by its parents, in addition to the maternal nourishment, which is generally continued for two years.

Children under twelve or fourteen years of age wear no clothing of any kind. When the family is travelling, the youngest child under two years old is carried on the mother's back beneath her rug, occasionally in company with a young dingo. When obliged to leave its comfortable pouch to make room for another arrival, it rides on its father's back for a year or two, with a leg over each shoulder, and both hands holding on to his front hair. In cold weather, the children, while sitting in the wuurn, are covered with a single kangaroo skin or a small opossum rug, thrown over their shoulders; but when they go outside they leave the skin or rug behind, as they prefer keeping them dry for inside comfort.

Boys have their food regulated and restricted to certain articles, and they are permitted to engage in fights only to the extent of picking up and returning spears and boomerangs to their friends. Girls have for their amusement a wooden doll covered with opossum skin, and furnished with a little basket on its back in imitation of the mother.

Large families of children are unusual among the aborigines. However many may be born, rarely more than four are allowed to grow up. Five is considered a large number to rear. Twins are as common among them as among Europeans; but as food is occasionally very scarce, and a large family troublesome to move about, it is lawful and customary to destroy the weakest twin child, irrespective of sex. It is usual also to destroy those which are malformed.

Malformations, however, were so rare before the arrival of the white man that no instances could be remembered. When a woman has children too rapidly for the convenience and necessities of the parents, she makes up her mind to let one be killed, and consults with her husband which it is to be. As the strength of a tribe depends more on males than females, the girls are generally sacrificed. The child is put to death and buried, or burned without ceremony ; not, however, by its father or mother, but by relatives. No one wears mourning for it. Sickly children are never killed on account of their bad health, and are allowed to die naturally.

No attention is paid to nævus marks on infants—which, in the aborigines show darker in colour than the surrounding skin—as these marks are attributed by them, not to the spells of enemies, but to frights, falls, or blows sustained by the mother.

Mischievous and thievish children are not personally punished by the individuals whom they may injure, as that would lead to quarrels, but the parents are held responsible ; and, should they refuse redress, they are dealt with according to the laws of the tribe.

Every person speaks the tribal language of the father, and must never mix it with any other. The mother of a child is the only exception to this law, for, in talking to it, she must use its father's language as far as she can, and not her own. At the same time, she speaks to her husband in her own tribal language, and he speaks to her in his ; so that all conversation is carried on between husband and wife in the same way as between an Englishman and a French-woman, each speaking his or her own language. This very remarkable law explains the preservation of so many distinct dialects within so limited a space, even where there are no physical obstacles to ready and frequent communication between the tribes. The only explanation which is given by the aborigines for this law is, that the attempt of one tribe to speak or to intone the language of another is a caricature of it, and is never made except in derision, with the intention of provoking a quarrel. Since the arrival of the Europeans this law has, to a certain extent, been disregarded, and individuals are now to be found who can speak three distinct languages, besides their own, and also very correct English. Yarruum Parpurr Tarneen, the very intelligent chiefess of the Morpor tribe, is an instance of this ; and she states that there are only four languages between Geelong and the South Australian boundary that she does not understand.

CHAPTER XIII.

NAMES OF PERSONS.

UNTIL a child is able to walk it is not distinguished by any individual name, and is called by the general term 'puupuup.' When it learns to walk, the father gives it a name. If the father is dead, the grandfather confers the name; and, failing him, the mother or nearest relative does so. The first child of either sex is called after its father, and the second, if a daughter, after its mother. If requested, the father will name his other children after friends, who call them 'laing,' meaning 'namesake,' and who are ever afterwards kind to them. In return, they address their godfathers by the same term. When children are not thus called after a friend, their names are taken from something in the neighbourhood, such as a swamp, rivulet, waterhole, hill, or animal; or from some peculiarity in the child or in its parents. Girls are sometimes named after flowers.

The name does not necessarily adhere to the individual during life. People sometimes exchange names as a mark of friendship. But as this would lead to confusion if it were done privately, it takes place only at one of the great meetings of the tribes, when the parties are full-grown, in order that every person may be informed of it, and may know that the chiefs and the parents give their consent, without which the exchange would not be permitted. The ceremony commences by the friends of each of the persons ranging themselves in opposite lines, with the principals in the centre facing each other, with firebrands in their hands. The chiefs inquire into the wishes of the parties, proclaim the names, and declare them exchanged for ever; and the principals then hand to each other their fire-sticks, weapons, and all other personal property. A man who wishes thus to express his love for a little boy two or three years old, or a woman who wishes to signify her affection for a little girl, can, with the consent of the parents and the chief, exchange names by tying strips of kangaroo skin round each of their own wrists, and the wrists of the children. These strips must remain till the transfer of rugs, personal property, and fire-sticks takes place at the first great meeting. Women's names are not changed by marriage; and they are always addressed and known by their maiden names, unless they are exchanged publicly.

Personal names are rarely perpetuated, as it is believed that anyone adopting that of a deceased person will not live long. This superstition accounts for the great number of unmeaning names in a tribe. When a dead man or woman is referred to, it is by the general term 'muuruukan '—' dead person ;' but when the time of mourning has expired, they can be spoken of by name, though still with very great unwillingness. If they need to be named by strangers during the period of mourning, it must be in whispers. As a great favour to the writer, references were made by name to deceased relatives ; but this was done with so much reluctance, that in several instances the inquiry had to be abandoned without obtaining the desired information ; and one man would not pronounce his own name because it was the same as that of his deceased brother. Not only is the name of a deceased person forbidden to be mentioned, but the names of all his near relatives are disused during the period of mourning, and they are mentioned only in general terms, as exemplified below. To call them by their own names is considered an insult to the deceased, and frequently leads to fighting and bloodshed.

EXAMPLES.

	Chaap wuurong dialect.	Kuurn kopan noot dialect.
When a man's father dies, the man is called	Palliin	Parrapeetch
When a man's mother dies, the man is called	Palliin	Kokætch
When a woman's father dies, the woman is called	Palliin kuurk	Parrapæheear
When a woman's mother dies, the woman is called	Palliin kuurk	Kokæheear
When a man's brother or sister dies, the man is called	Kæp gnunnæ	Kiiap mekunna
When a woman's brother or sister dies, the woman is called	Kæp gnunna kuurk	Kiiamma kunnaheear
When an uncle on father's side dies his nephew is called	Palliin	Parrapeetch

When an uncle on mother's side dies, his nephew is called	Kurm kurm kuurk	... Kun kun yaa
When an uncle on father's side dies, his niece is called	Palliin kuurk	... Parrapæheear
When an uncle on mother's side dies, his niece is called	Pitchæ kuurk	... Tætuyaar
When a male cousin dies, a male cousin is called ...	Gnullii yuurpeetch	... Parrap tow'will
When a female cousin dies, a female cousin is called ...	Gnullii yuurpee kuurk...	Parrap tow'will heear

A similar law regulates the names of animals and things after which a deceased person had been called. Thus, if a man is called after an animal, or place, or thing, and he dies, the animal, or place, or thing is not mentioned during the time of mourning by any member of the deceased person's tribe, except under another name, because it recalls the memory of the dead.

FOR EXAMPLE :—

The crow, waa, is called narrapart.
The magpie, or piping crow, kirræe, is called paalbaluum.
The common cockatoo, gniiyuuk, is called narrapart.
The black cockatoo, wilann, is called waang.
The grey duck, tuurbarnk, is called kulkuwæær.
The gigantic crane, or native companion, kuuront, is called kuuluur kuyætch.
The eagle, kneeangar, is called tiiro mænk.
The turkey bustard, barrim barrim, is called tillit tilliitsh.
The ringtail opossum, weearn, is called manuungkuurt.
The dasyure, or common native cat, kuppung, is called tulla meealeem.
The dingo, or wild dog, burnang, is called parroætch.
The kangaroo, kuuriin, is called warrakuul.
The carpet, or tiger snake, kuurang, is called killaweetch.
The black snake, mowang, is called kundareetch
Tussock grass, parræt, is called pallingii.
A swamp, yaang, is called warrumpeetch.

NAMES OF MEN.

The following are the names of men, with their meanings :—

Kaawirn kuunawarn   ...   ...   'Hissing swan'
(Chief of the Kirræ wuurong—'blood-lip'—tribe, named after the noise the swans
made when he robbed their nests.)

Wombeet tuulawarn...   ...   ...   'Rotten spear'
(From the old decayed spears his father carried.)

Gnuurnecheean	...	...	Hunting bag
Puunmuttal	...	...	Bite meat
Weerat kuyuut	...	...	Eel spear
Pundeet puulotong	...	...	Dragger out of fat
Teel meetch willa neung	...	...	Untied eel spear
Wittin yuurong	...	...	Strips of skin
Yambeetch	...	...	Swamp weed
Laaweet tarnæ	...	...	You eat my food
Wuromkil wuurong	...	...	Long lip
Purteetch wirrang ween	...	...	Fight with fire-stick
Wol muutang	...	...	Lightwood tree
Gnunnahiniitch	...	...	Bat
Peaalkoæ	...	...	Redgum tree
Wuruum kuurwhin	...	...	Long grass burning
Wuuro killink	...	...	Long waterhole
Nuurtekel wing	...	...	Deaf
Muuroæ wuulok	...	...	Seed of long grass
Tiyeer bariin	...	...	Spear knee
Puunmirng	...	...	Swamp—local name
Puunbat	...	...	Local name
Marrohmuuk	...	...	Swamp—local name
Puulepeetch	...	...	Bald head
Tuulirn beem	...	...	Red head
Naaweetch	...	...	Swamp water
Tumeetch puuruutch	...	...	Calves with large veins
Warrowill	...	...	Swamp—local name
Wombeetch puyuun	...	...	Decayed kangaroo
Wullæ merrii	...	...	Stony

Buundærang	...	...	... Leaf
Mæmamulga	...	...	... Repaired shield
Beeak ...	...	...	... Name of lake
Kurn kuyang	...	...	... Cry of the eel
Mirrenyarmin	...	...	... Not enough
Kon kon talliin	...	...	... Long tongue or boaster

Names of men without meanings :—

Pulornpuul	Meenkilwang
Karinn	Burkamukk
Puulaheuram	Tarrupiitch
Tumbo tumbo	Wuyuum karkorr
Peekum peekum	Tirrawuul
Tullum tullum	Bunkaruuk
Mirrin'gna min	Yuuruung kuyang
Meheaar yuluurn	Yaaheetch
Kaarin	Tuuruumbar
Mambupitt muuluung	Koong
Mirnmalk	Wat pareet parræœ

NAMES OF WOMEN.

Yarruun parpur tarneen	...	...	'Victorious'

(Chiefess of the Morporr tribe, named by her father after defeating his enemies in a great battle.)

Muulapuurn yurong yaar	...	...	Strips of kangaroo skin
Wuuriwuuriit	...	...	... Banksia tree
Warruum ...	...	...	... Bandicoot
Peecharn ...	...	...	... Blossom
Lærpeen tumbuur	...	...	... Singing woman
Bareetch churneen	...	...	... Cut
Poroitchol ...	...	...	... Scrubby place
Fatuurn yinheear	...	...	... Hanging root basket
Karndamaheear	...	...	... Upstanding
Walngeetch winyong	...	...	Ear
Tartuu tarneen	...	...	... Turn round
Meendeaar tuukuung	...	...	Dark body

Parputeen	Full
Yeetpuyeetch kamaruung	Breathless
Marrokeear tung an	Broken teeth
Purtkææræ	Knock dirt off tree
Gnaknii neear	Stutter
Koronn	Feather
Kuulern karrank	Wattle bloom
Peertob	Lake
Piik kuuruuk	Water weed
Tumbuurn	Native daisy
Moyuup	Flower (with edible root)
Nullor	Drosera
Peekirn	Flower of the yam
Mundarnin	Snap with mouth
Muinpa apuurneen	Kneading
Kummorntok	Name of bird
Weeitcho tærinyaar	Playful leaves
Tuppuun	Water lily

Names of women, without their meanings :—

Meen baaburneen	Kuulandarr
Nirræmeetch kuuronong	Buung'guæ
Wiitpurneen	Yatneetch pillæruung
Poatpoteen	Yillin tuupeheaar
Puunameen	Kuumarneen
Luppirnin nullohneung	Kunning juung
Yerrkombeen	Morpræwirngnong
Luupir purneen	Peeka
Yaabuur	

The distinction of gender between these proper names, though not recognizable by the white man, is discerned at once by the aborigines.

Besides proper names, some men are nicknamed after peculiarities in their persons, or habits, such as—

Kuunjeetch	Blind
Kiiam mirng	One eye

Warn mirng	...	...	Squint eye
Pappakupee yanmeetch	...	...	Hopping
Gnuttcheep gnuttcheep	...	...	Cripple leg
Mærng barriin	...	...	Crooked knee
Muulpæn ...	...	...	Leg cut off below knee
Porrgnomæt	...	...	Deformed ankle
Tinnang wuumpmæt	...	...	Club foot
Wuurk gnaato	...	...	Broken arm
Morrdilwuurk	...	...	Arm cut off at shoulder
Morrwhork	...	...	Arm cut off at elbow
Tinning tinning turam	...	...	Stout man

The nicknames of women are distinguished by the feminine affix, such as—

Kuunjee heear	...	...	Blind female
Kiiam minyaar	...	...	One-eyed female
Warn minkgneear	..	...	Squint-eyed female
Pappakupee yanmeheear	...	...	Hopping female
Gnuttcheep gnuttcheep heear ...		...	Cripple leg female
Mæring barring heear	...	...	Crooked knee female
Porrgnomæheear	...	...	Deformed ankle female
Tinnang wuumpmæheear	...	...	Club foot female
Wuurkna heearong ...	...	...	Broken arm female
Morrkilwuurk heear	...	...	Arm cut off at shoulder female
Morrwhork heear	...	...	Arm cut off at elbow female
Tinning tinning turam gneear...		...	Stout female

White people are also named after their peculiarities, or after localities, such as kuurn wirndill, 'little bottle,' from the person carrying a flask of spirits while travelling.

Teeri yeetch beem	...	...	Red head
Pæteritt	...	...	Lapwing

(In consequence of the person having a habit of running like that bird.)

Meheaar kapuung	...	...	Big nose
Wullang ...	...	...	Wide walker
Meheaar talliin	...	...	Loud voice

Tachwirring   ...   . Eat ghost
Kuurpeen mumkilling   ...   ... Live beside waterhole
Konngill   ...   . Doctor
Narrakebeen   ...   . No meaning
Luppertan tullineann   ...   ... Speaker of native language

Dogs are generally named after their owners, and when the latter are addressed the dogs recognize the names, and wag their tails. Other names are—

Wirng an ...   . ' Ear mine '
Peechilakk...   ...   .
Puunmirng...   ...   . Name of swamp
Waameetch cheearmart   ...   ... Swelled chest
Kæræreetch   ...   .
Howlæluya   ...   . Hallelujah
Karlo   ...   . Name of Barrukills dog
Puunmæn ...   . Name of swamp

CHAPTER XIV.

SUPERSTITIONS AND DISEASES.

IN investigating the superstitions of the aborigines, every care has been taken to exclude any superstitious notions which might have been impressed on their minds since they came in contact with the white race; and those from whom information was obtained were fully aware of the necessity of adhering strictly to the beliefs they entertained before they knew of the existence of Europeans.

It was ascertained that they believe in supernatural beings—celestial, infernal, and terrestrial.

The good spirit, Pirnmeheeal, is a gigantic man, living above the clouds; and as he is of a kindly disposition, and harms no one, he is seldom mentioned, but always with respect. His voice, the thunder, is listened to with pleasure, as it does good to man and beast, by bringing rain, and making grass and roots grow for their benefit. But the aborigines say that the missionaries and government protectors have given them a dread of Pirnmeheeal; and they are sorry that the young people, and many of the old, are now afraid of a being who never did any harm to their forefathers.

The bad spirit, Muuruup, sometimes called 'Wambeen neung been-been aa,' 'maker of bad-smelling smoke,' is always spoken of with fear and bated breath, as the author of every misfortune. He visits the earth in the form of lightning, knocking trees to pieces, setting fire to wuurns, and killing people by 'striking them on the back.' At times he assumes the form of a large ugly man, frequenting scrubs and dense thickets; and, although not provided with wings, like the white man's devil, he flits and darts from place to place with the rapidity of lightning, is very mischievous, and hungers for the flesh of children. The natives are not much afraid of Muuruup in the daylight, but have a great dread of him in the dark. They say that he employs the owls to watch and give notice when he may pounce upon any unfortunate straggler from the camp. Hence their hatred of owls, as birds of evil omen. When one of these birds is heard screching or hooting, the children immediately crawl under their grass mats. If children are troublesome at any time, they are hushed by their mother calling out 'kaka muuruup,' 'Come here, devil.' None of the Kuurn kopan noot tribe ever saw the Muuruup, but believe he was once seen by two natives of the Chaap wuurong tribe at Merrang, on the Hopkins River, when that country was first occupied with live stock; and they described him as a huge black man, carrying a great many spears, with a long train of snakes streaming behind him, 'like smoke from a steamboat.'

The Muuruup lives deep under the ground in a place called Ummekulleen, and has under his command a number of inferior spirits, who are permitted to visit the surface of the earth occasionally. No human being has ever returned to tell what kind of place Ummekulleen is. There is a belief, however, that there is nothing but fire there, and that the souls of bad people get neither meat nor drink, and are terribly knocked about by the evil spirits.

A spirit lives in the moon, called Muuruup neung kuurn tarrong'gnat, meaning 'devil in the moon.' Children are sometimes threatened, when they are bad, that this Muuruup will be sent for to take them to the moon.

Of terrestrial spirits there are devils, wraiths, ghosts, and witches, the differences between them being somewhat indefinite.

There are female devils, known by the general term Gnulla gnulla gneear. Buurt kuuruuk is the name of one who takes the form of a black woman 'as tall as a gum tree.' She has for a companion the dark-coloured bandicoot. If this animal be killed and eaten by a native, he is punished by misfortunes and by nightly visitations from Buurt kuuruuk. There is a legend that she carried off a woman from near the mouth of the Hopkins River to her wuurn on the top of the Cape Otway mountains, and compelled her to eat raw opossums for six moons. Various parts of the country are supposed to be haunted by these female devils; but none are so celebrated for their great size as those frequenting the Cape Otway ranges. The aborigines do not believe in any devils belonging to the sea.

Every person over four or five years of age has a spirit or ghost, which, although dormant through life, assumes a visible but undefined form after death; and, for a time, haunts the spot where a corpse is interred or placed in a tree. Although it is considered to be quite harmless, it is regarded with fear. It is said to be seen sitting on the grave or near the body, but it sinks into the ground or disappears if anyone approaches. As the friends of the deceased are very unwilling to go near the place, it is seldom seen and never examined. For its comfort a large fire is kept burning all night near the corpse. The recent custom of providing food for it is derided by the intelligent old aborigines, as ' white fellow's gammon.'

It is a remarkable coincidence with the superstition of the lower orders in Europe, that the aborigines believe every adult has a wraith, or likeness of himself, which is not visible to anyone but himself, and visible to him only before his premature death. If he is to die from the bite of a snake, he sees his wraith in the sun ; but in this case it appears in the form of an emu. If, in the evening, after sunset, a person walking with a friend sees his own likeness—'muuruup man,' and, if a woman, 'muuruup yernan,'—the friend says, 'Something will happen to you, as you have seen your wraith.' This so preys on the mind of the individual that he falls into low spirits, which he tries to relieve by recklessness and carelessness in battle.

After the disposal of the body of a good person, its shade walks about for three days ; and, although it appears to people, it holds no communication with them. Should it be seen and named by anyone during these three days, it instantly disappears. At the expiry of three days it goes off to a beautiful country above the clouds, abounding with kangaroo and other game, where life will be enjoyed for ever. Friends will meet and recognize each other there ; but there will be no marrying, as the bodies have been left on earth. Children under four or five years of age have no souls and no future life. The shades of the wicked wander miserably about the earth for one year after death, frightening people, and then descend to Ummekulleen, never to return. There was a belief current among the aborigines, that the first white men seen by them were the embodied spirits or shades of deceased friends. Whether this belief originated with the tribes of Port Phillip, or was transmitted from the Sydney district, it is now impossible to ascertain ; but there is no doubt that it did exist among the aborigines of Victoria at the time of its first occupation by the white man.

Some of the ideas described above may possibly have originated with the white man, and been transmitted from Sydney by one tribe to another.

On the sea coast, opposite Deen Maar—now, unfortunately, called Julia Percy Island—there is a haunted cave called Tarn wirring, ' road of the spirits,' which, the natives say, forms a passage between the mainland and the island, When anyone dies in the neighbourhood, the body is wrapped in grass and buried ; and if, afterwards, grass is found at the mouth of the cave, it is proof that a good spirit, called Puit puit chepetch, has removed the body and everything belonging to it through the cave to the island, and has conveyed its spirit to the clouds ;

and if a meteor is seen about the same time, it is believed to be fire taken up with it. Should fresh grass be found near the cave, when no recent burial has taken place, it indicates that some one has been murdered, and no person will venture near it till the grass decays or is removed.

Witches appear always in the form of an old woman, and are called kuin'gnat yambateetch, meaning 'solitary,' or 'wandering by themselves.' No one knows where they come from or where they go to; and they are seldom seen unless at great meetings. They are dressed in an old ragged kangaroo skin rug, sewn together with rushes, and carry on their backs a worn-out basket containing various charms, and bits of the flesh of opossums and bandicoots. They belong to no tribe, and have no friends; and, as everyone runs away on their approach, they neither speak to anyone nor are spoken to. They are considered harmless.

There is a belief in prognostication of dreams. If a man dreams he will find a swan's nest in some particular spot, he visits the place with the expectation of finding it. If he dreams that something serious happens to him, as, for example, that he is mortally wounded in battle, and if, afterwards, he is wounded, he says, 'I knew that this would take place, for I dreamt it;' and so deeply is he impressed with the idea of approaching death, that he rushes wildly into the fight. If a man is told by a friend that he had a bad dream about him, this will make him very miserable and ill for a long time. If a dog shows agitation while asleep, that is a sign that he dreams of hunting kangaroos, and that he will kill one next day; and so confident is his master in the dog's dream, that he will go out with him the next day to help him.

The aborigines have superstitious ideas connected with certain animals. The grey bandicoot belongs to the women, and is killed and eaten by them, but not by the men or children. Boys are not allowed to eat any female quadruped. When they are caught eating a female opossum, they are punished by their parents, as it makes them peevish and discontented. The common bat belongs to the men, who protect it against injury, even to the half-killing of their wives for its sake. The fern owl, or large goatsucker, belongs to the women, and, although a bird of evil omen, creating terror at night by its cry, it is jealously protected by them. If a man kills one, they are as much enraged as if it was one of their children, and will strike him with their long poles. Children are severely punished if they kill and eat the magpie lark, for it makes their hair prematurely white. The shepherd's companion belongs to both men and women, and is never killed, because it attacks snakes, and gives warning of their approach. The pelican and its eggs are never eaten, but only because they are too strongly flavoured and fishy.

Kokok, the powerful owl, is a bird of evil omen, smells death in the camp, and visits the neighbourhood of a dying person, calling 'Kokok-kokok.' It is therefore hated by men, women, and children. It is of a fierce disposition, vigorously attacking anyone who approaches its nest; and, as it has a strong spur on the carpal joint of the wing, a blow from it is not pleasant. It is also disliked because it kills opossums, flying squirrels, and small animals, the food of the natives. The kokok builds its nest of reeds and sedges in the blackwood tree, and lays three eggs, which are sought after and eaten.

A porcupine ant-eater coming near a dwelling is a sign that someone in it will die before long. The cries of the banksian and white cockatoos announce the approach of friends. An itchy nose indicates a visit from a friend.

If a person imagines that he sees the planet Venus set twice in one night, it warns him of his death before morning. With this exception the aborigines do not predict events from the position of the stars.

The cause of an echo is not understood, but it is supposed to be something mysterious mocking the speaker.

The mantis belongs to the men, and no one dare kill it. Women are not permitted to eat the flesh or eggs of the gigantic crane, or of the emu, till they are old and greyheaded. If a baby is taken near the dead body of a gigantic crane, it is certain to break out in sores.

Pork is generally rejected by the natives because they believe it produces skin disease; but, as swine were unknown before the arrival of the white men, the idea of their flesh being unclean and unhealthy must have been impressed on them by the first settlers, and probably as a means of protecting from depredation their pigs, which were always allowed to run at large.

Strange spears and weapons are reluctantly touched, as it is believed they communicate sickness, and might cause death. It was with difficulty that some of the aborigines could be prevailed upon to take hold of spears, arrows, and clubs from the Society Islands. When the spear or weapon of an enemy has killed a friend, it is always burnt by the relatives of the deceased; but those captured in battle are kept, and used by the conquerors.

Fire caused by lightning is called 'Pillætuung murndall gnat'—'supernatural fire belonging to thunder'—and is shunned, because there is a belief that the lightning hangs about the spot, and would kill anyone going near it. However much the natives may be in want of a firestick in travelling through the bush, they will not take a light from a strange fire unless they observe the footprints of human beings near it, indicating that it has been kindled by man. Neither will they take a light from a funeral pyre.

There is a tradition that fire, such as could be safely used, belonged exclusively to the crows inhabiting the Grampian Mountains; and, as these crows considered it of great value, they would not allow any other animal to get a light. However, a little bird called Yuuloin keear—'fire-tail wren'—observing the crows amusing themselves by throwing firesticks about, picked up one, and flew away with it. A hawk called Tarrakukk took the firestick from the wren, and set the whole country on fire. From that time there have always been fires from which lights could be obtained.

There is a superstition, called Wuurong, connected with the tracking and killing of kangaroos. In hot weather a doctor, or other person possessed of supernatural powers, looks for the footprints of a large kangaroo. On finding them he follows them up, putting hot embers on them, and continues the quest for two days, or until he tracks it to a water-hole, where he spears it. He then presents portions of the body to his nearest neighbours, and takes the head home to his own wuurn. There seems to be no special meaning attached to this custom.

The aborigines believe that if an enemy get possession of anything that has belonged to them—even such things as bones of animals which they have eaten, broken weapons, feathers, portions of dress, pieces of skin, or refuse of any kind—he can employ it as a charm to produce illness in the person to whom they belonged. They are, therefore, very careful to burn up all rubbish or uncleanness before leaving a camping-place. Should anything belonging to an unfriendly tribe be found at any time, it is given to the chief, who preserves it as a means of injuring the enemy. This wuulon, as it is called, is lent to any one of the tribe who wishes to vent his spite against any one belonging to the unfriendly tribe. When used as a charm, the wuulon is rubbed over with emu fat mixed with red clay, and tied to the point of a spear-thrower, which is stuck upright in the ground before the camp fire. The company sit round watching it, but at such a distance that their shadows cannot fall on it. They keep chanting imprecations on the enemy till the spear-thrower, as they say, turns round and falls down in the direction of the tribe the wuulon belongs to. Hot ashes are then thrown in the same direction, with hissing and curses, and wishes that disease and misfortune may overtake their enemy.

As a mark of affection, locks of hair are exchanged by friends, and are worn round the neck, tied to the necklace. Should one of these be lost, most diligent search is made for it, as it is considered very unlucky to lose or give away a keepsake. If it be not found, the person who holds possession of the other lock of hair is asked to undo the exchange by returning it. If this were not done, the loser of the lock would die. So strong is this belief, that people in such circumstances often fall into bad health, and sometimes actually die.

The aborigines had among them sorcerers and doctors, whom they believed to possess supernatural powers. In the Kolor tribe there was a sorceress well known in the Western district under the name of White Lady, who was the widow of the chief, and whose supernatural influence was much dreaded by all. As an emblem of her power, she had a long staff resembling a vaulting pole, made of very heavy wood, and painted red. This pole, which she said was given to her by the spirits, was carried before her by a 'strong man' when she visited her friends or attended a meeting. On occasions of ceremony, it was dressed up with feathers of various colours, and surmounted by a bunch of the webs of the wing feathers of the white cockatoo. The pole-bearer, whose name was Weereen Kuuneetch, acted also as her servant. After ushering her to the meeting, he hid the pole at a short distance from the camp, while singing and amusements were going on, as it was too sacred to be exposed to common inspection. At bedtime he brought it into the circle by her direction, and held it upright before the fire, as a signal of retirement for the night. At her death the pole was carried off by the spirits, and no one has seen it since.

In order to support her pretensions to supernatural power, she would, on some moonlight night, leave the camp with an empty bag made of netted bark cord, and return with it full of snakes. These she said were spirits. No one, therefore, dare go near them or look at them. She described one as pure white, another black; the rest were young ones. She emptied the bag near the fire and made them crawl around it, by pointing with a long stick, and speaking to them. On another occasion, having left the camp for awhile on a moonlight night, she pretended, on her return, that she had been to the moon; and, in proof of her visit, produced a tail of a lunar kangaroo—an old fur boa which she had got from the whites. Besides this boa she had a number of charms round her neck, and, in her bag portions of the bones of animals, beads, pieces of crockery, bits of brass and iron, and strangely-shaped stones, each having its particular spell, and capable of producing good or evil, as suited her interests. This clever old witch was very much annoyed when any white person scrutinized and exposed the contents of her bag; but the natives, though the more sensible of them were not sorry to see her powers and mysterious charms ridiculed, were too much afraid of her to smile, or join in any mirth at her expense.

White Lady was an honorary member of the teetotal society, and carried a temperance badge suspended from her neck, which she said told her 'not to drink spirits.' When an opportunity occurred, however, to get a drop of rum, she took off the badge and hid it in the ground, and, when sober, put it on again. She also had a cross suspended in the same way, which she said 'yabbered,' 'do not tell lies,' 'do not kill anybody,' 'do not steal potatoes;' but, when hunger prompted a raid on a potato field, the cross was temporarily buried in like manner. This cunning woman possessed such power over the minds of her tribe that anything she fancied was at once given to her. When she died, at Kangatong, her death was followed by the usual wailing and scratching of faces amongst her friends during the whole night; but, as she had been such a terror to her tribe on account of her reputed powers for evil, there was more form than sincerity in their professions of grief. The following day her body and all her property, consisting of clothing, opossum rug, ornaments and spells, were placed on a bier made of saplings, and silently carried off by the friends and relatives, and interred in a grave two feet deep. Her head, however, and portions of the legs and arms were buried in a cave near Mount Kolor, where she was born.

Every tribe has its doctor, in whose skill great confidence is reposed; and not without reason, for he generally prescribes sensible remedies. When these fail, he has recourse to supernatural means and artifices of various kinds.

The following remedies are those most commonly used. In cases of pain in one spot the skin is scarified, and the blood allowed to flow freely. When the pain is general, and arises from severe cold or rheumatism, a vapour bath is produced by kindling a fire in a hole in the ground, covering it with green leaves, and pouring water on them. The sick person is placed over this, and covered with an opossum rug, and steamed till profuse perspiration takes place. He is then rubbed dry with hot ashes, and ordered to keep warm. Another cure for rheumatism is an infusion of the bark of the blackwood tree, which is first roasted, and then infused while hot. The affected part is bathed with the hot infusion, and bandaged with a cord spun from the fur of the flying squirrel, or ringtail opossum, with a piece of opossum rug as a covering. Severe headaches of long continuance, requiring strong remedies, are cured by burning off the hair and blistering the skin of the head. Earaches are treated by pouring water on hot stones placed in a hole in the ground, and holding the ear over the steam. For pains in the joints, fresh skins of eels are wrapped round the place, flesh side inwards. The same cure is very common in Scotland for a sprained wrist. Sow thistles are eaten raw to soothe pain and induce sleep. The gum of the eucalyptus, or common white gum tree, is a cure for toothache. It is stuffed into the hollow of the tooth. Teeth are never extracted unless they are loose enough to be removed by the finger and thumb. For indigestion, the small roots of the narrow-leafed gum tree, or the bark of the acacia, are infused in hot water, and the liquor drunk as a tonic. When a child gorges itself with food, its mother gathers yellow leeches from underneath dry logs, and bruises them up along with the roasted liver of kangaroo, and sow thistles, and compels it to eat the mess, which is called kallup kallup. It acts as a strong emetic. Adults, when ill from overfeeding, are sometimes induced to take this dose, in ignorance of its composition ; and it affects them strongly, but beneficially. Wood ashes are applied to wounds and cuts. Burns are covered with fat. Running sores which are difficult to heal, are rubbed with the fat of the powerful owl, which dries them up quickly. The fat of large grubs is used for anointing the skin of delicate children. Women unable to nourish their newly-born infants have their breasts bathed with lime-water, which is made by burning the shells of fresh-water mussels and dissolving them in water. Every married woman carries several shells in her basket, which are commonly used as spoons.

If diseases will not yield to these ordinary remedies, the doctor invokes the aid of spirits. Visiting his patient in the evening, and finding that the case is beyond the reach of the ordinary remedies, the doctor goes up to the clouds after dark, and brings down the celebrated spirit, 'Wirtin Wirtin Jaawan,' who is said to be the mate of the 'good spirit, pringheeal.' When he is expected to arrive, the women and children are sent away from the camp, and the men sit in a circle of fifty yards in diameter, with a banksia tree in the centre. The doctor and spirit alight on the top of the tree, and jump to the ground 'with a thud like a kangaroo.' The spirit gives his name ; and, after the doctor has felt all over the body of his patient, they both go up to the clouds again. It is supposed that the patient must get well. Occasionally the doctor brings down with him the spirit of the sick man, in the form of a doll wrapped in an opossum rug. This doll produces a moaning noise. The sick person is placed sitting in the middle of a circle of friends, supported behind by one of them, and the doctor presses the rug containing the doll to the patient's chest for some minutes, and then departs.

If the sick person is a chief or a chief's wife, or of superior rank, and the doctor, on visiting him at sunset, finds it beyond his power to remove the disease in the usual way, he goes up to the clouds after dark, and fetches down ten spirits. These he places at a distance of fifty yards from the sick person. He then has a conversation with his patient, and, after kneading him all over to ascertain the seat of the disease, he informs the spirits, and they tell him what to do. Having received his instructions, he warms his right hand at the fire and rubs it over the affected spot. The spirits then depart, with a croaking noise 'like the cry of the heron.' The doctor repeats the rubbing for three nights, and then, telling the patient he will soon be well, he departs for his home, with his followers. If, at the first meeting thereafter, his patient is cured, the doctor receives presents of food, rugs, and weapons; but if he dies the doctor gets nothing.

Spirits were very plentiful before the arrival of the white man. A spring of fine water near Mount Kolor, called Lurtpii, was their favourite resort, and they were to be found there at all times by the doctor, who alone had the power to make them appear. He summoned them, however, only in summer time, while the tribes were having their meetings and amusements. The men are not much afraid of these spirits in the daytime, but the women and children are terrified at them, and nobody runs the risk of seeing them after sunset.

Sometimes, when a korroboræ has ended, the doctor of the tribe calls on three or four female spirits to come down from the clouds and dance round the fire; and, when accosted, each gives its name as that of a deceased member of the tribe. Any person may look at them, but no one except the doctor can speak to them, and nobody dares to run away.

When the white men came to Victoria, there was one doctor of great celebrity in the Western District, Tuurap Warneen, chief of the Mount Kolor tribe. So celebrated was he for his supernatural powers, and for the cure of diseases, that people of various tribes came from great distances to consult him. He could speak many dialects. At korroboræs and great meetings he was distinguished from the common people by having his face painted red, with white streaks under the eyes, and his brow-band adorned with a quill feather of the turkey bustard, or with the crest of a white cockatoo. Tuurap Warneen was unfortunately shot by the manager of a station near Mount Kolor; and his death caused much grief to all the tribes far and near.

On one occasion, when the tribe had a great meeting at a lake called ' Tarræ Yarr,' to the north of Mount Kolor, doubts were expressed as to his power to summon spirits, and make them appear at mid-day. To show he could do this, he went up to the clouds and brought down a gnulla gnulla gneear, in form of an old woman, enveloped in an opossum rug, tied round her waist with a rope of rushes. In order to thoroughly frighten the people, he held her tethered with a grass rope like a wild beast, as though to prevent her chasing and hurting them. He did not allow her to go nearer to the wuurns than about fifty yards. After exhibiting her for half an hour, he led her off. Everyone was intensely terrified at the gnulla gnulla gneear, and the doctor found her a profitable invention, as he received numerous presents of weapons, rugs, and food to keep her away. When he was in want of a fresh supply, he could always command it by a threat of another visit from the gnulla gnulla gneear.

The doctor pretends to cure pains of every description, and makes his patients believe—not unwillingly—that he extracts foreign substances from the body by sucking the sore places. He actually spits out bits of bone, which he had previously concealed in his mouth. He also, by rubbing, apparently makes stones jump out from the affected part.

To cure toothache, a cape made of the basket rush is worn over the shoulders and round the neck, and is laid aside when the pain is gone—its name is weearmeetch. Another remedy is the application of a heated spear-thrower to the cheek. The spear-thrower is then cast away, and the toothache goes with it in the form of a black stone, about the size of a walnut, called karriitch. Stones of this kind are found in the old mounds on the banks of the Mount Emu Creek, near Darlington. The natives believe that when these stones are thrown into the stream at a distance from their residence, they will return to the place where they were found; and as they are considered an infallible remedy for toothache, they are carefully preserved. They are also employed to make an enemy ill, and are thrown in the direction of the offending tribe, with a request to punish it with toothache. If, next day, the stones are found where originally picked up, it is believed that they have fulfilled their mission. Not far from the spot where these stones are plentiful, there is a clump of trees called karriitch —meaning toothache—and the natives of the locality warn their friends never to go near it, for if they do they will be sure to get toothache. Stones of a similar description are found in the sand hills on the sea coast, and are put into a long bag made of rushes, which is fastened round the cheek. The doctor always carries these stones in his wallet, and lends them to sick people without fee or reward.

Sunstroke is not common, although the natives never wear any head-dress ; but the effect of the sun's rays are known to be injurious to the brain, and to cause death. The rays of the moon are also believed to be hurtful; and, when the moon is looked at too long by any person, ' the devil in it makes them whirl round, and tumble helplessly into the fire.'

The aborigines were not subject, in former times, to pulmonary complaints, though they were very much exposed to the weather. At all seasons of the year the men, while travelling in a strange country, slept among bushes or long grass, often quite destitute of clothing. This was necessary to prevent surprise by enemies, who would be attracted by the smoke of a fire. Since the introduction of European clothing, however, they are very liable to affections of the lungs. The reason for this seems to be that, however much they may clothe and perspire during the daytime, they still very generally keep up the custom of throwing off their clothing when they go to sleep, with the exception of a kangaroo skin or an opossum rug in cold nights, or a little dry grass as a covering in hot weather.

The aborigines have been visited on several occasions by epidemics, which were very fatal. The first occasion which the natives remember was about the year 1830, and the last in 1847. The very small remnant of old aborigines now alive who escaped the first of these epidemics describe it as an irruptive fever resembling small-pox. They called it Meen warann—' chopped root.' They have still a very vivid recollection of its ravages, and of the great numbers cut off by it in the Western District. In remembrance of it they still chant a wail called Mallæ mallææ, which was composed in New South Wales, where the disease first broke out, and is known to all the tribes between Sydney, Melbourne, and Adelaide. The malady spread with rapidity from tribe to tribe, in consequence of the infection being carried by the messengers who were sent forward to communicate the sad news of its ravages. It was considered to be so infectious and deadly, that when anyone sickened and refused food, and when pustules appeared on the body, the tribal doctor gave them up at once, and the friends deserted them, leaving beside them in the wuurn a vessel of water to drink. When they died, the body was allowed to decay where it was ; and, long afterwards, when all infection was supposed to be gone, and nothing left but bones, some of the relatives returned, and burned the wuurn and the remains. If a mother was affected by the disease, her child was immediately removed and given to a female relative to rear, while the mother was left to die. The aborigines say that the Meen warann came from the west in form of a dense mist; and that the chief places of mortality were round the Moyne Lagoon, and on the sand hummocks to the east of Port Fairy.

At the last of these visitations, also, great numbers died near the sea coast, and were buried in the hummocks at Mill's Reef, two miles east of Port Fairy. The skeletons were exposed some years ago by the drifting of the sand, and were found to be buried in pairs. This proves that the deaths were not then considered to be caused by any contagious disease, else the relatives would have abandoned the bodies, and only returned to burn the bones. It may be here said that there was a considerable slaughter of the natives at the same place by the white men, and the natives say that those who had escaped returned after some short time and buried their dead; but they did not bury these in pairs. The writer saw, about the year 1844, an aboriginal of the Hopkins River tribe as thoroughly marked with the small-pox as ever he saw a white man.

For scabies the natives have no cure, and they treat an infected person as though he had the leprosy. They will not touch him; and, although they supply him with food and water, they remove their wuurns to a distance, for fear of infection. On the death of the person—for the natives say that they do die of it—the body and everything near it is burned.

Scrofula is uncommon, and traces of it are seldom observable on their persons.

Cases of insanity are very rarely met with, but the aborigines believe that there is more of it since the use of intoxicating liquors was introduced, and especially since they began to disregard their laws of consanguinity in marriage. When a case of insanity occurs, a consultation is held among the relatives; and, as they have a very great dread of mad people, the afflicted person is put to death.

Children born with any deformity or defect attributable to close consanguinity, and likely to render them an encumbrance to their parents in their wanderings about the country, are destroyed. In an instance of two dumb children, which was attributed to this cause, the tribes would have put them to death but for the British law.

CHAPTER XV.

DEATH AND BURIAL.

DYING persons, especially those dying from old age, generally express an earnest desire to be taken to their birthplace, that they may die and be buried there. If possible, these wishes are always complied with by the relatives and friends. Parents will point out the spot where they were born, so that when they become old and infirm their children may know where they wish their bodies to be disposed of.

When old people become infirm, and unable to accompany the tribe in its wanderings, it is lawful and customary to kill them. The reasons for this are— that they are a burden to the tribe, and, should any sudden attack be made by an enemy, they are the most liable to be captured, when they would probably be tortured and put to a lingering death. When it has been decided to kill an aged member of the tribe, the relatives depute one of their number to carry out the decision. The victim is strangled with a grass rope, and the body, when cold, is burned in a large fire kindled in the neighbourhood. All his property is burned with him except rugs, weapons, and implements. In this cremation the sons and daughters and near relatives take part; and two or three friends collect the necessary firewood and attend to the fire. This custom is recognized as a necessity. There is, therefore, no concealment practised with regard to it. Very often the poor creatures intended to be strangled cry and beg for delay when they see preparations made for their death, but all in vain. The resolution is always carried out.

Suicide is uncommon; but if a native wishes to die, and cannot get any one to kill him, he will sometimes put himself in the way of a venomous snake, that he may be bitten by it. An instance is given of a determination to commit suicide. A man having killed his wife while he was intoxicated, was so sorry, on discovering what he had done, that he besought the tribe to kill him. As he was a general favourite, no one would do it. He resolved, therefore, to starve himself to death on the grave of his deceased wife. His friends, seeing his determination, at last sent for the tribal executioner, Pundeet Puulotong, who pushed a spear through him, and the body was burned.

Natural deaths are generally—but not always—attributed to the malevolence and the spells of an enemy belonging to another tribe.

When a person of common rank dies under ordinary circumstances, and without an enemy being blamed, the body is immediately bound, with the knees upon the chest, and tied up with an acacia bark cord in an opossum rug. Next day it is put between two sheets of bark, as in a coffin, and buried in a grave about two feet deep, with the head towards the rising sun. All the ornaments, weapons, and property of the deceased are buried with him. Stone axes are excepted, as being too valuable to be thus disposed of, and are inherited by the next of kin. If there is no time to dig a grave—which occasionally happens in hot weather— or if the ground is too hard, the body is placed on a bier and removed by two men to a distance of a mile or two. There the relatives prepare a funeral pyre, on which the body is laid, with the head to the east. All the effects belonging to the deceased are laid beside the body, with the exception of stone axes. Two male relatives set fire to the pyre, and remain to attend to it till the body is consumed. Next morning, if any bones remain, they are completely pulverized and scattered about. When a married woman dies, and her body is burned, the husband puts her pounded calcined bones into a little opossum-skin bag, which he carries suspended in front of his chest until he marries again, or till the bag is worn out, when it is burned.

When two persons die in a wuurn at the same time, if they are brothers or sisters, they are interred close together in separate graves. If they are not so related, one of the bodies is tied with the knees to the face, and buried with the head towards the rising sun, in a shallow hole, or in a deserted mound; the other is put up in a tree till nothing remains but skin and bones, when it is taken down and burned.

The bodies of children between the ages of four and seven years are wrapped in an opossum rug, and put in a sheet of bark rolled up into a tube. This is pushed up into a hollow tree till the remains are quite dry, when they are taken down and burned. The bodies of children under four years of age, who have died a natural death, are kept a day and a night, and are then interred or burned without any ceremony. Infants who have been put to death by their parents, in accordance with the customs of the tribe, are burned without ceremony.

Under ordinary circumstances a corpse is kept in the wuurn one night; in very hot weather it is kept only a few hours; and, immediately on its removal, a large fire is kindled on the spot, and the wuurn and all the materials connected with it are burned. Even the grass and the leaves, if dry enough, are carefully gathered and consumed.

Before the minds of the aborigines were poisoned by the superstitions of the white people, they had not the slightest dread of the dead body of a friend, nor had they any repugnance to remain beside it. Indeed, it often occurred that, while awaiting the arrival of friends from a distance, they kept watch constantly for six days beside the corpse, and in the same wuurn; by turns sleeping and wailing, and protecting the body from the flies by green boughs of trees. They have their own superstition, however, connected with this watching; for they believe that should the corpse open its eyes and stare at any one, that person will not live long.

The approaching death of a chief causes great excitement. Messengers are sent to inform the neighbouring tribes, and all his relatives and friends come and sit around him till he expires. They then commence their mourning. They enumerate the good qualities of the deceased, and wail and lacerate their foreheads. Messengers are sent, with their heads and faces covered with white clay, to inform the tribes of his death, and to call them to attend his funeral obsequies.

Immediately after his death the bones of the lower part of the leg and of the fore-arm are extracted, cleaned with a flint knife, and placed in a basket; the body is tied with a bark cord, with the knees to the face, and wrapped in an opossum rug. It is then laid in a wuurn filled with smoke, and constantly watched by friends with green boughs to keep the flies away.

When all the mourners, with their faces and heads covered with white clay, have arrived, the body is laid on a bier formed of saplings and branches, and is placed on a stage in the fork of a tree, high enough from the ground to be out of the reach of wild dogs. Everyone then departs to his own home. The adult relatives and friends of the deceased visit the spot every few days, and weep in silence. No children accompany them, as 'they are frightened.'

At the expiry of one moon, the relatives and the members of his own and the neighbouring tribes come to burn the remains. The body is removed from the tree. Each chief, assisted by two of his men, helps to carry it, and to place it on the funeral pyre; while the relatives of the deceased sit in a semicircle to windward of the pyre, and each tribe by itself behind them. The fire is lighted and kept together by several men of the tribe, who remain till the body is consumed, and till the ashes are sufficiently cool to allow the fragments of small bones to be gathered. These are then pounded up with a piece of wood, and put into the small bag prepared for them. The widow of the deceased chief, by first marriage, wears the bag of calcined bones suspended from her neck, and she also gets the lower bones of the right arm, which she cleans and wraps in an opossum skin. This she puts in a long basket made of rushes, and ornamented with kangaroo teeth, emu feathers, cockatoos' crest feathers, red paint, and a lock of hair of the deceased. These relics she carries for two years, and keeps them under cover, with great care. She cannot marry while she carries these. Should she resolve to be married before the two years are out, she delivers the basket and bones to her deceased husband's next widow, or widows, in succession; failing them, to his mother; but should she also be dead, she gives them to his mother's sister, if she has a family; or, lastly, to his eldest daughter, if she is married and has a family. If the deceased has left no such relatives, the widow ultimately buries the bones in a deserted mound and burns the basket.

The eldest sister of the deceased chief gets the lower bones of the left arm, and his aunts get the lower bones of the legs, which are treated in the same way. Failing sisters and aunts, the nearest female relatives, to the degree of first cousins, take their place. The only reason one can assign for the observance of this custom is to induce the relatives of chiefs to keep them alive as long as possible; for the task of carrying dead men's bones for two years cannot be an agreeable one.

The body of a chiefess is treated like that of a chief, and the bones are carried about in a basket in the same way. When the body is burned, at the termination of one moon, if the deceased was greatly beloved by her husband, he gathers the calcined bones, pounds and puts them into a small bag made of opossum skin, which he wears suspended in front of his chest for twelve moons. They are then buried. Until these relics of his wife are buried he cannot marry again. The bodies of the adult sons and daughters of chiefs are disposed of in like fashion, and their bones carried about for the same period by their mother, and other relatives in succession.

If a chief dies of disease which is attributed to the spell of an enemy, his body is put up in a tree and watched all night by a dozen or more of his friends, who conceal themselves behind a log near the body. One of them in a low tone of voice calls on the spirits to appear. Sparks like "lighted matches" then come out of the ground, followed by several spirits. The most conspicuous of these spirits represents the person who bewitched the deceased. They then disappear for ever. Some time ago an aboriginal man named Buckley was found dead near Camperdown: his body was put up in a tree and watched. The aborigines declared that the spirits came, but nothing was done to avenge his death.

A widower mourns for his wife for three moons. Every second night he wails and recounts her good qualities, and lacerates his forehead with his nails till the blood flows down his cheeks, and he covers his head and face with white clay. He must continue to mourn and wear the white clay for other nine moons, unless he shall succeed in taking a human life in revenge for her death. If he cease wearing the clay before the expiry of three moons without taking a life, his deceased wife's relatives say 'he has told a lie,' and they will attempt to kill him. If the woman left a child, it is taken from its father and given to its grandmother or grandfather to rear; but if its father succeeds in taking a life, he has a right to take it back. When the husband has had a great affection for his wife, and is anxious to give expression to his grief, he burns himself across the waist in three lines with a red-hot piece of bark.

A widow mourns for her husband for twelve moons. She cuts her hair quite close, and burns her thighs with hot ashes pressed down on them with a piece of bark, till she screams with agony. Every second night she wails and recounts his good qualities, and lacerates her forehead till the blood flows down her cheeks. At the same time she covers her head and face with white clay. This she must do for three moons, on pain of death. The white clay is worn for twelve moons. Sometimes, towards the end of the period of mourning, one or two stripes of pale brown are painted across the nose and under the eyes, and near the end of the time the colour is changed to red.

For the same period, and in like manner, adults mourn for a father or mother, and parents mourn for their children if over three moons old. Children are not allowed to paint their heads and faces, but are obliged to show their grief by lacerating their brows and crying. While parents are mourning for their children, they live in a separate wuurn away from their friends. In their lamentations and wailings for the dead, the aborigines always enumerate all the good qualities of the deceased; and they appear to mourn sincerely.

The relatives—as far as cousins—of a deceased chief must mourn for him for twelve moons. The other members of the tribe must also mourn for the same period; but if an enemy has been blamed for the death, and they succeed in killing a man of another—but not a contiguous—tribe, they at once remove the clay and paint from their heads and faces, and their mourning is ended. It is the same with a deceased chiefess; but the mourning for her lasts only six moons, and the person to be killed for her must be a woman.

The widow of a chief can return to her own tribe, but she cannot take her children with her, as they belong to the tribe of their father. If they are left with it by their mother, their nearest relatives are obliged to support and take care of them.

After the dead are finally disposed of, no amusements are permitted among the relatives of the deceased for two or three days; and if any levity is observed among them by the next of kin, he is entitled to take the life of one of them. Even hunting for food is not allowed until the brother or nearest male relative grants permission.

A very strange and revolting custom is practised in connection with the disposal of the bodies of those who have lost their lives by violence; and this custom has given rise to the idea that the aborigines are cannibals.

There is not the slightest doubt that the eating of human flesh is practised by the aborigines, but only as a mark of affectionate respect, in solemn service of mourning for the dead. The flesh of enemies is never eaten, nor of members of other tribes. The bodies of relatives of either sex, who have lost their lives by violence, are alone partaken of; and even then only if the body is not mangled, or unhealthy, or in poor condition, or in a putrid state. The boy is divided among the adult relatives—with the exception of nursing or pregnant women—and the flesh of every part is roasted and eaten but the vitals and intestines, which are burned with the bones. If the body be much contused, or if it have been pierced by more than three spears, it is considered too much mangled to be eaten. The body of a woman who has had children is not eaten. When a child over four or five years of age is killed accidentally, or by one spear wound only, all the relatives eat of it except the brothers and sisters. The flesh of a healthy, fat, young woman, is considered the best; and the palms of the hands are considered the most delicate portions.

On remarking to the aborigines that the eating of the whole of the flesh of a dead body by the relatives had the appearance of their making a meal of it, they said that an ordinary-sized body afforded to each of numerous adult relatives only a mere tasting; and that it was eaten with no desire to gratify or appease the appetite, but only as a symbol of respect and regret for the dead.

CHAPTER XVI.

AVENGING OF DEATH.

A DYING person, who believes that sorcery and incantations are the cause of his illness, intimates to his friends the number of persons in the suspected tribe whom they are to kill. Sometimes the individual who is believed to be the cause of his illness is named by the dying person.

When the offending tribe is not otherwise revealed, the question is decided, after the body has been put up into the tree, by watching the course taken by the first maggot which drops from the body and crawls over the clean-swept ground underneath. If the body has been buried, the surface of the grave is swept and smoothed carefully; then the first ant which crosses it indicates the direction of the tribe which caused the death of the deceased. If possible, one of the members of that tribe must be killed.

A consultation takes place, and when an individual is fixed upon as the cause of the death, he receives warning that his life will be taken. If he escapes for two moons, he is free. Immediately after the warning, a small party of the male friends and relatives of the deceased prepare themselves by eating sparingly for two or three days, and getting together, each for himself, a supply of cooked food. When ready to start, they paint and disguise themselves, that they may not be recognized by the friends of the person whom they intend to kill. They proceed, well armed, by night to the vicinity of the residence occupied by their intended victim. It is difficult to surprise a camp, owing to the watchfulness and ferocity of the dogs belonging to it. The attacking party, therefore, form a wide circle, and gradually close round the wuurn, guiding each other by uttering cries in imitation of nocturnal animals. At the dawn of day, which is the time of the deepest sleep with the aborigines, and when it is sufficiently light to distinguish the person they wish to kill, they rush on their victim, drag him out of his bed, and spear him without the slightest resistance from himself or his friends, who, paralyzed with terror, lie perfectly still. After the departure of the attacking party, the friends cut up the body and burn it. No reason is given for this custom.

When the person who has been named by the deceased, and who has been warned of his intended fate, seeks safety by keeping away from his tribe, his enemies search for him for two moons; and, as he must hunt for food, he is sometimes discovered. When his enemies see him, they all keep out of sight except one man, who approaches him in a friendly way, and, in course of conversation, directs his attention to something up a tree, or in the distance. Being off his guard, he is suddenly knocked down. The others, who have been watching, immediately rush on their victim, catch him by the throat, throw him on his face, and hold him down, while one cuts open his back with a sharp flint knife, and pulls out the kidney fat, afterwards stuffing the hole with a tuft of grass. A piece of the fat is rolled up in grass and thrown over the shoulder of the operator, who then seats the man against a tree with a burning stick in his hand, and, retiring backwards with his eyes fixed on him, picks up the fat, which he wraps in opossum skin and carries away. This kidney fat is afterwards presented to his chief, who fixes it on his spear-thrower, as a charm to ensure his spear going straight and fatally. After a while the wounded man walks home, with the grass still in the wound, and, as his case is hopeless, no effort is made to remove it, and nothing is done for him. He walks about for a day or two, and eats his food as if nothing had happened, but soon dies.

Sometimes the enemy is killed by strangling. He is watched by three or four men, who are provided with a tough rope, made of the inner bark of the stringybark tree. A running noose is made on the rope; they throw the noose over his head, and pull—one man at each end of the rope—till he is choked.

Intending murderers always disguise themselves with coloured clay; their victim cannot, therefore, easily recognize them. But as, if he do not die immediately, he is expected to name his murderers, he often fixes on the wrong persons. When these are killed in retaliation, a feud is begun; and thus there is kept up a constant destruction of life. If the attack upon the supposed spell-thrower should take place near a camp, and he should be killed, his murderer is at once chased by every able-bodied man present, and, if caught, is put to death on the spot. Every pursuer thrusts four spears into his body, and leaves them there. His friends, who have been watching the result at a distance, wait till the pursuers go away, and then burn the body and all the spears which were thrust into it, and which are sometimes so numerous as to be likened to 'spines in a porcupine.' The body of the supposed spell-thrower is removed to the camp, to be eaten according to the custom described in the previous chapter.

This ends the feud, as life has been taken for life; but if the murderer should escape, and should be known to the friends of the deceased, he gets notice to appear and undergo the ordeal of spear-throwing at the first great meeting of the tribes.

If he pay no attention to the summons, two 'strong, active men,' called Pææt pææts, accompanied by some friends, are ordered by the chief to visit the camp where he is supposed to be concealed, and to arrest him. They approach the camp about bedtime, and halt at a short distance from it. One of the Pææt pææts goes to one side of the camp, and howls in imitation of a wild dog. The other, at the opposite side, answers him by imitating the cry of the kuurku owl. These sounds bring the chief to the door of his wuurn to listen. One of the Pææt pææts then taps twice on a tree with his spear, or strikes two spears together, as a signal that a friend wishes to speak to him. He then demands the culprit; but, as the demand is generally met by a denial of his being there, they return to their friends, who have been waiting to hear the result. If they still believe him to be concealed in the camp, they surround it at peep of day, stamping, and making a hideous noise, to frighten the people in the camp. In the meantime the chief, anticipating the second visit, has very likely aided the culprit to escape while it is dark. When the Pææt pææts and their friends discover that the man is not in the camp, they freely express their anger and disappointment; but, without attempting to injure anyone, they start off at once on the track of the fugitive.

The deaths of adults caused by epidemics are not avenged, nor are the natural deaths of boys before they have beards, or of girls before entering womanhood, or of those who have lost their lives by accident, such as drowning, falling off trees, snake bite, &c.

When the body of an adult is found with the muscles of the back of the neck 'slack,' and marks of blows on the breast, it is concluded that death has been produced by strokes from a heavy club of quandong wood, called 'yuul marrang,' 'wild hand.' A club of this kind is kept among the associated tribes for the express purpose of killing criminals, and, as the quandong does not grow in the Western District, this club is borrowed by the chiefs around when needed, and especially when they visit tribes with the expectation of avenging death. When a man has been killed by this club, the body is brought home and examined by his relatives, and disposed of according to the laws regulating mourning and the eating of human flesh, which are described in the previous chapter.

The friends examine the footprints of the murderers, and follow them sufficiently far to indicate the direction from which they came. If they are unable to follow up the track, they console themselves by expressing the wish that some evil may befall the murderer. If they have been able to follow up the track, they return home and collect as many men as possible, and make an attack on the suspected tribe; and, should they succeed in killing a member of the tribe—even though it be a woman, or only a child—they are satisfied, and the two tribes are again friendly. But if one of an innocent tribe should be killed, retaliation is sought, and probably another life sacrificed.

When a number of men have been implicated in a murder or other crime, they disguise their track by walking backwards in line over ground likely to retain the impressions of their feet; and they hide their numbers by stepping in each other's footprints. This they continue as long as they are in country belonging to another tribe. When lying in wait for an enemy they lay their ears near the ground, but not touching it, and listen attentively. They can hear the sound of footsteps on the soft sward at a distance of one hundred yards; those of a horse at two or three hundred.

Friendship is seldom allowed to interfere with the sacred duty of revenge. A man would consider it his bounden duty to kill his most intimate friend for the purpose of avenging a brother's death, and would do so without the slightest hesitation. But if an intimate friend should be killed, he would leave revenge to the relatives of the deceased. In all cases, if they fail to secure the guilty person, they consider it their duty to kill one of his relatives, however ignorant he may have been of the crime.

This law holding every member of the tribe responsible for the conduct of each individual in the tribe is doubtless founded upon the necessities of the case, and entails upon each one the duty of controlling the violent passions, not only of himself, but also of the others.

CHAPTER XVII.

GREAT MEETINGS.

GREAT meetings are held periodically in summer, by agreement among the friendly tribes. But any two chiefs have the power of sending messengers and commanding the attendance of the tribes at an appointed time and place, in order that matters of dispute may be arranged. Sometimes, instead of dispatching men to give notice of a meeting, a signal smoke is raised by setting fire to a wide circle of long grass in a dry swamp. This causes the smoke to ascend in a remarkable spiral form, which is seen from a great distance. The summons thus given is strictly attended to. Or, if there is not a suitable swamp, a hollow tree is stuffed with dry bark and leaves, and set on fire. Or, a fire is made on a hill top.

Each tribe, on its arrival, erects its wuurns, and lights its fires in front of them, on the side of the camp next their own country. When all are assembled, proceedings commence after sunset, or before sunrise next morning. As soon as the families of the different tribes are seated in rows on the ground, the chief of each tribe, accompanied by the other chiefs, walks along and taps everyone on the head with a piece of bark, asking the name of his tribe, his personal name, and his class. If anything of importance has to be discussed, a circular open space, of one hundred or one hundred and fifty yards in diameter, is reserved in the centre of the camp, into which the chiefs advance by turns, and speak in a loud voice, that everyone may hear what is said.

When a chief has a matter of great importance to settle, and desires the advice and assistance of friendly tribes, he dispatches two messengers to the nearest chief with a message-stick. This message-stick is a piece of wood about six inches long and one inch in diameter, with five or six sides, one of these indicating by notches the number of tribes to be summoned, and the others the number of men required from each. The messengers are not allowed to explain the business of the proposed meeting. Immediately on a chief receiving the message-stick, he sends for his principal men, who pass their hands down the stick and ascertain the number of men required from the tribe. They then decide who are to be sent. The stick is next forwarded by messengers from their tribe to the nearest chief, who sends it on to the next, and so on until all are summoned. The most distant tribe starts first, and, joining the others in succession, all arrive in a body at the camp of the chief who sent for them. They are accompanied by their wives, but not by children or by very old persons. In the evening, when the children of the tribe and the women have gone to bed, the chief who convened the meeting gives his reason for doing so. After consultation, the chiefs decide what is to be done; each chief tells his people what is required, and all retire for the night.

The spear-thrower is also used as a message-stick; but, when so employed, it is specially marked to indicate its purpose. The writer has in his possession a specimen which was made by Kaawirn Kuunawarn, the chief of the Kirræ Wuurong tribe, and which is a *fac-simile* of a summons issued by him long ago to three tribes, to meet his own tribe at a favourite swamp and camping-place called Kuunawarn, on the east side of the River Hopkins, and represents their approach to his camp. In the centre of the flat side of the spear-thrower is a carved circle of about an inch and a quarter in diameter, which represents the camp of Kaawirn Kuunawarn. Near it are three notches on the edge of the stick, and two lines and two dots on the flat side, pointing to the camp, which form his signature; and, at the hooked end of the stick, three lines in shape of the letter Z indicate his presence. Four rows of notches, extending from each end of the stick to the camp, indicate the numbers of individuals of the two tribes approaching from opposite directions. On the other side of the spear-thrower, in the centre, there are two circles of a smaller size, and pointing to them is a small, rudely carved figure of a hand—the word for 'hand,' munya, also means a 'meeting.' From each end of the stick six lines of notches represent the numbers of individuals of other two tribes approaching from opposite directions. As each notch indicates an individual, there must have been a thousand at this meeting. Kaawirn Kuunawarn was then a very young chief; and as he is now a man considerably over sixty years of age, the meeting must have been held immediately previous to the occupation of the country by the white man. Of those who attended it there are only four individuals now alive, viz., Kaawirn Kuunawarn, Jamie Ware, Jim Crow, and Helen Crow.

Occasionally, a distant and distrustful tribe will send two men to test the friendship of a meeting. On arrival, they announce the name of their tribe and their own names, and then retire to the wuurn of an acquaintance. He ties a feather to the point of one of their spears, and fixes the spear upright at his door. When the attention of a chief is called to this, he transfers the spear to the middle of the camp. Two or three men come and draw their hands down it, and retire to their wuurns ; no objection having been made, the chief takes the spear to the two strangers and lays it down beside them, remarking that it belongs to them, and is returned as a sign of friendship and welcome. If the friendship of their tribe is not desired, a hint is given to them to go away. Three or four young women at sunset will pretend to go for water, carrying pieces of smouldering bark hidden in their buckets. These pieces of bark they give to the strangers to make their fire on their journey home. The men immediately set off, carrying the pieces of lighted bark under their rugs till they are out of danger of pursuit.

Messengers are attached to every tribe, and are selected for their intelligence and their ability as linguists. They are employed to convey information from one tribe to another, such as the time and place of great meetings, korroboræs, marriages, and burials, and also of proposed battles ; for, if one tribe intends to attack another, due notice is always honourably given. Ambuscades are proceedings adopted by civilized warriors. As the office of messenger is of very great importance, the persons filling it are considered sacred while on duty ; very much as an ambassador, herald, or bearer of a flag of truce is treated among civilized nations.

To distinguish them from spies or enemies, they generally travel two together, and they are painted in accordance with the nature of the information which they carry. When the information is about a great meeting, a korroboræ, a marriage, or a fight, their faces are painted with red and white stripes across the cheeks and nose. When the information relates to a death, their heads, faces, and hands, their arms up to the elbows, and their feet and legs up to the knees, are painted with white clay. Thus the appearance of the messengers announces the nature of their news before they come to the camp. If their appearance indicates a death, lamentation and disfigurement begin immediately. On arriving at the camp they sit down without speaking, apparently unobserved ; and, after a little time, one of them delivers the message in a short speech with intoned voice.

There are also teachers attached to each tribe, whose duty is to instruct the young in the use of weapons, and in other needful information. Sometimes a messenger is also a teacher.

The fine old chief of the Spring Creek tribe, Weeratt Kuyuut—'Eel spear,' occasionally called Morpor, after his tribe and country, and believed to have been upwards of eighty years of age—was both a messenger and a teacher. As a messenger he generally travelled by himself. In his younger days he was a great warrior, and in more mature years was considered such an honourable, impartial man, that he was selected on all occasions as a referee in the settlement of disputes. When a great battle was to be fought, he was sent for by the contending chiefs, who placed him in a safe position to see fair play. In reward for his services he returned home laden with presents of opossum rugs, weapons, and ornaments.

As a teacher he taught the young people the names of the favourite planets and constellations, as indications of the seasons. For example, when Canopus is a very little above the horizon in the east at daybreak, the season for emu eggs has come ; when the Pleiades are visible in the east an hour before sunrise, the time for visiting friends and neighbouring tribes is at hand; if some distant locality requires to be visited at night, it can be reached by following a particular star. He taught them also the names of localities, mountain ranges, and lakes, and the directions of the neighbouring tribes.

As Weeratt Kuyuut had the reputation of being an expert warrior, besides being well known as a messenger, he travelled unmolested all over the country between the Grampian ranges and the sea, and between the rivers Leigh and Wannon ; and was received and treated everywhere with kindness and hospitality.

In his travels towards Geelong—which at that time was the name of the bay and not of the land—he heard of Buckley as a chief who had 'died and jumped up whitefellow,' and who on that account was treated with marked consideration and respect. There is little doubt that Buckley owed his life to this idea, which was very likely encouraged by him to enable him to retain his influence over the tribes with which he mingled.

Among the associated tribes a public executioner was employed to put criminals to death when ordered by the chiefs to do so. The natives have a vivid recollection of a bloodthirsty savage named Pundeet Puulotong, 'dragger out of kidney fat,' who acted in that capacity, and who was so fond of doing cruel deeds that he solicited the office himself. He killed his victims with a club called yuul marrang, 'wild hand,' made of quandong wood, and kept for the purpose.

Pundeet Puulotong was a great fighting man. On killing one of a neighbouring tribe, he would show himself to the relatives of his victim, and challenge them to spear him. None, however, dared to meddle with him. On asking members of his tribe how many lives he had destroyed, the reply was that he took one at almost every meeting. When he was seen approaching a meeting the women wept, as they were certain he would put someone to death before he left. If he received a scratch, or had blood drawn from him, he would kill some person in revenge. The old savage grew quite blind and helpless in his old age, and the natives say, that, instead of putting him to death, which they could easily have done, they left his blindness to punish him for his innumerable murders and cruelties.

Persons accused of wrong-doing get one month's notice to appear before the assembled tribes and be tried, on pain of being outlawed and killed. When a man has been charged with an offence, he goes to the meeting armed with two war spears, a flat light shield, and a boomerang. If he is found guilty of a private wrong he is painted white, and—along with his brother or near male relative, who stands beside him as his second, with a heavy shield, a liangle, and a boomerang—he is placed opposite to the injured person and his friends, who sometimes number twenty warriors. These range themselves at a distance of fifty yards from him, and each individual throws four or five gneerin spears and two boomerangs at him simultaneously, 'like a shower.' If he succeeds in warding them off, his second hands him his heavy shield, and he is attacked singly by his enemies, who deliver each one blow with a liangle. As blood must be spilt to satisfy the injured party, the trial ends on his being hit. After the wound has been dressed, all shake hands and are good friends. If the accused person refuses to appear and be tried, he is outlawed, and may be killed; and his brother or nearest male relative is held responsible, and must submit to be attacked with boomerangs. If it turns out that the man was innocent, the relatives have a right to retaliate on the family of the accuser on the first opportunity.

Should a person, through bad conduct, become a constant anxiety and trouble to the tribe, a consultation is held, and he is put to death. Liars are detested; and should anyone, through lying, get others into trouble, he is punished with the boomerang and liangle. Women and young people, for the same fault, are beaten with a stick.

Long ago the Bung'andætch natives, who inhabited the Mount Gambier district, were looked upon as wild blacks and very malevolent, for they sent lightning and rain to injure the associated tribes. In retaliation, the latter challenged the Bung'andætch natives to fight at Coleraine ; but, as they never could get them to stand and give battle, they chased them to their own country. According to the account of a native who accompanied his father on such occasions, the fires of the associated tribes at the Wannon falls, 'Tuunda beean,' were like the lights of Melbourne at night.

Quarrels between tribes are sometimes settled by single combat between the chiefs, and the result is accepted as final. At other times disputes are decided by combat between equal numbers of warriors, painted with red clay and dressed in war costume; but real fighting seldom takes place, unless the women rouse the anger of the men and urge them to come to blows. Even then it rarely results in a general fight, but comes to single combats between warriors of each side ; who step into the arena, taunt one another, exchange blows with the liangle, and wrestle together. The first wound ends the combat. This is often followed by an encounter between the women, who begin by scolding, and rouse each other to fury, tearing each other's hair, and striking one another with their yam-sticks or muurong poles. There is no interference by the men, however severely their wives may punish each other. Both men and women, when quarrelling, pace about, tossing up the dust with their toes, stamping, and making a hissing noise like 'ishew,' or 'eeshwuur.' Every license is allowed to the tongue. They wish each other all kinds of evil in the coarsest and most violent language. The mildest imprecations are such as—'May your teeth project, and your eyes squint and be closed with small pox; ' 'May you lose your hair and be completely bald;' 'May you have a deformed nose;' 'May you break your neck and become a skeleton, for you should have died long ago ;' and 'May many assist in putting you to death.' Words failing to produce the desired effect, they will spit in each other's faces.

Sometimes a fight takes the form of a tournament or friendly trial of skill in the use of the boomerang and shield. Ten or twelve warriors, painted with white stripes across the cheeks and nose, and armed with shields and boomerangs, are met by an equal number at a distance of about twenty paces. Each individual has a right to throw his boomerang at anyone on the other side, and steps out of the rank into the intervening space to do so. The opposite party take their turn, and so on alternately, until someone is hit, or all are satisfied. Every warrior has a boy to look after his boomerang, which, on striking a shield, flies up and falls at a considerable distance. As the boomerang is thrown with great force, it requires very great dexterity and quick sight to ward off such an erratic weapon, and affords a fine opportunity for displaying the remarkable activity of the aborigines. This activity is, no doubt, considerably roused by fear of the severe cut which is inflicted by the boomerang. Mourners are not allowed to join in these tournaments, as it would be considered disrespectful to the dead. Women and children are generally kept at a safe distance. The chiefs and aged warriors stand by to see fair play, and to stop the proceedings when they think they have gone far enough.

At the periodical great meetings trading is carried on by the exchange of articles peculiar to distant parts of the country. A favourite place of meeting for the purpose of barter is a hill called Noorat, near Terang. In that locality the forest kangaroos are plentiful, and the skins of the young ones found there are considered superior to all others for making rugs. The aborigines from the Geelong district bring the best stones for making axes, and a kind of wattle gum celebrated for its adhesiveness. This Geelong gum is so useful in fixing the handles of stone axes and the splinters of flint in spears, and for cementing the joints of bark buckets, that it is carried in large lumps all over the Western District. Greenstone for axes is obtained also from a quarry on Spring Creek, near Goodwood; and sandstone for grinding them is got from the salt creek near Lake Boloke. Obsidian or volcanic glass, for scraping and polishing weapons, is found near Dunkeld. The Wimmera country supplies the maleen saplings, found in the mallee scrub, for making spears. The Cape Otway forest supplies the wood for the bundit spears, and the grass-tree stalk for forming the butt piece of the light spear, and for producing fire; also a red clay, found on the sea coast, which is used as a paint, being first burned and then mixed with water, and laid on with a brush formed of the cone of the banksia while in flower by cutting off its long stamens and pistils. Marine shells from the mouth of the Hopkins River, and freshwater mussel shells, are also articles of exchange.

Attendance at these great meetings is compulsory on all. As an instance of the obedience paid to the usual summons, a very faithful native, who had charge of a flock of sheep at Kangatong, gave notice that he had received a message directing him to attend a meeting at Mount Rouse, whenever he saw the signal smoke, or a reflection in the sky of a fire in that direction. As there was at that time a very great scarcity of shepherds, in consequence of the rush to the goldfields, permission to go was refused. Some days afterwards the signal was seen. Next morning Gnaweeth was away, leaving his flock in the fold. Having thus broken his engagement, he considered he had forfeited all claim to payment for the work which he had before faithfully performed; and, therefore, deposited at the back door of the house a bundle containing his clothing, blankets, gun, and every other article that had been given to him for his long services. He gave up all his property rather than disobey the summons. Many months passed over ere he was heard of; and it was only after repeated invitations and assurances of welcome that he returned. He then explained, that, had he neglected the summons to attend the meeting, his life would have been forfeited.

When it had been agreed by the chiefs of the associated tribes to have a grand battue, messengers were sent all round to invite everybody to join. As each tribe left its own country, it spread out in line, and all united to form a circle of fifteen or twenty miles in diameter. By this means the kangaroos and emus were enclosed, in order to be driven to an appointed place—usually on Muston's Creek, a few miles from its junction with the River Hopkins. To this place the old people, women, and children of the several tribes had previously gone, and were there encamped. At a fixed time the circle was perfected by arranging the men so that they stood about two hundred yards apart. The circle then began to contract. As they drew near to the central camp both young and old joined them, and formed a line too compact to allow the escape of the game; which, frightened and confused with the yells and shouting all around, were easily killed with clubs and spears. In the evening a grand feast and korroboræ ended the day's sport. Next morning the game was fairly divided, and each tribe started homewards, with the usual 'wuwuurk, wuwuurk,' farewell, farewell.

CHAPTER XVIII.

AMUSEMENTS.

THE leading amusement of the Australian aborigines is the karweann, or korroboræ, which somewhat resembles pantomime, and consists of music, dancing, and acting.

Little can be said in favour of the aboriginal music. The airs are monotonous and doleful, and there is no such thing as harmony. Men and women join in singing. The women commence, each one accompanying her voice with regular beats of the open hand on a rolled-up opossum rug, which sometimes contains shells, to produce a jingling sound; the men strike in with their voices and with their music sticks. These sticks are made of hard wood, and are about nine inches long and an inch and a half in diameter, rounded, and tapering at each end to a point. The one is held stationary, and is struck with the other. The sound produced is clear and musical, and can be heard at a great distance.

Many songs having appropriate airs are universally known. Very often complimentary or descriptive songs are composed on the instant, and are sung to well-known airs, the whole company joining in the chorus. A lament called 'Mallæ malææ,' composed in New South Wales in commemoration of the ravages of small-pox, is known all over the Australian colonies, and is sung in a doleful strain, accompanied with groans and imitations of a dying person. The following is a song in the Chaap wuurong language, with its translation. It is said to have been composed in the neighbourhood of Sydney by one of the aborigines of that country, and to have been translated into the different languages as it became known. In singing it the last two lines are repeated three times.

CHUUL'YUU WILL'YUU.

Chuul'yuu Will'yuu
Wallaa gnoræeæ.
Chillæ binnæ aa gna
Kinuuaa gnuuraa jeeaa,
Chiæbaa gnuutaa.
Kirrægirræ, kirrægirræ, kirrægirræ,
Leeaa gnaa.

THE PORCUPINE.

Porcupine spikes
Burn like heat of fire.
Someone pinching me
When I am up high,
With affection like a sister.
Grinning, grinning, grinning,
Teeth mine.

When a korroboræ is held, all are dressed in their best attire. The chiefs are painted red over and under the eyes and on the cheeks; a twisted band of the tuan squirrel fur surrounds the head; in this band, over the right temple, is stuck a plume made of the webs of a swan's dark quill feather, which are tied to the barrel of a long white quill feather from the swan's wing; in the hair are fastened several incisor teeth of the large kangaroo; and the tail of a wild dog hangs from the hair down the back; the arms are adorned with armlets of tuan fur rope. The common men wear round the head a plaited band about two inches broad, made of the inner bark of the stringy-bark tree, coloured red; over this band is a thick rope of ring-tailed opossum skin with its fur outside; and in the band, above the right temple, is stuck a white quill feather of the swan, with its webs torn half way down, so as to flutter in the wind. Both chiefs and common men wear necklaces. The usual necklace is formed of from eighty to one hundred kangaroo teeth, tied by their roots to a skin cord. This necklace hangs loosely round the neck, and displays the teeth diverging towards the shoulders and breast. Another kind of necklace is composed of short pieces of reeds strung in eight or ten rows on bark cords. A third kind of necklace is formed of numerous threads spun from opossum fur. The usual apron is worn, with the addition of an upright tuft of emu neck feathers fastened to the belt behind, and somewhat resembling the tail of a cock.

The women wear the usual opossum rug, and have their heads bound with a plaited bark band and an opossum skin rope. A few kangaroo teeth are fastened among their back hair. Above each ear, and projecting beyond the forehead, is a thin piece of wood with various coloured feathers tied to the end of it. Over the forehead there is stuck in the brow band a bunch of white cockatoo crest feathers. A short piece of reed is worn in the cartilage of the nose, and flowers in the slits of the ears. They also wear reed or kangaroo teeth necklaces, and anklets of green leaves. The wives of chiefs are distinguished by two red stripes across the cheeks.

Both men and women are ornamented by cicatrices—which are made when they come of age—on the chest, back, and upper parts of the arms, but never on the neck or face. These cicatrices are of a darker hue than the skin, and vary in length from half an inch to an inch. They are arranged in lines and figures according to the taste or the custom of the tribe. The operator cuts through the skin with a flint knife, and rubs the wounds with green grass. This irritates the flesh and causes it to rise above the skin. By repeated rubbings, the flesh rises permanently, and the wounds are allowed to heal. About the same age, nearly every person has the cartilage of the nose pierced to admit some ornament. The hole is made with the pointed bone of the hind leg of the kangaroo, which is pushed through and left for a week. A short tube, made of the large wing bone of the swan, is then introduced to keep the hole open, and is turned round occasionally while the nose is kept moist by holding the face over a vapour bath, produced by pouring water over hot stones. When the wound is quite healed, the ring is removed. On occasions of ceremony, a reed about eighteen inches long is pushed through the opening and worn as an ornament.

Before the korroboræ commences—which is immediately after sunset—large quantities of dry bark, branches, and leaves are collected, and the young people are ordered to light the fire and attend to it. The men and well-grown boys retire to prepare themselves for the dance. They paint their bodies and limbs with white stripes, in such a manner as to give them the appearance of human skeletons; and they tie round their ancles a number of leafy twigs, which touch the ground, and make a rustling noise as they move. Each dancer wears the reed ornament in his nose. When they stand in a row these reeds have the appearance of a continuous line.

The women do not join in the dance, but sit in a half-circle behind the fire, and sing, accompanying their song with the sound of beating on opossum rugs, as described under the head of music. Some of the men stand beside the fire, beating time with the music sticks.

After the music has begun, one of the dancers emerges from the darkness into the open ground, so as just to be seen ; and, with a stamp, sets himself with arms extended, and legs wide apart and quivering, his feet shuffling in time to the music, and the twigs round his ankles rustling at each movement. He remains thus for a few seconds, and, turning round suddenly, disappears in the darkness with a rustling sound. Another dancer takes his place, and goes through the same movements, and disappears in the same way. Then two or three come forward, and dance in a line, and disappear in the darkness. At length all the dancers are seen in a row, quivering and making a great rustling in time to the music, and advancing nearer and nearer to the fire until they come quite close, when a simultaneous loud groan is suddenly given, and the dance is over. The bright light of the fire shining on the white stripes of the dancers against a pitch-dark background, produces a very striking effect. The different tribes dance by turns; they never mingle.

The interludes between the dances are filled up by the buffoonery and jesting of one or two clowns, called ' chipperuuks,' chosen for their powers of humour, ready wit, and repartee. These clowns do not perform altogether voluntarily, owing to the manner in which they are treated previous to the korroboræ. They are caught by the orders of the chiefs, and are compelled to live apart in a separate wuurn, without any covering to keep out the cold, but are supplied with plenty of food. The hair of the chipperuuk is cropped off both sides of his head, which are plastered with white clay, leaving a crest of hair along the ridge like the hog-mane of a horse. A stripe of white paint extends from the top of the brow down the nose, mouth, chin, and neck to the waist; and the same behind, from the crown of the head down the spine; another stripe extends down the inside of each leg, terminating in an arrow-point above the ankles. The arms are encircled with three white stripes between the shoulder and wrist. He wears the usual apron and the tail of emu feathers. The chipperuuk enters the circle between the dances, and amuses the people with jokes, and with ludicrous movements in imitation of the gambols of emus, native companions, and other animals. Sometimes he puts on a mask formed of a kangaroo pouch, painted white, and having holes for the eyes, nose, and mouth. These are pulled over the head and face, and are often used to frighten children when they misbehave. After the amusements are finished, the chipperuuks visit each wuurn, with a bark torch, and a basket to receive presents of food, which are liberally bestowed.

It is now almost impossible to ascertain whether or not the korroboræs held among the tribes referred to, previous to the advent of the Europeans, were attended with indecencies; but the aborigines now alive—and many of them are very truthful and intelligent—declare that there was nothing indecent permitted, and that when anything contrary to strict propriety was attempted, it was instantly stopped, and the offenders reprimanded, and threatened with punishment if it were repeated.

Since the aborigines have been gathered together under the immediate care of Government officials, and other protectors, the korroboræ is discountenanced ; and, as little or nothing in the form of amusement is substituted, the weary monotony, restraint, and discipline of these tutelary establishments have a very depressing effect on the minds and health of the natives, and impel them to seek relief in the indulgence of intoxicating drinks. And who can blame them ?

Another amusement, called 'Tarratt' in the Kuurn kopan noot language, and 'Wittchim' in the Chaap wuurong and Peek whuurong languages, consists in stalking a feather, in imitation of hunting an emu. The feather is tied to the end of a long stick, which is held by a man in the centre of a large circle of natives. A man, who has dressed himself in korroboræ costume, enters the circle with shield and boomerang, and moves round the circle for fifteen or twenty minutes with his eye upon the feather, now crouching, and then running, in imitation of stalking game, and finishes by stooping and touching the feather. His place is taken by another, and so on, until four or five competitors have gone through the same movements. The ceremony is conducted with so much gravity, that if a spectator should laugh, or in any way ridicule the actor, the latter would be entitled to throw his boomerang at him with impunity. The chiefs then decide who has performed best, and they present him with the feather. In the evening, after several korroboræ dances have been gone through, the winner of the feather, who has kept out of sight, comes into the circle in korroboræ costume, and by order of the chiefs repeats his movements round the feather. He then presents it to the other competitors in the game, out of compliment, and with a view to remove any feeling of jealousy.

Games are held usually after the great meetings and korroboræs. Wrestling is a favourite game, but is never practised in anger. Women and children are not allowed to be present. The game is commenced by a man who considers himself to be a good wrestler challenging any one of his own or another tribe. His challenge being accepted, the wrestlers rub their hands, chests, and backs with wood ashes, to prevent their hold from slipping ; they then clasp each other and struggle, but do not trip with their feet, as that is not considered a fair test of strength. After one of them has been thrown three times, he retires. Other two men then engage, and so on. When all competitors have had a trial, the conquerors are matched; and the last couple decide the championship. The event is followed by a promiscuous wrestling, and the game terminates with shouting, just as among white people.

One of the favourite games is football, in which fifty, or as many as one hundred players engage at a time. The ball is about the size of an orange, and is made of opossum-skin, with the fur side outwards. It is filled with pounded charcoal, which gives solidity without much increase of weight, and is tied hard round and round with kangaroo sinews. The players are divided into two sides and ranged in opposing lines, which are always of a different 'class'—white cockatoo against black cockatoo, quail against snake, &c. Each side endeavours to keep possession of the ball, which is tossed a short distance by hand, and then kicked in any direction. The side which kicks it oftenest and furthest gains the game. The person who sends it highest is considered the best player, and has the honour of burying it in the ground till required next day.

The sport is concluded with a shout of applause, and the best player is complimented on his skill. This game, which is somewhat similar to the white man's game of football, is very rough; but as the players are barefooted and naked, they do not hurt each other so much as the white people do; nor is the fact of an aborigine being a good football player considered to entitle him to assist in making laws for the tribe to which he belongs.

The throwing of spears at a mark is a common amusement. Young people engage in the pastime with toy spears. A number of boys will arrange themselves in a line: one of the party will trundle swiftly along the ground, about ten yards in front of them, a circular piece of thick bark about a foot in diameter, and, as it passes them, each tries to hit it with his toy spear. They amuse themselves also with throwing wands, fern stalks, and rushes at objects, and at each other.

The toy boomerang is much lighter and more acute in the angle than the war boomerang, and has a peculiar rounding of one of its sides, which has the effect of making it rise in the air when thrown along the ground, and return to the thrower when its impetus has been expended. It requires much skill, and study of the wind, to throw it aright. On dark nights this boomerang will sometimes be lighted at one end and thrown into the air, with an effect very like fireworks. This boomerang is also thrown into flocks of ducks, parrots, and small birds, among which it commits great havoc—occasionally cutting off their heads as with a knife.

The wuæ whuuitch is also used as a toy. It is a tapering wand about two feet long, with a pear-shaped knob on the thick end. It is held by the small end, whirled round the head, and projected with force along the ground, where it skips for a considerable distance. It is also used for throwing at birds. This toy is used in the games after great meetings. Like football, it is played by opposing classes—kuurokeetch against kirrtuuk, kappatch against kartpærup, &c.—and the award is given to those who throw it to the greatest distance.

CHAPTER XIX.

WEAPONS.

THE spear is the chief and most formidable weapon amongst the aborigines. There are seven kinds of spears, each of which is used for a special purpose. The longest and heaviest are the war spears, which are about nine feet long, and made of ironbark saplings reduced to a uniform thickness. They are variously named from the way in which they are pointed. The 'tuulowarn' has a smooth point. The 'tungung'gil' is barbed on one side for six inches from the point. The 'wurokiigil' is jagged for six inches on each side of the point, with sharp splinters of flint or volcanic glass, fixed in grooves with the same kind of cement which is employed to fix the handles of stone axes. The hunting spear, 'narmall,' is about seven feet long, and is made of a peeled ti-tree sapling, with a smooth, sharp point; to balance the weapon it has a fixed buttpiece formed of the stalk of the grass tree, about two feet long, and with a hole in the pith in its end to receive the hook of the spear-thrower; but, as the hook of the spear-thrower would soon destroy the light grass tree, a piece of hard wood is inserted in the end, and secured with a lashing of kangaroo sinew. Although the narmall is chiefly used for killing game, it is the first spear thrown in fighting, as it can be sent to a greater distance than the heavy war spears, which are only used in close quarters.

The spear-thrower is a piece of wood about two feet and a half long, and three-quarters of an inch thick. It is two or three inches broad in the middle, and tapers off into a handle at one end and a hook at the other. Its object is to lengthen the arm, as it were, and at the same time balance the spear by bringing the hand nearer its centre. The hook of the spear-thrower is put into the hole in the end of the hunting-spear, and the other end is grasped with the hand, which also holds the spear above it with the finger and thumb. With this instrument a spear is sent to a much greater distance than without it.

The 'gnirrin' spear is made of a strong reed, about five feet long, with a sharp point of ironbark wood, and is used only for throwing at criminals, as mentioned in the chapter on great meetings. The eel spear is formed of a peeled ti-tree sapling, of the thickness of a little finger and about seven feet long, pointed with the leg bone of the emu, or with the small bone of the hind leg of the large kangaroo ground to a long, sharp point, and lashed to the shaft with the tail sinews of the kangaroo. The spear called ' bundit '—which name means ' bite '—is made of a very rare, heavy wood from the Cape Otway mountains, and is so valuable that it is never used in fighting or hunting, but only as an ornament. It is given as a present in token of friendship, or exchanged for fancy maleen spears from the interior.

Spears are warded off with the light shield, which is a thin, oblong, concave piece of wood about two and a half feet long, nine inches broad in the centre, and tapering towards the ends. It has a handle in the middle of the hollow side, which is grasped by the hand when in use, and the convex side is ornamented with the usual diagonal cross lines.

The aborigines never heard of poisoned spears, or the use of poison for the destruction of life.

The liangle is a heavy, formidable weapon, about two and a half feet long, with a sharp-pointed bend, nine inches in length, projecting at a right angle. It is used in fighting at close quarters; and the blows are warded off by the heavy shield, which is a strong piece of triangular wood, three feet long by five or six inches broad, tapering to a point at each end; with a hole in the centre, lined with opossum skin, for the left hand. In grappling, the shields are thrown away, and the combatants deliver their blows on each other's backs with the sharp point of the liangle, by reaching over their shoulders. The liangle is not ornamented in any way, but the front of the shield is covered with the usual diagonal lines.

There are several kinds of clubs, varying in size from a walking-stick, which the natives term a ' companion,' up to one of a formidable size, called a wuæ whuitch, which is always made of heavy wood, and is about two feet and a half long, with a broad almond-shaped end, about a foot long, terminating in a sharp point. The war boomerang is much heavier and more obtuse in the angle than the toy boomerang, and on being thrown it does not return. The natives generally carry a weapon resembling a war boomerang, but longer and heavier, and somewhat like a scimitar in shape. It is used as a scimitar.

CHAPTER XX.

ANIMALS.

THE dingo—the wild dog of Australia—deservedly holds the first place in the estimation of the aborigines. Previous to the advent of the white man, though every wuurn had its pack of dogs, they were so very rare in their wild state—at least in the inhabited parts of the country—that one 'would not be seen in many days' travel.' This scarcity is attributed by the aborigines to the want of food. They were usually bred in a domesticated state, and no puppies were ever destroyed. Wild young ones also were caught and domesticated. The dogs were trained to guard the wuurns, which they did by growling and snarling. Dingoes never bark. As they would not sleep or take shelter under the roof of their master, a separate place was generally erected for them. In watching they were vigilant and fierce. They would fly at the throats of visitors; and strangers had often to take refuge from them by climbing into a tree. They were also trained to hunt, which was their principal use. They were active and skilful in killing kangaroos, and seldom got cut with the powerful hind toes of these animals. When they killed one, they yelped to let their master know where they were. Some well-trained dogs would even come home and lead their owners to the dead game. In some of the mountainous parts of Victoria, but especially in the Otway ranges, the dingoes were so very numerous and fierce, and hunted in such large packs, that the natives were afraid to venture among them, and often had to take refuge in trees. Since the introduction of the European dog the dingo is not used, notwithstanding its superiority in several respects to the former, which is preferred on account of its affectionate and social disposition.

The forest kangaroo is generally hunted by stalking, and is killed with the hunting spear. If the kangaroo is grazing on open ground, where there is no cover to conceal the hunter, he makes a circular shield of leafy branches, about two or three feet in diameter, with a small hole in the centre to look through; and, with this in front, he crawls towards the kangaroo while its head is down, remains motionless if it looks up, and, when he has got within throwing distance, transfixes it with a spear which he has dragged after him between his toes. The brush and wallaby kangaroos, unlike the foresters, frequent scrubby valleys and patches of brushwood, and are hunted with dogs and spears.

The common opossum supplies the aborigines with one of their principal articles of food, and the skin of this animal is indispensable for clothing. It lives in holes in the trunks of trees, and also in the ground and among rocks. Before the occupation of the country by the white man, opossums were only to be found in the large forest trees; and they were so scarce that the hunter required to go in search of them early in the morning, before the dew was off the grass, and track them to the trees, which were then marked and afterwards visited during the day. Now, since the common opossums have become numerous, in consequence of the destruction of animals of prey by the settlers, the hunter does not look for their tracks among the grass, but examines the bark of the trees; and, if recently-made scratches are visible on it, he immediately prepares to swarm up the bole. It may be seventy or one hundred feet in height without a branch, but he ascends without difficulty, by cutting deep notches in the thick bark with his axe. In these notches he inserts his fingers and his toes, and climbs with such skill and care that very few instances of accident are known. On reaching the hole where the opossum has its nest, he introduces a long wand and pokes the opossum till it comes out. He then seizes it by the tail, knocks its head against the tree, and throws it down. Occasionally several opossums occupy one cavity. When it is too deep for the wand to reach them, a hole is cut in the trunk of the tree opposite their nest.

The ring-tailed opossum—so the aborigines say—formerly made its nest in the holes of trees; but, since the common kind has increased so greatly in numbers, they have taken possession of the holes, and compelled the ring-tails to build covered nests in low trees and scrub, somewhat similar to those of the European magpie and squirrel. In corroboration of the change in the habits of the ring-tail opossum, the writer may state that he has observed their nests in both situations, in low shrubs and also in hollow stumps of trees. As a further proof of this, the aborigines have no name for the nest of the ring-tail opossum when it is built in a bush.

The wombat, being a nocturnal animal, cannot be caught by daylight; and, being a deep burrower, cannot be got by digging, except where the ground is soft. The burrow sometimes extends a long distance; but, as it is large enough to admit a man, the hunter crawls into it till he reaches the animal—which is harmless—and then taps on the roof to let his friend above ground know its position; a hole is then sunk, and the wombat dragged out. Should the burrow be under a layer of rock, the hunter lies quietly above its mouth, and, when the wombat comes out after sunset to feed, he jumps into the hole and intercepts the frightened animal on its retreat to its den. The flesh of a fat wombat is considered very good to eat. No use is made of the skin.

The bear, or 'sloth bear of Australia,' forms a substantial article of food; and it is easily discovered by the hunter, as it does not hide itself in holes, but sits all day long in the fork of a tree. On a native ascending the tree, it gradually climbs for safety to the top of a branch so slender that it bends with its weight. As the climber dare not venture so far, he cuts the limb, and with it sends the bear to the ground. But, as nature appears to have given tree-climbing animals immunity from injury from falls of even hundreds of feet, the bear immediately scrambles up the nearest tree, unless someone is ready to secure it. No use is made of the skin of the bear.

The emu, the turkey bustard, and the gigantic crane are stalked by means of a screen made of a bunch of plants held in front of the hunter. The plant used is the shepherd's purse, and a bunch of it is indispensable to every hunter on the open country, where branches of trees are not easily got. The hunter, concealed from view behind this screen, creeps up towards the game, and carries exposed to view as a lure a blue-headed wren, which is tied alive to the point of a long wand, and made to flutter. When the game approaches to seize the bait, it is killed with a waddy; or it is caught with a noose fixed on the point of the wand, which the hunter slips over its head while it is trying to catch the wren.

The turkey bustard is sometimes killed without stalking, as it has a habit, when anyone approaches, of lying down and concealing itself among long grass, like the grouse and partridge. In this way the hunter gets near enough to kill it with a waddy. In the breeding season no respect is paid to birds hatching. When a turkey's nest is discovered, the great object of the hunter is to secure the mother as well as the eggs; and, for that purpose, he suspends a limb of a tree across the nest, supported at one end with a short stick, to which a long string is attached. This string reaches to a hole in the ground, which the hunter digs, and in which he sits, covered with bushes and dry grass. When the turkey returns to her nest, and seats herself in it, the string is pulled, and she is crushed by the log.

Emus are frequently run down with dogs. They are sometimes trapped, during the dry weather, by digging a hole in a nearly dried-up swamp, where the birds are in the habit of drinking. The hole is about twenty feet in diameter, and made very muddy and soft, with a little water in the centre. When the birds wade in to drink, they get bogged, and are easily captured. If not actually smothered, they are very much exhausted with struggling. This trap, if at a distance from the camp, is visited every two or three days to remove the birds. The feathers are highly prized for making ornaments, the fat for anointing the body and hair, and the flesh for food. Emu is considered the greatest delicacy. It is eaten, however, only by the men and grey-haired women; young women and children are not allowed to partake of it. No reason is given for this rule. When the time for the emu to lay her eggs has arrived—which is marked, as has been elsewhere observed, by the star Canopus appearing a little above the horizon in the east at daybreak—every member of a tribe must return home, and no eggs must be taken from the grounds of a neighbouring tribe. If any person is caught trespassing and stealing the eggs, he or she can be put to death on the spot. The aborigines say that the emu is very ready to desert her nest, and if she observes yellow leeches crawling over her eggs before she lays the usual number, she immediately commences a new one, which accounts for many abandoned nests with only two or three eggs in them, instead of the usual dozen. The first egg of the emu is called 'purtæ wuuchuup,' meaning 'youngest,' because it is not only the smallest but the last to hatch, and is always at the bottom of the nest, covered by the others. The eggs are considered a great treat, and are cooked in hot ashes.

The aborigines have a tradition respecting the existence at one time of some very large birds, which were incapable of flight, and resembled emus. They lived long ago, when the volcanic hills were in a state of eruption. The native name for them is 'meeheeruung parrinmall'—'big emu,' and they are described, hyperbolically, as so large that their 'heads were as high as the hills,' and so formidable that a kick from one of them would kill a man. These birds were much feared on account of their extraordinary courage, strength, and speed of foot. When one was seen, two of the bravest men of the tribe were ordered to kill it. As they dared not attack it on foot, they provided themselves with a great many spears, and climbed up a tree; and when the bird came to look at them, they speared it from above. The last specimen of this extinct bird was seen near the site of Hamilton. In all probability, skeletons will be some day found, corroborating the statements of the aborigines with regard to this bird, which seems to have resembled the gigantic moa of New Zealand.

Swans are killed in marshes, by the hunter wading among the tall reeds and sedges, and knocking the birds on the head with a waddy. When the nullore blossoms, the swans commence laying. The eggs are generally eaten raw, especially by the men while wading in the cold swamps, as they believe an uncooked egg keeps them warm. The penalty for robbing a swan's nest in a marsh belonging to a neighbouring tribe is a severe beating. Ducks and the smaller waterfowl are captured among the reeds and sedges with a noose on the point of a long wand. The hunter approaches them under the concealment of a bunch of leaves, and slips the noose over their heads, and draws them towards him quietly, so as not to disturb the others.

In summer, when the long grass in the marshes is dry enough to burn, it is set on fire in order to attract birds in search of food, which is exposed by the destruction of the cover; and, as the smoke makes them stupid, even the wary crow is captured when hungry. Sometimes a waterhole is surrounded with a brush fence, in which an opening is left. Near this opening a small bower is made, in which the hunter sits; and, when the birds come to drink, he nooses them while passing. Pigeons are caught in great numbers in this way; and, as they come regularly to drink at sunset, the hunter has not long to wait for them. The quail is captured during the breeding season only, for then it is readily attracted by imitating the call of its mate; and the hunter, concealed by a bush shield and provided with the long wand and noose, has no difficulty in catching it among the long grass. Small birds are killed with a long, sharp-pointed wand by boys, who lie in thickets and attract them by imitating their cries. When a bird alights on a bush above their heads, they gently push up the wand and suddenly transfix the animal.

The eagle is hated on account of its readiness to attack young children. The natives mention an instance of a baby having been carried off by one, while crawling outside a wuurn near the spot where the village of Caramut now stands. On the discovery of an eagle's nest—which is always built on the top of a high tree—the natives wait the departure of the old birds, and, while one man watches for their return, the other climbs up and digs a hole through the bottom of the nest, and removes the eggs. If it contains young birds, too strong to be handled, he sets fire to the nest with a lighted stick, which he carries between his teeth. This so terrifies them that they jump out, and fall to the ground. While the old birds are present no native will venture up to their nest, for a blow from their wing would make him lose his hold, and death would be the consequence.

Fish are caught in various ways, but the idea of a hook and line never appears to have occurred to the natives of the Western District. Large fresh-water fish are taken by tying a bunch of worms, with cord made of the inner bark of the prickly acacia, to the end of a long supple wand like a fishing-rod. The bait is dipped into the pool or stream, and, when swallowed by the fish, it is pulled up quickly before the fish can disgorge it. Fishing baskets, about eight or ten feet long, made of rushes in the form of a drag-net, are drawn through the water by two persons. Various kinds of fish are thus captured. The small fish, 'tarropatt,' and others of a similar description, are caught in a rivulet which runs into Lake Colongulac, near Camperdown, by damming it up with stones, and placing a basket in a gap of the dam. The women and children go up the stream and drive the fish down ; and, when the basket is full, it is emptied into holes dug in the ground to prevent them escaping. The fish thus caught are quickly cooked by spreading them on hot embers raked out of the fire, and are lifted with slips of bark and eaten hot.

Eels are prized by the aborigines as an article of food above all other fish. They are captured in great numbers by building stone barriers across rapid streams, and diverting the current through an opening into a funnel-mouthed basket pipe, three or four feet long, two inches in diameter, and closed at the lower end. When the streams extend over the marshes in time of flood, clay embankments, two to three feet high, and sometimes three to four hundred yards in length, are built across them, and the current is confined to narrow openings in which the pipe baskets are placed. The eels, proceeding down the stream in the beginning of the winter floods, go headforemost into the pipes, and do not attempt to turn back. Lake Boloke is the most celebrated place in the Western District for the fine quality and abundance of its eels ; and, when the autumn rains induce these fish to leave the lake and to go down the river to the sea, the aborigines gather there from great distances. Each tribe has allotted to it a portion of the stream, now known as the Salt Creek ; and the usual stone barrier is built by each family, with the eel basket in the opening. Large numbers are caught during the fishing season. For a month or two the banks of the Salt Creek presented the appearance of a village all the way from Tuureen Tuureen, the outlet of the lake, to its junction with the Hopkins. The Boloke tribe claims the country round the lake, and both sides of the river, as far down as

Hexham, and consequently has the exclusive right to the fish. No other tribe can catch them without permission, which is generally granted, except to unfriendly tribes from a distance, whose attempts to take the eels by force have often led to quarrels and bloodshed. Spearing eels in marshes and muddy ponds is a favourite amusement. Armed with two eel-spears, the fisher wades about, sometimes in water up to his waist, probing the weeds and mud, at the same time gently feeling with his toes. On discovering an eel under his feet, he transfixes it with one spear pushed between his toes, and then with another, and by twisting both together he prevents its escape, and raises it to the surface. He then crushes its head with his teeth, and strings it on a kangaroo sinew tied to his waist. In instances where old men have very few or bad teeth, it is amusing to see them worrying the heads, while the tails of the eels are wriggling and twisting round their necks. If the marsh is shallow, the eel can be seen swimming in the water. It is followed to its hole in the ground. The fisher probes the spot with an eel-spear, and, feeling that he has transfixed the eel, he treads in with his heel a round portion of the mud and weeds, lifts the sod to the surface of the water, and removes the eel. Sometimes two spears are needed to secure the fish. In summer, when the swamps are quite dry on the surface, but moist underneath, eels are discovered by their air-holes, and are dug up.

For night fishing in deep waterholes, a stage is formed of limbs of trees, grass, and earth, projecting three or four feet from the bank, and close to the surface of the water. A fire is lighted on the bank, or a torch of dry bark held aloft, both to attract the fish and give light. The fisher, lying on his face, spies the fish through a hole in the middle of the stage, and either spears or catches them with his hand. In shallow lakes and lagoons fish are caught during very dark nights with torch and spear. The torch is made of dried ti-tree twigs, tied in a bundle. The fishers wade through the water in line, each with a light in one hand and a spear in the other. Fish of various kinds are attracted by the light, and are speared in great numbers.

Crayfish and crabs are caught by wading into the sea, and allowing them to lay hold of the big toe, which is moved about as a bait. The fisher then reaches down and seizes the animal by the back, pulls off its claws, and puts it into a basket, which is slung across his shoulders. Freshwater mussels are found in the rivers. When the water beetle is seen swimming on the surface of the water in great numbers, it is a sign that there are 'plenty of mussels there.' Hence the water beetle is called the 'mother of mussels.' Tortoises abound in the

River Hopkins. The aborigines believe that thunder causes them to come out of the water and lay their eggs. These they deposit in the sand, and cover with a layer of soft mud, about the size of the mouth of a tea cup. This indicates their position to the fisher, who digs them up with a stick. They are roasted in hot ashes, and are considered very good eating.

Snakes are very much dreaded by the aborigines, who, from their primitive habits, are peculiarly exposed to danger from these reptiles. Only two instances, however, of death from snake-bite are known to the present generation of the tribes mentioned in this book; and there is no recollection of any death of a child from this cause. There are eight kinds of snake, including boas, most of which are venomous; and their poison is considered to be just as virulent when they are in a semi-torpid state as when they are in full activity. There is only one variety—the carpet or tiger snake—which will attack a man without provocation, and this is the most deadly of all the Victorian snakes. The death-adder of the interior of Australia, whose bite is said to kill a large dog in fifteen minutes, is unknown in the Western District of Victoria. On the Mount Elephant Plains there is a small kind of snake, called 'gnullin gnullin,' which is about eighteen inches long, and one-third of an inch in diameter, of uniform thickness, and terminating abruptly at the tail. It resembles the English blind-worm, and, like it, is harmless. With the exception of this and the boas, the bite of any of the snakes will produce temporary indisposition. When, therefore, a person is bitten by a snake, and has not been able to discern the species to which it belongs, he is made to look at the sun, and, if he see an emu in it, the case is considered hopeless: he has seen his spectre, and must shortly die. If nothing be seen in the sun, there is hope of recovery. The only remedy used is rubbing the wound with fat. They have no idea of sucking the wound, or scarifying it. They have a very correct idea of the nature of snake-bite, for they believe that the poison is contained in a bag behind the eye, and is projected into the wound through a hollow in the fang. They say that one poisonous snake can kill another.

Boa snakes are not so plentiful as the others. There are two kinds, a larger and a smaller. Of the larger kind, individuals have been killed ten feet long. They are of a dark mottled leaden colour, and have small heads, with large teeth. The smaller kind is the more dangerous of the two. It will attack a human being readily and unprovoked. When it has laid hold of its victim, it cannot easily be removed. It winds itself tightly round the body until it reaches the crown of the head, and then waves its head to and fro. When irritated, or when calling to its mate, it emits a sound like 'kæ, kæ, kæ.' It is the only snake that makes any sound. Pundeet Puulotong said, that, when he was a little boy, a boa snake attacked a man at the Salt Creek, and squeezed his neck so severely that he died the same day. The boy saw the reptile spring on its victim, but was afraid to go near it, and ran home to tell his friends, who came too late to assist the man. He was dead, and the snake was gone. Near Mount Rouse two men were attacked by a boa, which sprang on one of them and wound itself round his body; the other was too frightened to help his companion, and kept at a distance. The snake, on reaching his head, 'whistled' and brought its mate, which also wound itself round the man. He, knowing the habits of the boa, remained quite still. The other man then ran for assistance. The friends came, but only to watch; knowing that the boas, if disturbed, would probably bite the man as well as squeeze him, and, if let alone, might leave their victim alone. After a while they did so, but the man had been nearly frightened to death.

At Kangatong, an aboriginal was attacked by a boa, which got up his leg, underneath his blue shirt as far as his belt, and began to squeeze him. He threw himself on the ground, and rolled backwards and forwards till it released him. When he came to the house at Kangatong and told the story, it was at first discredited; but on examining the dead snake and the marks of the struggle, and knowing the thoroughly reliable character of the man—who was blue with fright, and scarcely able to walk—there was no longer room to doubt of the truth of his statement. Long previous to this occurrence the natives had often pointed to a stony rise, and said that there a snake had seized and squeezed a man; but the story had been misbelieved. This later occurrence, coming more under the cognizance of the white people, obtained credit for the former statements, and showed that the boas of Victoria will attack human beings, and are dangerous.

CHAPTER XXI.

METEOROLOGY AND ASTRONOMY.

GREAT reliance is placed by the natives on certain signs, as indicating a change in the weather; and, even when a white person might not observe symptoms of an approaching storm, the natives are made aware of it by signs well known to them. They notice the appearance of the sun, moon, stars, and clouds, the cries and movements of animals, &c. A bright sunrise prognosticates fine weather; a red sunrise, rain; a red sunset, heat next day; a halo round the sun, fine weather; a bright moon, fine weather; the old moon in the arms of the new, rain; the new moon lying on its back, dry weather; a halo round the moon, rain; a rainbow in the morning, fine weather; a rainbow in the evening, bad weather; a rainbow during rain, clearing up; when mosquitoes and gnats are very troublesome, rain is expected; when the cicada sings at night, there will be a hot wind next day. The arrival of the swift, which is a migratory bird, indicates bad weather. The whistle of the black jay, the chirp of the little green frog, the creak of the cricket, and the cry of the magpie lark indicate bad weather; wet weather is more likely to come after full moon. It is a sign of heat and fine weather when the eagle amuses itself by towering to an immense height, turning its head suddenly down, and descending vertically, with great force and with closed wings, till near the earth, then opening them and sweeping upwards with half-closed wings to the same height. This movement it repeats again and again, for a long time, without exertion and with apparent pleasure. The aborigines call this movement 'warroweean,' and always expect warm weather to follow it.

They believe that, in dry weather, if any influential person take water into his mouth and blow it towards the setting sun, saying, 'Come down, rain,' the wind will blow and the rain will pour for three days. When they wish for rain to make the grass grow at any particular place, they dig up the root of the convolvulus, called 'tarruuk,' and throw it in the direction of the place, saying, 'Go and make the grass grow there!'

Although the knowledge of the heavenly bodies possessed by the natives may not entitle it to be dignified by the name of astronomical science, it greatly exceeds that of most white people. Of such importance is a knowledge of the stars to the aborigines in their night journeys, and of their positions denoting the particular seasons of the year, that astronomy is considered one of the principal branches of education. Among the tribes between the rivers Leigh and Glenelg, it is taught by men selected for their intelligence and information. The following list was obtained from Weerat Kuyuut, the sagacious old chief of the Moporr tribe, and from his very intelligent daughter, Yarrum Parpur Tarneen, and her husband, Wombeet Tuulawarn :—

The sun is called 'tirng,' meaning 'light,' and is of the feminine gender.

The moon, 'meeheaarong kuurtaruung,' meaning 'hip,' is masculine.

The new moon, 'taaruuk neung,' is masculine.

The larger stars are called 'kakii tirng,' 'sisters of the sun,' and are feminine.

The smaller stars, 'narweetch mæring,' 'star earth.'

The milky way, 'barnk,' 'big river.'

The coal sack of the ancient mariners—that dark space in the milky way near the constellation of the Southern Cross—is called 'torong,' a fabulous animal, said to live in waterholes and lakes, known by the name of bunyip, and so like a horse that the natives on first seeing a horse took it for a bunyip, and would not venture near it. By some tribes the coal sack is supposed to be a waterhole ; and celestial aborigines, represented by the large stars around it, are said to have come from the south end of the milky way, and to have chased the smaller stars into it, where they are now engaged in spearing them.

The larger Magellanic cloud, 'kuurn kuuronn,' 'male native companion,' or 'gigantic crane.'

The smaller Magellanic cloud, 'gnærang kuuronn,' 'female native companion.'

Jupiter, 'Burtit tuung tirng,' 'strike the sun'—as it is often seen near it at midday—feminine.

Venus, 'Wang'uul,' 'twinkle,' feminine ; also 'Paapee neowee,' 'mother of the sun.'

Canopus, 'Waa,' 'crow'—masculine.

Sirius, or the dog star, 'Gneeangar,' 'eagle'—masculine.

Antares, 'Butt kuee tuukuung,' 'big stomach'—masculine. The two stars near Antares, one on each side, are his wives, and the three stars underneath are called 'kuukuu narranuung,' 'nearly a grandfather.' The glow-worm took its light from Butt kuee tuukuung.

Stars in tail of Scorpio, 'Kummim bieetch,' 'one sitting on the back of the other's neck'—masculine.

Pleiades are called 'kuurokeheear,' 'flock of cockatoos,' by the Kuurn kopan noot tribe, and are feminine. The Pirt kopan noot tribe have no general name for the Pleiades; but there is a tradition that the stars in it were a queen called Gneeanggar, and her six attendants; and, that, a long time ago, the star Canopus—'Waa,' 'crow'—fell in love with the queen, but was so unsuccessful in gaining her affections that he determined to get possession of her by stratagem. Shortly after her refusal to become his wife, he discovered by some means that the queen and her six attendants were going in search of white grubs, of which they were very fond. On hearing of this, 'Waa' at once conceived the idea of transforming himself into a grub; and in this form he bored into the stem of a tree where he was certain to be observed by the queen and her servants. He was not long in his hiding-place before he was discovered by one of them, who thrust into the hole a small wooden hook, which women generally use for extracting grubs. He broke the point of the hook. He did the same with those of the other five attendants. The queen then approached, and introduced a beautiful bone hook into the hole. He knew that this hook was hers; he therefore allowed himself to be drawn out, and immediately assumed the form of a giant, and ran off with her from her attendants. Ever since the loss of the queen there have been only six stars in the Pleiades, representing her six servants.

Some doubt having been expressed by friends to whom the manuscript was shown with regard to the authenticity of this story, which shows a very remarkable coincidence with tales of Grecian mythology, the strictest inquiry has been made through Mr. William Goodall, the superintendent of the Framlingham Aboriginal Station; and the result of this inquiry has been to confirm the story, and to show that it is well known in the Western District, and, with some variation, in South Australia also.

The three stars in the belt of Orion are called 'Kuppiheear' and are the sisters of Sirius, who always follows them.

A yellowish star in the constellation of Orion is called 'Kuupartakil;' and another, of a red colour, is called 'Moroitch,' 'fire'—masculine.

Southern Cross, 'Kunkun Tuuromballank,' 'knot or tie'—masculine.

Centauri, the pointers, 'Tuulirmp,' 'magpie larks'—masculine.

Mars, 'Parrupum'—masculine.

Fomelhaut, 'Buunjill'—masculine.

Hydra, 'Barrukill,' is a great hunter of kangaroo rats. On his right, and a little above him, are two stars—the rat, and his dog 'Karlok;' above these again are four stars, forming a log; underneath are four other stars, one of which is his light, and three form his arm. The dog chases the rat into the log; Barrukill takes it out, devours it, and disappears below the horizon. Hydra is of great service to the aborigines in their night journeys, enabling them to judge the time of the night and the course to be taken in travelling.

A comet, 'Puurt Kuurnuuk,' believed to be a great spirit.

A meteor, 'Gnummæ waar,' 'deformity.'

The crepuscular arch in the west in the morning is called 'Kullat,' 'peep-of-day.'

The upper crepuscular arch in the east at sunset is called 'Kuurokeheear' puuron,' 'white cockatoo twilight.'

The under arch, 'Kappiheear puuron,' 'black cockatoo twilight.' The natives say this arch comes from the constellation Orion.

The crepuscular rays in the west after sunset are called 'rushes of the sun.'

The Aurora Australis, 'Puæ buæ,' 'ashes.'

For the names of the cardinal points of the compass, and of the various winds, see the vocabulary at the end of the book.

The aborigines appear to be well acquainted with the effects of earthquakes. Besides one which they say rent the ground and formed 'Taap heear'—a waterhole in Spring Creek, near Minjah House—they have a vivid recollection of another which occurred about forty years ago. Puulornpuul, who described it, was a little boy when it occurred. Three tribes were encamped on the lower Hopkins River, and were holding a korroboræ after sunset; they had their fires lighted round a waterhole, and were in the midst of their dancing, when a strange sound, 'like the galloping of horses,' approached from the north-west, accompanied with a violent shaking of the ground, which, according to Puulornpuul, 'ran about and pushed up blackfellows,' and was immediately followed by a hurricane. This may have been the same earthquake which upset one of Major Mitchell's drays while his party was encamped between the Hopkins and Geelong.

Some names of places indicate the existence of heat in the ground at a former period; but no tradition exists of any of the old craters, so numerous in the Western District, ever having thrown out smoke or ashes, with the exception of 'Bo'ok,' a hill near the town of Mortlake. An intelligent aboriginal distinctly remembers his grandfather speaking of fire coming out of Bo'ok when he was a young man. When some of the volcanic bombs found among the scoriæ at the foot of Mount Leura were shown to an intelligent Colac native, he said they were like stones which their forefathers told them had been thrown out of the hill by the action of fire.

CHAPTER XXII.

NATIVE MOUNDS.

NATIVE mounds, so common all over the country, are called 'pok yuu' by the Chaa wuurong tribe; 'po'ok,' by the Kuurn kopan noot tribe; and 'puulwuurn' by the Peek whuurong tribe; and were the sites of large, permanent habitations, which formed homes for many generations. The great size of some of them, and the vast accumulation of burnt earth, charcoal, and ashes which is found in and around them, is accounted for by the long continuance of the domestic hearth, the decomposition of the building materials, and the debris arising from their frequent destruction by bush fires. They never were ovens, or original places of interment, as is generally supposed, and were only used for purposes of burial after certain events occurred while they were occupied as sites for residences—such as the death of more than one of the occupants of the dwelling at the same time, or the family becoming extinct; in which instance they were called 'muuru kowuutuung' by the Chaa wuurong tribe, and 'muuruup kaakee' by the Kuurn kopan noot tribe, meaning 'ghostly place,' and were never afterwards used as sites for residences, and only as places for burial. There is an idea that when two persons die at the same time on any particular spot, their deaths, if not attributed to the spell of an enemy, are caused by something unhealthy about the locality, and it is abandoned for ever. It is never even visited again, except to bury the dead; and the mounds are used for that purpose only because the soil is loose, and a grave is more easily dug in them than in the solid ground. The popular notion of their having been ovens is refuted, not only by the unanimous testimony of all the old aborigines, but also by a careful examination of the structure and stratification of the mounds. On opening a very perfect circular mound, sixty-five feet in diameter and five feet high, and intersecting it by parallel trenches dug at intervals of three feet, down to the original surface soil, and through that and a bed of gravel to the clay, not the slightest sign was observed of the ancient alluvial soil having been disturbed. Had an oven ever existed there, it would have been distinctly visible in the floor of the wuurn, as native ovens are always formed by digging deep holes in the ground. In cutting through these mounds, a complete history of their growth was exhibited. Layers of yellow ashes, mixed with small pieces of charred wood, alternated with the earthy debris of the old dwellings ; and the numerous saucer-shaped, ashy hollows in the strata of the mounds showed where the fires had been. No stones larger than a walnut were found ; which is another proof that the fireplaces were never used as ovens. Several mounds, not more than a foot high, on being intersected in every direction, showed the remains of only one fireplace, and that always on the eastern side of the mound. In every large mound, and in some of the smaller ones, human skeletons were found about eighteen inches below the surface, lying on the side, with the head to the west, and the knees drawn up to the chest—a mode of sepulture not uncommon among the aboriginal inhabitants of England.

CHAPTER XXIII.

ANECDOTES.

THE first white man who made his appearance at Port Fairy (a locality named after a small vessel called the *Fairy*) was considered by the aborigines to be a supernatural being; and, as he was discovered in the act of smoking a pipe, they said that he must be made of fire, for they saw smoke coming out of his mouth. Though they were very ready to attack a stranger, they took good care not to go near this man of fire, who very probably owed the preservation of his life to his tobacco-pipe. Shortly afterwards a tipsy man was seen. He was considered mad, and everyone ran away from him.

The first ship which was descried by the aborigines was believed to be a huge bird, or a tree growing in the sea. It created such terror that a messenger was immediately sent to inform the chief of the tribe, who at once declared the man to be insane, and ordered him to be bled by the doctor.

When the natives first saw a bullock, they were encamped at the waterhole Wuurong Yæring in Spring Creek, near the spot where the village of Woolsthorpe now stands, and were engaged in fishing. The animal, which was evidently a stray working bullock from some exploring party, and which had a sheet of tin tied across his face to prevent him from wandering, came down to the waterhole to drink. The natives, who had never in their lives heard of such a large beast, instantly took to their heels. In the night time the bullock came to the encampment and walked about it bellowing, which so terrified the people in the camp that they covered themselves up with their rugs and lay trembling till sunrise. In the morning they saw what they believed to be a Muuruup, with two tomahawks in his head; but no one dared to move. Immediately after the departure of this extraordinary and unwelcome visitor, a council of war was held; and the brave men, accompanied by their wives and children—who could not, under such alarming circumstances, be left behind—started in pursuit. The animal was easily tracked, as such footprints had never been seen before. They were followed four or five miles in a north-easterly direction. The bullock was at length discovered grazing in an open part of the forest. The bravest of the warriors went to the front, and, with the whole tribe at their back, approached the animal. They asked if he was a whitefellow, and requested him to give them the tomahawks he carried on his head ; whereupon the astonished bullock pawed the ground, bellowed, shook his head, and charged. This so terrified the 'braves' that they fled headlong, and in their precipitate retreat upset men, women, and children, and broke their spears. The natives afterwards told this story with great glee. It used to be narrated in a very humorous way by Gnaweeth, who was mentioned in a previous chapter, and afforded the women many a laugh at the expense of the men. It was also told more recently by Weeratt Kuuyuut, when he was considerably over seventy years of age ; and he described it as having occurred when he was a newly married man, which makes the date of the incident to have been about 1821 or '22.

THE FIRST FORMATION OF WATERHOLES.

One very dry season, when there was no water in all the country, and the animals were perishing of thirst, a magpie lark and a gigantic crane consulted together. They could not understand how it was that a turkey bustard of their acquaintance was never thirsty ; and, knowing that he would not tell them where his supply of water was obtained from, they resolved to watch and find out where he drank. They flew high into the air, and saw him go to a flat stone. Before lifting the stone, the turkey, afraid of his treasure being discovered, looked up and saw the two birds, but they were so high, and kept so steady, that he took them for small clouds. He lifted the stone, therefore, and drank from a spring running out of a cleft in a rock. When he replaced the stone and flew away, the two spies came down and removed it, and took a drink and a bath, remarking, 'King gnakko gnal'—'We have done him.' They flapped their wings with joy, and the water rose till it formed a lake. They then flew all over the parched country, flapping their wings and forming water-holes, which have been drinking-places ever since.

THE TORTOISE AND THE SNAKE.

Long ago the tortoise was a venomous beast, and bit people while they were drinking at waterholes and streams. To avoid being bitten, they adopted the plan of scooping up the water with their hands and throwing it into their mouths. This precaution so disappointed the tortoise, that he asked the snake to allow him to transfer his deadly venom to it; and argued that, since the natives had adopted another mode of drinking, he had no opportunity of destroying them, but that the snake had many opportunities of biting them in their wuurns and among the long grass. The snake agreed to the proposal, and ever afterwards the tortoise has been harmless. This method of drinking, however, which was adopted to avoid the bite of the tortoise, still continues.

THE BLUE HERON.

Once upon a time, while a large meeting was being held at a place near Dunkeld, and the natives were encamped under a wide-spreading red gum-tree, and were enjoying a feast of small fish, one of their number was so displeased because he did not get the whole of the fish to himself, which had been distributed to his tribe, that he took the form of a heron, and, lighting on the tree, knocked it down and killed nearly the whole of the tribe. Those who escaped ran off and told the other tribes who were encamped in the neighbourhood what had happened. When they came to the spot, they found that the heron had eaten all the fish. In revenge they laid upon him the curse that his spirit would fly about for ever in the form of a blue heron, and then they killed him.

THE NATIVE COMPANION AND THE EMU.

A native companion and an emu, each with a brood of young ones, went to a swamp to get sedge roots, which are very good to eat. They kindled a fire on the bank in which to cook the roots, and then waded into the water to get a supply. The native companion pulled up a number of roots, and returned to the fire, provided with a long pole, with which she pushed the roots into the fire, and had them all covered up, and the pole hidden, before the emu returned with her supply. The emu had only a very short stick, which was soon burnt in trying to push her roots into the fire. She used first one foot and then the other. Both got scorched. She tried her wings next, then her bill, and had them scorched likewise. She ran to the swamp to cool her burns. On her return she found the native companion and her young ones digging the roots out of the fire with the long pole, and eating them. The emu was very ill pleased at the trick, but resolved to be revenged at a future opportunity. Some time afterwards they went again to the swamp for roots, kindled a fire on the bank, and left the young emus only at it to watch the fire. The young native companions accompanied their mother. The emu came home first, fed her young ones with roasted roots, and hid all her brood except two. The native companion returned with her young ones, and, on inquiring what was being roasted in the fire, was told by the emu that, as she could not find any roots, and was very hungry, she was cooking all her young ones except the two which were running about. Thereupon the native companion killed all her young ones except two, and put them into the fire to roast. After they were eaten, the emu called her brood from their hiding-place, and, addressing the native companion, said, ' Now I have served you out for deceiving me on a former occasion, and ever after this you will have no more than two young ones at a time, instead of a dozen as I have, and as you had before playing this trick on me.'

THE BUNYIP.

The following story was told by the old chief, Morpor, to his daughter and her husband :—Long ago two brothers—one of them so tall that he looked down on everybody, and the other of ordinary size—went to a swamp near Mount William to get swans' eggs. They found a great many ; and, while roasting some of them on the bank of the lagoon, the smaller of the brothers said that he must get some more from the swamp. The taller one forbade him to go alone. However, he did go. He found a nest in the middle of the lagoon, and took the eggs. When returning to the shore, he heard a rush of water behind him, and saw the water-fowls in front of him hurrying along the water as if frightened. At the same time, the bottom of the marsh became so soft that he stuck in the mud, and could not go forward. A great wave overtook him and carried him back to the nest, where a large bunyip caught him in its mouth. It held him so high that his brother saw him. Some hours afterwards the water became calm. The tall brother then took a sheet of bark and put a fire on it, and, approaching the nest, saw his brother in the mouth of the bunyip. Speaking to the bunyip, he said—'Be quiet, and let me take my brother.' The bunyip gnashed its teeth and gave him up ; but he was dead, and his entrails had been devoured. The brother took the body ashore and laid it near the fire, and wept. He then went for his friends, who came and carried the corpse to their home. After he had watched it for two days, the relatives put it in a tree for one moon, and then burned it, with the exception of the leg and arm bones, which were given to the friends of the deceased.

THE GHOST.

A man, travelling in the country of a friendly tribe, came upon a deserted habitation. Above the doorway he saw the usual crooked stick, pointing in the direction which the family had taken; and, all round about the place, pieces of bark covered with white clay, indicating a death. He found tracks leading to a tree, in which he soon discovered a dead body. Anxious to know who had died, he laid down his rug and weapons at the foot of the tree, and ascended it. On removing the opossum rug from the face, he found that it was a friend. He wept for a long time, then came down and went away; but he had not gone far before he heard some magpies making a great noise, as though they saw something strange. He turned round to see what it was, and, to his horror and amazement, saw the ghost of the deceased come down and follow him. He became so terrified that he could not move; and, addressing it, said—'Why do you frighten me, when I have come to see you, and never did you any harm?' It never spoke, but followed him for a considerable distance, scratching his back meanwhile with its nails, and then returned to the tree. When he reached his friends he told them what had happened, and showed them his back, lacerated and bleeding; and said that he had a presentiment that something bad would befall him before long. At the next meeting of the tribes he was speared through the heart.

THE METEOR.

A friend communicates the following anecdote as illustrative of the cleverness of the aborigines. 'On one occasion, having tried in vain to get an old man—known about Camperdown as Doctor George—to understand something of the Christian religion, I turned the conversation to the subject of a large meteor which had appeared a few months previously, and asked him if he had seen it. After a little he caught my meaning, and said—"Yes! me see him, like it fire; him go 'ff 'ff," pointing with his finger its path along the sky. I asked him what he thought it was. He answered, carelessly, "Borak me know." Then suddenly brightening up, and putting on a slyly grave countenance, he said:

" Me think, great big one master "—pointing to the sky—" want smoke him pipe. Him strike him match," suiting the action to the words, " and puff, puff," pretending to smoke. Then he made a movement as though he slowly dropped a match through the air. The comical assumption of gravity with which this was said, and the quickness with which the impromptu explanation was invented, showed that if he did not understand my religious teaching, it was certainly not from lack of intelligence.'

BUCKLEY'S WIDOW.

The following account has been kindly communicated by Mr. Goodall, the Superintendent of the Aboriginal Station at Framlingham, who has in several other ways assisted the writer in obtaining information from the aborigines under his charge :—

There is, at the Aboriginal Station at Framlingham, a native woman named Purranmurnin Tallarwurnin, who was the wife of the white man Buckley at the time he was found by the first settlers in Victoria. She belonged originally to the Buninyong tribe, and was about fifteen years old when she became acquainted with Buckley. She says that one of the natives discovered immense footprints in the sand hummocks near the River Barwon, and concluded that they had been made by some unknown gigantic native—a stranger, and therefore an enemy. He set off at once on the track and soon discovered a strange-looking being lying down on a small hillock, sunning himself after a bath in the sea. A brief survey, cautiously made, was sufficient. The native hurried back to the camp and told the rest of the tribe what he had seen. They at once collected all the men in the neighbourhood, formed a cordon, and warily closed in on him. When they came near he took little or no notice of them, and did not even alter his position for some time. They were very much alarmed. At length one of the party finding courage addressed him as muurnong guurk (meaning that they supposed him to be one who had been killed and come to life again), and asked his name, " You Kondak Baarwon?" Buckley replied by a prolonged grunt and an inclination of the head, signifying yes. They asked him a number of other questions, all of which were suggested by the idea that he was one of themselves returned from the dead, and to all the questions Buckley gave the same reply. They were highly gratified, and he and they soon became friends. They made a wuurn of leafy branches for him, and lit a fire in front of it, around which they all assembled. He was then recognized as one of the tribe. The news spread rapidly, and he was visited by large numbers of natives from different parts of the colony, who always showed great fear of him at first. The children especially would hide themselves from him, or call to their mothers to keep them from the Muuruup.

When ships visited the coast to get wood and water, Buckley never sought to make himself known to any of them. On several occasions ships were wrecked on the coast and all hands perished. From the wrecks Buckley and his tribe secured a large quantity of blankets, axes, and other articles, which he taught them how to use.

When Batman arrived at Geelong, Buckley was fishing in the river Barwon— in which pursuit he excelled—and the news was conveyed to him by a number of natives, who brought him several articles which they had received as presents from Batman and his friends, such as biscuits, sugar, bread, &c., which he at once recognized and partook of. He was asked by the tribe to take his fish (of which he had a large quantity) and all his war accoutrements, and go down to the " big ships." When he arrived he was met by Batman and " all the other big fellows," who were well pleased to see a white man among the natives. Buckley could not at first understand what they said, having completely forgotten his own language. He looked so puzzled while he was endeavouring to recall his mother tongue. Several days passed before he could converse with any freedom. Batman and his companions were not long in getting Buckley thoroughly washed and shaved, and in cutting his hair, which had grown to a prodigious length. When he was taken away in the ship the natives were much distressed at losing him, and when, some time after, they received a letter informing them of his marriage in Hobart Town, they lost all hope of his return to them, and grieved accordingly.

Buckley arrived at Port Phillip in 1802 as a convict, and in 1803 made his escape into the bush. After wandering about for one year he joined the aborigines, and lived with them till 1835. For thirty-two years he had not conversed with a white man. He had no children, and died in Tasmania in 1856.

CONVEYANCE BY PRINCIPAL CHIEFS TO BATMAN OF 100,000 ACRES BETWEEN GEELONG AND QUEENSCLIFF.

THE lithograph opposite to this page is a *fac-simile* of a parchment conveyance of certain land near Geelong to John Batman from eight chiefs, who affixed their marks, or signatures, to the deed, and at the same time symbolized the transfer of the land by taking up some of the soil and handing it to Batman. The original document is in the custody of Messrs. Taylor, Buckland and Gates, who have kindly given their permission to its publication. The heading is not in the original document.

Another conveyance of 500,000 acres between Geelong and the Yarra was made to Batman. A copy of this conveyance is to be found in the Record Office, in the Van Diemen's Land Correspondence, and has been published by Dr. Lang, by Mr. Bonwick, by Mr. Arden, and by Mr. Labelliere, in their several accounts of the early settlement of Victoria.

Both of the transactions represented by these documents were disallowed by the Colonial Secretary, in London.

The marks made by the chiefs on the parchment were their genuine and usual signatures, which they were in the habit of carving on the bark of trees and on their message sticks. The reader will be interested in these traces of civilization among a people who have hitherto been considered the least civilized of all nations.

Know all Persons

that We *Three Brothers,* *Coolooock, Bubej*

at and near *Port Phillip* called by ...

hereinafter mentioned for and in consideration of *Twenty Pair of Blankets, Thir*

Fifty Handkerchiefs — Twelve Red Shirts — Four Flannel Jacke

by *John Batman* residing in *Van Diemens Land* Esquire but at presen

Give Grant Enfeoff and confirm unto the said *John Batman* h

of *Port Phillip* known by the Name of *Indented Head*

about due south for *Ten miles* more or less to the *Heads.*

and containing about *One Hundred Thousand* ———— Acres as the same ha

according to the custom of our *Tribe* by certain marks made upon the

said *Tract of Land* with all advantages belonging thereto unto and

Intent that the said *John Batman* his Heirs and Assigns may ...

Yielding and delivering to Us and our Heirs or Successors the ...

Fifty Pair Scissors Fifty Looking Glasses Twenty

We *Jagajaga, Jagajaga, Jagajaga, the Three Principal Chiefs,* and a

the Chiefs of the said Tribe have hereto affixed our Seals to these ...

this *Sixth* day of *June* One thousand eight hundred

Signed Sealed and Delivered in the presence of Us the same having
been fully and properly interpreted and explained to the said Chiefs

James Gumm

Alexander Thompson

Wm Todd

Jagajaga, Jagajaga, Jagajaga, being the Principal Chiefs, and also
..arie, Yanyan, Moowhip, Mommamalar
..being the Chiefs of a certain Native Tribe called Dutigallar, situate
..s the above mentioned Chiefs Iramoos & Geelong being possessed of the Tract of Land
..y Knives, Twelve Tomahawks, Ten looking Glasses Twelve Pair Scissors
..te Four Suits of Cloths and Fifty pounds of Flour delivered to Us
..& sojourning with Us and our Tribe Do for ourselves and our Heirs and Successors
..s Heirs and Assigns **All that** Tract of Country situate and being in the Bay
.., but called by us Geelong, extending across from Geelong Harbour
..of Port Phillip taking in the whole neck or Track of Land
..th been before the execution of these presents delineated and marked out by Us
..e Trees growing along the boundaries of the said Tract of Land **To Hold** the
..To the Use of the said John Batman his heirs and Assigns for ever To the
..ccupy and possess the said Tract of Land and place thereon Sheep and Cattle
..yearly Rent or Tribute of Fifty Pair of Blankets Fifty Knives, Fifty Tomahawks
..Suits of Slops, or Clothing and Two Tons of Flour **In Witness** whereof
..ls Cooloolock, Bungarie, Yanyan, Moowhip, Mommamalar
..resents and have signed the same Dated according to the Christian Era
..and thirty five

Jagajaga
Jagajaga
Jagajaga
Cooloolock
Bungarie
Yanyan
Moowhip
Mommamalar
John Batman

Be it Remembered That on the day and Year
within written possession and delivery of the tract of
Land within mentioned was made by the within
named Jagajaga, Jagajaga, Jagajaga,
Cooloolock, Bungarie, Yan Yan Moowhip Mommamalar
Chiefs of the Tribe of Natives called Dutigallar
Geelong to the within named John Batman
by the said Chiefs taking up part of the Soil of
the said tract of Land and delivering the same
to the said John Batman in the name of
the whole

                     Jagajaga his ⦚⦚⦚ mark

In presents of   Jagajaga his ⦚⦚⦚ mark

James Gumm   Jagajaga his ⦚⦚⦚ mark

Alexander Thompson Cooloolock his ⦚⦚⦚ mark

W.m Todd   Bungarie his ⦚⦚⦚ mark

                  Yan Yan his ⦚⦚⦚ mark

                  Moowhip his ⦚⦚⦚ mark

             Mommamalan his ⦚⦚⦚ mark

VOCABULARY OF WORDS IN THREE LANGUAGES.

English.	Chaap wuurong (broad lip).	Kuurn kopan noot (small lip).	Peek whuurong (kelp lip).
A, this, that ...	Mank	Deen	Teenang
Aborigines, generally	Kuulæ	Maar	Maar
Above	Keyukun yu puuree o	Kunnæ puuræ	Kunn hatnenuung
About, here and there	King winja	Deen wuunda	Teenunuung
Acacia tree, common	Tunlin	Karrank	Karrank
Acacia tree, black	Warrarakk	Pareetcheerang	Nullawurt
Across	Kutjæerang kuurtang	Kunpillækuurt	Kilkurtin
Acid	Kirritch	Lapeetch	Gnumee chaar
Acrid	Chuutch	To'ot	To'ot
Active	Tullapuucha ...	Tulapp	Moreitch
Adultery	Yuurmelann	Yuurnonong	Yuurnonong
After	Gneokuurndeetch	Kullækitto	Kullo
Afternoon	Mirma neow wee, 'playful sun'	Kiilkan tirng, 'go down sun'	Puuron katto, 'going down'
Against, to lean against...	Purpuuna	Wambuur an	Wattum kitnan
Agrimony	Challarp	Narrak wuurong, 'hairy lip'	
Air	Motælung	Gnarnpeann	Gnuurnduuk
Air vessel of seaweed	Kuumbuuk	Gnapanyuung, 'teat or nipple'	Gnapanyuung
Algæ, fresh water	Kurambuul	Wuurnarkuæ	Wuurnarkue
Algæ, salt water	Peekoæ	Peekoæ	Peekoe
All ...	Kan kan baa	Kiangjeetch	Takuurt gnatuuk knatt
Amusement	Gnuyam charrang gno	Kulmba wan	Millin bukkan
Ancestor	Murtæ kuulæ	Allam meen	Allam meen
And	Baa	Baa	Baa
Anger	Pirnawuchuup	Warrakealeek	Watee leek
Animal	*Only specific*	*Only specific*	*Only specific*
Ankle	Puulin	Parn	Parn

i

a

English.	Chaap wuurong (broad lip).	Kuurn kopan noot (small lip).	Peek whuurong (kelp lip).
Answer	Gneerr na gneen	Lirtang	Kueaa
Ant	Only specific	Only specific	Only specific
Arm, right	Tukchukk	Tumbit	Tumbit
Arm, left	Warram	Warram	Warram
Arm, upper	Tukchukk	Mille work	Mille wuurk
Arm, fore	Ka'yuk Ka'yuk	Ka'yuuk Ka'yuuk	Ka'yuuk ka'yuuk
Artery	Gnullma	Gnullman	Puunpuun mung'an
Ashes	Paræe	Paliin	Paliin
Asleep	Kuumba gnu	Yuwan	Yuwakuea
Ask	Keeyalla gnano	Kuetkartawan	Kiitpurta g'nin
Attendant boy on warrior	Tumbaka	Tumbakko	Tumbakko
Aurora Australis	Pii	Puebuae	Puebuae
Autumn	No term	No term	No term
Awake	Pil'kneango mirnk, 'open eyes'	Lirpeeteann	Mirtan, 'jump up'
Axe, iron axe	Tartakarm	Bart bart kuurt	Purtpakuurt
Axe, stone celt	Buuraku	Mochæær	Mochæær
Axe, large stone celt	Wang'itch	Wung'itt	Purukuutch
Bachelor, old	Knallum mutchuum	Kueenat yuwatnætch	Pakeetch
Bachelor, young	Knulla yan yan kiapp	Kueenatt yan yan butteetch	Kneenatt yan yan butteetch
Back	Gnarnkuyerk	Gnawuurn	Wirk
Backbone	Kalkwirp	Turitt	Pukkiin wirk
Bad	Pirnaewuuchuup	Warrakeek laæk	Gnumeen char
Bag	Only specific	Only specific	Only specific
Bag, net bag for back	Warrak	Kuuræer	Kuuræer
Bag, water-bag	Ko'wapp	Ko'wapp	Ko'wapp
Bag, game-bag	Gnuunyee	Gnuurneen	Gnuurneen
Bag, made of kangaroo pouch			
Bag for carrying calcined human bones	Piinteuk	Paanung	Paanung
Bald head, totally	Wæet	Walluutch	Walluutch
Bald crown of head	Turkaepuurp	Pukkuitch beem	Tiinbeetch
Ball, foot ball	Challepuurp	Tulliin beem	Tulliin beem
Ball, hand ball	Min'gorn	Man'guurt	Yuumkuurt
	Man guurmp	Man'guurt	Yuumkuurt

English	Chaap wuurong (broad lip).	Kuurn kopan noot (small lip).	Peek whurrong (kelp lip).
Ball players	Beiin	Beiin	Millim beeyeetch
Band round the head	Marak kulla	Marak kullim	Yarndnul
Banksia tree	Wuurak	Weeriitch	Weeriitch
Bark of dog	Yapuunya	Yap	Luukirnin
Bark of tree	Gninakk	Tuurong	Moroitch
Bark of acacia for making cord and netting	Waakong	Wiitko	Wiitko
Bark for pegging skins on	Gninakk	Tuurong	Moroitch
Bark for producing fire	Meetenk dulang ak	Muurnong kurang at	Muluteung kurang at
Barter or exchange	Yulkuumjerrang	Yulkuurnban	Yulkuurnban
Basalt	La'aa	Marrii	Marrii
Basin made of bark	Gnunnak	Turong	Turong
Basket made of rushes	Paalk	Bun'gar	Kuirn
Basket for carrying human bones	Kulk kulk	Wiin wiin	Wiin wiin
Basket for cooking in	Pillerbirr	Milleweetch	Puurpuur
Basket for fishing	Kalwill	Moall	Moall
Basket work for back	Yalern	Pirakk	Pirakk
Battle, general fight	Gnullang	Gnullang	Gnullang
Battle between two chiefs	Puuleitcha gnerneetch	Puuleitcha wungit	Puuleitcha wungit
Beard	Knunye	Gnarin	Gnarin
Beat	Tukkuk	Burteen	Purtaa
Bed for sleeping on	Po hneugnak	Pop kanann	Pop kanann
Before	Chuumbuuk	Tuumbuuk	Tuumbuuk
Behind	Wurteea gnurak	Wurkat hatnaen	Wurk hatnaen
Belle, or handsome woman	Marrine bang bang guurk	Marrine tambuur	
Below	Kang'ok	Kang'giyu	Waenyu
Bend	Wandak	Wandako	Warnda
Beside	Lunbelang	Lunpeen chuutnan	Peenba kitnan
Betrothed boy, on a visit to his intended wife's relations	Tannat muuchelap	Kuumagnat wumbeetch	Kuumagnat wumbeetch
Betrothed girl, on a visit to her intended husband's relations	Tannat yanballup kuurk	Kuumagnat yanburtaheear	Kuumagnat yanburtaheear

English.	Chaap wuurong (broad lip).	Kuurn kopan noot (small lip).	Peek whuurong (kelp lip).
Betrothed man	Karrin yah, 'reared together'	Karræ kundar, 'reared together'	Karræ kundar, 'reared together'
Betrothed woman	Karrinup kuraak, 'reared together'	Karrinmikeearr, 'reared together'	Kuurndeepikkeearrgnan, 'reared together'
Between	Bukkar yu	Bukkur æ	Bukkur æ
Bewitched	Baak chinakk	Piet teean	Piet teean
Beyond	Kugun yuuk	Kunnæ gnuung	Puuree
Bier made of branches	Wallo walott	Wallo whalott	Wallo whalott
Big	Martuuk	Meheaaruung	Lingkill
Big mouth	Martee wuurong	Meheaar gnulang	Wuurong eaar
Big nose	Martuuk kaar	Meheaar kapuung	Murkil kapuung
Big log	Martuuk wee	Meheaar ween	Nullo neung
Bill of bird	Kaaneu	Kapuun'yuung	Kapuunyuung
Bill of platipus	Wuroitneuk	Woroitnong	Woroitnong
Bird, general term	Yowwir	Muttal	Muttal
Birthplace	Chukknat, 'ground mine'	Meering an, 'ground mine'	Wuurk gnan, 'ground mine'
Bite	Puundak	Puundake	Puunta
Bitter	Kaeriit	Lapetch	Lapætch
Black	Woke	Meeng	Meen
Black-foot, or matchmaker	Gnaterambula	Gnapunda	
Black wattle tree	Wararakk	Pareetcheerang	Gnullawurt
Blackwood tree	Miutchung	Mutang	Mutan
Bladder	Charraka kok	Palleen neung	Tarrakuk
Blanket	Martuuk knular	Gnular	Gnular
Blaze or flame	Churonia wee	Torro wan	Pipkæta
Blear eye	Kuurke mirng, 'blood eye'	Kirræ kirræ mink, 'blood eye'	Wawa meen yuung, 'sore eye'
Bleeding	Kang kneelang kuurk, 'spill blood'	Towarteean kuureek, 'spill blood'	Wayeen kirrikan, 'spill blood'
Blind	Kneem kneem	Kuunjeetch	Kuunjeetch
Blister by sun	Meitch gnuurak	Yurrara unnin	Yurrara unnin
Blood	Kuurk	Kaerik	Kaerik
Blow, a stroke	Tukkuk	Partang	Partaa
Blow, to blow	Porn geen	Puimbeen	Puumba
Blue	Wo'ok	Wuulok	Wuulok
Blunt	Turnup	Mo'ort	Mort mittin
Blush	Yallucham	Yatneyan	
Boat	Wartæpuuk gnanakk	Kuurnong turong, 'small ship'	Turong

iv

English.	Chaap wuurong (broad lip).	Kuurn kopan noot (small lip).	Peek whuurong (kelp lip).
Bodkin of bone	Kirndeen	Kirndeen	Kirndeen
Body	Pengneeung uratt	Turang muttnaen	Turang muttnaen
Boil, to boil	No term	No term	No term
Bone	Kulku	Pukkiin	Bukkiin
Bone, ribs	Lun'yin	Yeeyeer	Yeeyeer
Bone of upper arm	Kun'kun'tutchuk	Millaewuurk	Millaewuurk
Bone of lower arm	Tutchakuuk	Wuurhmeong	Wuurhneung
Bone of hand	Kulkeea	Pukkiin marrang, 'bone hand'	Bukkiin marrank, 'bone hand'
Bone of leg, general term	Kulkeea nurak	Pirn	Pirn
Bone of thigh	Kulkin karipp	Pukkiin karipp	Muulo
Bone of lower leg	Karnuuk	Pirnuung	Pirnuung
Bone of foot	Warteep kulk	Pukkiin dinnang, 'bone foot'	Bukkiin tinnang, 'bone foot'
Bones, custom of carrying human bones	Wiindeetch	Wiin wiin	Chirt titt
Bones, calcined human bones, worn in bag	Cheaet chaet	Taeet taet	Taeet taet
Bone in point of spear	Killaepuuk	Killipneung	Kilaepneung
Boomerang, general term	Littum littum	Laede laedim	Laede laedim
Boomerang, 'companion stick'	Paang geetch	Paang geetch	Paang geetch
Boomerang, which returns	Peenyarra gnapp	Whatannomeetch	Whatannomaa
Boomerang, which does not return	Pungo gnapp	Bungo neetch	Pungo naen
Boot	W,emajinna	Walla whallop dinnang	Wirn dinnang
Bottle	Tuunduum beawir	Wirndill	Wirndill
Bower, of bower-bird	Larnokk	Yurohneung	Lorrotch
Bowels	Warteepuup kuuna	Kuurn kuurn kuurnang	Piuloin neung
Boy	Watcheepuuk	Warran warran	Warran warran
Boy whose beard is beginning to grow	Kaetnaetch	Kutnaet	Kutnaet
Box-tree	Taak	Weetcheerin	Karran
Brain	Mirtpuurp	Turuchar beem	Tulo'choae
Branch of tree	Tutchakukk	Wuurhneung	Taerang
Brave	Tititwuuchuup	Pinnukillik	Likkaetuung
Break	Puku g'nak	Kirndeen	Kirnda

English.	Chaap wuurong (broad lip).	Kuurn kopan noot (small lip).	Peek whuurong (kelp lip).
Breath	Gnang guutch	Gnaawuurn kupa wan	Gniindepawan
Bride	Jankuurk	Keeyan	Keeyan
Bridegroom, before marriage	Witchikk	Wirrek	Wirrek
Bridegroom, after marriage			
Bridesmaid	Kuumban gneelang	Yuwitneetch	Parketch
Bride man, or best man	Muit chillup kuurk	Wambekeear	Yung'ameeteear
Bring	Muit chilaawill	Wambekill	Yung armekill
Brood, general term	Miuutcha ka	Wambake	Wambake
Brood of young ducks	Puupuup kaleek	Tukuae tukuae	Gnarrakitta tukuaeyuung
Brood of young emus	Popop gnae	Tempatæt	Wætuurbank
Brush, paint brush	Wortok	Wætong	Wætong
Bucket, made of wood	Purot purot	Parrit parrit	Tærewirriitch
Bucket, made of bark	Popeer yu	Popeer	Keekeetch
Buffoon or clown	Yuruum	Yuruum	Yuruum
Build	Chippateuk	Chipparuuk	Chipparuuk
Bull	Parpak	Marng'gakkae	Meng'aa
Burr	Buul	Buul	Buul
Burn	Moroe gnuum	Moroe gnuum	Moroit muutch
Burial place	Walpa	Bawann	Powaa
Bury, to	Neep pargat, 'ghostly place'	Miuruup kakee, 'ghostly place'	Muuraka, 'ghostly place'
Bush	Gnippa'gnu	Miurokan	Miuruukukan
Bush fire	Poroitcholl	Piitpurong	Piitpurong
Butt piece of spear	Piikourda	Mirtapuurtan karwhin	Muitpeetch
Buttercup flower	Bukkup	Kaaween	Kaaween
Butterfly, all kinds	Na'heeeak mirnk, 'seeing eye'	Na'heeangmaing, 'seeing eye'	Wa'ang
Buzz	Ballumbar	Ballumbii	Pallumbii
Calf of leg	Muurnda	Muurnbann	Miuurnba
Call, name of	Kuurn muurk	Kapuul	Puuroitch
Call, to call	Karnda	Karnda	Karnda
Call or visit	Watekaa	Kii	Kowæee
Calm	Gneeakatto wunjinaen	Gnakuuna mako kullo	Gnakokoten
Camomile, native	Titcherik kuma	Kuurkuurtaban	Wurtpaa
	Nareetch	Nareetch	Nareetch

English.	Chaap wuurong (broad lip.)	Kuurn kopan noot (small lip).	Peek whuurong (kelp lip).
Camp or village	Yartma kœra ...	Pareen been ...	Wiitpee wuurn
Canoe, made of bark	Gnunnak ...	Torrong ...	Torrong
Canopus planet	Wœœ, 'crow' ...	Waa, 'crow' ...	Murhearong wœœ, 'large crow'
Carry ...	Tuurta ...	Walateen ...	Walatta
Catch ...	Kurkak ...	Mummakee ...	Manna
Catching men with noose	Worm match chinnin	Gnorm gnorm ...	Porkopa
Catching wild turkey or pigeon with noose	Parrem ...	Patkœyan ...	Patkœyan
Catching waterfowls with noose	Kœram bakk ...	Tœrang bukkœ ...	Tœrang bukkœ
Cave ...	Yeitchmir, 'close the eyes'	Yatmiruk, 'close the eye'	Yuluurn
Celt, or stone axe	Buuroku ...	Mochœœr ...	Mochœœr
Cement for celt handles...	Puuropiitch ...	Puuropanuut ...	Puuroputt
Cement for spears and buckets	Chuulim ...	Tuulemuul ...	Tuulemuul
Ceremony ...	Only specific ...	Only specific ...	Only specific
Chickweed ...	Kœramukka ...	Tœramukkar ...	Mukkar
Chief ...	Gnern neetch ...	Wung'it ...	Wung'it
Chief, when addressed ...	Nannœyok, 'chief mine'	Wung'it nan ...	Wung in hnœn
Chiefess ...	Gnun kuutchup mutchong	Piniitchong mullert	Piniitchong mullert
Chiefess, when addressed	Gnannœkuurk ...	Wangin heear ...	Wang in heear
Child ...	Pupuwuuk ...	Tukuœ ...	Pupuup
Child, illegitimate ...	Kœearn kuurk ...	Keearn ...	Keearn
Childbirth ...	Narram ...	Moœkorn ...	Moœkorn
Children ...	Pupuup kaleek ...	Tukuœ tukuœ ...	Porpong
Childless ...	Alla pupuup, 'no children'	Bang pupuup, 'no children'	Bang&heeartukuœ, 'no children'
Chin ...	Gnun'yee ...	Narriin ...	Gnarriin
Chirp of small bird	Wurika yarwirra yarwirr	Wuingjun kuurn kuurn muttal	Lurkun tokoe muttal
Chisel, made of bone	Pilœœr ...	Pikœœr ...	Tirn tirn
Chisel, made of stone	Kannœwil ...	Puin puin ...	Kannakil
Claw of bird ...	Tinanyuuk ...	Tinan yuang ...	Phrœnnung
Clay ...	Peek ...	Pupall ...	Yuum
Clay, white ...	Peek ...	Martang ...	Martang
Clay, red ...	Chuulim ...	Tuulirn ...	Tuulirn
Clever ...	Murpillup munya, 'making hand'	Muuyuup marrang, 'making hand'	Muuyuupeen marrang, 'making hand'

vii

English.	Chaap wuurong (broad lip).	Kuurn kopan noot (small lip).	Peek whuurong (kelp lip).
Climatis	Charuuk	Taruuk	Taruuk
Climb up	Warwaak	Warrandak	Kunbaa
Climber of trees	Turt turt willa	Part bart	Part bart
Cloud	Marn	Muurnong	Muurnong
Cloud, red	Kuurke marn	Kirrae kirra muurnong, 'blood cloud'	Kirrae kirre muurnong, 'blood cloud'
Club, or 'company stick'	Chulluk kanne	Malinya kunnuk	Kannak
Club, executioner's club	Yuul munya, 'wild hand'	Yuul marrang, 'wild hand'	Yuul marrang, 'wild hand'
Club, heavy club for fighting	Wue wuitch	Wue wuitch	Wuae wuitch
Club for throwing at game	Muunyuup	Muunyuup	Muunyuup
Club with knob at end	Pirp pen	War war	War war
Club, walking-stick	Kunnuk	Kunnuk	Kunnuk
Coal-sack in Milky Way	Bun'yipp	Torong	Kapeen
Cock nose	Warnka	Warn kapuung	Warn kapuung
Cold	Mutae	Palla pitta	Kuunketeetch
Come back, or return	Pirndaega	Wattake	Wattah
Come here	Pirnaega	Wattake	Wattae
Comet	Taandan	Puurt kuurnnuuk	
Conglomerate stone	Kuurwharram	Korwharram	Korwharram
Consanguinity	Tow'wil guurk	Tow'wil yerr	Tow'wil yerr
Constellation	*Only specific*	*Only specific*	*Only specific*
Contempt	Yatching ballingkuutcha	Gnumme gnummae ku'gnan	Gnumme gneaar
Contentment	Tulkuuk bang yaa, 'pleased am I'	Gnueet puun an, 'pleased am I'	Gnueet puun an, 'pleased am I'
Convolvulus root	Gneumbeet	Tarruuk	Taaruuk
Cook, to cook	Walpap	Bawaku	Muurtpa
Cord of bark or hair	Tulang	Wung'ar	Weerang an
Cord for tying umbilical cord	Gnarram	Puuroitch	Puuroitch
Corpse	Knutcha	Weering	Kalpurneetch
Cough	Kunyan kan	Kunnar pan	
Country, my country	Cha knaek	Maeering an	Maeering
Count, to count	Gnuurteen gnan	Gnutaku	Gnutang in
Courage	Tititwuchuup	Pinnakillik	Likkaetuung
Courtship	Charnda	Keearndann	Keearndabaa

English.	Chaap wuurong (broad lip).	Kuurn kopan noot (small lip).	Peek whuurong (kelp lip).
Cousin, general term	Yuurpeeya	Towwill	Towwill
Covering head custom	Gnulluun kuurk	Gnulluun yarr	Gnulluun yarr
Coward, or cowardice	Pamba muum, 'frightened back'	Kuunin muum, 'show your back'	Kunin muum, 'show your back'
Cramp	Wiinjahgnee buur buuro	Mirrkurot	Mekuurith
Crash	Pueetka	Yirndabuurtee	Pokirta
Crater	Kuulkuurt	Gnapuuruung	Kuulkuurt
Crawl, like a snake	Yukkelang	Woounteeyun	Woountiin
Crawl on game	Kaeram bung'u	Chaeran baawan	Chaeran ba'wan
Crepuscular, upperpurple arch in the east after sunset	Kiiyakka guurk	Kuurokeheear puuron, 'white cockatoo twilight'	Not known
Crepuscular, lower blue arch in the east after sunset	Kappi kuurk	Kappiheear puuron, 'black cockatoo twilight'	Not known
Crepuscular, rays in the west after sunset	Pung a ruuk neowee gna 'rushes of sun'	Weearmeetchuung, 'rushes'	Puung'ortuung munnanat, 'rushes'
Crest of cockatoo	Gnarraneuk	Peereeneung	Peereeneung
Crest of Gang Gang parrot	Perring guuk	Butkueewan, 'project'	Lapaeetch
Cripple, natural	Wamp wuutcha	Wamp	Gnumme kuurtnin
Cripple from wounds	Wirpkeetch	Mingjeetch	Gnachepa
Croak of large frog	Cheenyapp	Dinupp	Dinupp
Crooked	Ween ween	Warwhart	Wawaa
Crosscut saw	Tillaelapp wee, 'cut wood'	Parrithae ween, 'cut wood'	Tirrekuun tirrekuun
Crowd	Larbargirrar	Wuurt ba daerang	Gnarra kittuung
Cruel	Takaelup	Burteetch	Gnummejaar
Cry, to weep	Yeereeya	Luung an, or Weepa	Weepa
Cry of infant	Yeereeya	Luung an' or Wirpa	Wirpa
Cry of cockatoo	Keenjeea	Keenjan	Naeek kuya
Cry of crow	Waee	Waa	Waa
Cry of laughing jackass	Wiiakaa, 'laugh'	Weeitchkan, 'laugh'	Weeitchkan, 'laugh'
Cry of Gang Gang parrot	Nilma	Gniilman	Kiwuurtin
Cry of snake	Ka ka	Ka ka	Ka ka
Crysolis of bark	Tringkup	Kurpeetch	Wuurlnong tokoinert
Cure	Tulku'gnak	Gnuitch pu gmakee	Gnuitch pu guang in
Cut, to divide	Kalpurakk	Mumbortann	Kulkirta

English.	Chaap wuurong (broad lip).	Kuurn kopan noot (small lip).	Peek whuurong (kelp lip).
Cut flesh	Tullak	Pareetchakee	Towakk
Daisy, wild daisy	Gnullo	Puulomell	Patteratt mink, 'lapwing eye'
Dance, name of	Yappan neaa	Karweean	Kurween
Dance, to dance	Yappan neitch	Karweean neut	Kurween
Dance of gigantic crane	Gnuyeelang	Yakeeapeann	Kurween
Dandy, or fop	Marrinae kuule	Marrinae maar	
Dark, pitch dark	Titit wuuma	Kuurowulok	Kuurowulok
Daughter	Pupuwee	Gnarn	Gnaart
Daughter-in-law	Naluun kuuree	Naluun heaar	Naluun heaar
Day, midday	Naluuke neow wee, 'shine sun'	Naluuka-tirng, 'shine sun'	Kiiappa gnunnung, 'one sun'
Day after to-morrow	Perpchuun yuuk	Malee neung	Mung æ neung
Deaf	Moart wirnkbuul, 'shut ear'	Nuurteean wirng o, 'shut ear'	Gnuurteetch wirng, 'shut ear'
Death, or dead	Weeka	Kalperann	Kalpirna
Death of woman by sentence	Weegurrk	Wirreyerr	Wirreyerr
Decay	Purngkuekalk	Puunoitch	Puunoitch
Destroy	Yatchang bulling kuung at	Gnummae gnumme kuukna war	Gnummae gnumme kuukna war
Devil, general term	Muuruup	Muuruup	Tambuur
Devil, male devil	Muutcheyok porta, 'maker of bad smoke'	Wambeen neung been been aa, 'maker of bad smoke'	Tambuur
Devil, female devil	Buurt kuuruuk	Buurt kuuruuk	Weaar
Devil in the moon	Kuurnok billy	Muuruup neung kuurn taarong gnat, 'Devil of moon'	Muuruup neung yaheear gnat, 'Devil of moon'
Dew	Kuutchall	Mikuur	Mikuur
Dialect	Challing in, 'tongue'	Taaliin, 'tongue'	Taaliin, 'tongue'
Dig	Tuurna kutcha	Pundanuung maering, 'bite the ground'	Punda maering, 'bite the ground'
Discontent	Gnumartii an	Waliit pan o	Waliit pang in
Disrespect	Yatchang	Gnummae gullin	Gnummeenjar
District, area of tribe	Cha kneek, 'ground mine'	Maering an, 'ground mine'	Maering, 'country or ground'
Dive	Lukaera	Nuur meen been gnan, 'down go I'	Puro wirta, 'down go I'
Diversion, or sport	Gnuyam chungnanu	Kulmba wan	Kulmba wan
Divorced man	Winnakum, 'left off'	Wanna'gnum, 'left off'	Gnummaekuupa, 'left off'

English.	Chaap wuurong (broad lip).	Kuurn kopan noot (small lip).	Peek whuurong (kelp lip).
Divorced woman	Winnakum kuurk, 'left off wife'	Wanna'gnumheear, 'left off wife'	Yuunyuunda, 'left off'
Do, to do anything	Talkugnak	Muyubakkae	Muyuparrin
Doctor	Lunyewil	Kuurnuukbuul	Kuun'gill
Doorway of dwelling	Wuuro laar	Wuro wuurn	Wuro wuurn
Down of bird	Nuurtknok	Nuurtnong	Nuurtnong
Down, to tumble down	Puitkan	Yarndapuurtee an	Yuungkin
Drag	Tirndak	Wireenjakae	Wireenjan
Dray	Ka'att	Barrang'guurt	Barrang'guurt
Dream, or dreaming	Ya ya yellang	Yarkeen	Yakinno
Drink, to drink	Kuupalann	Tuttakawann	Tutta kuyerk
Drive of game	Paayaar wuung'iitch	Gnummang kuuknanuut	Gnummang kuuknanuut
Dropsy	Purpelang	Purpeean	Purpeen
Drum, made of opossum rug	Paelp	Murn	Murn
Drumming noise	Kurnda pelp	Kurndun murn	Kurndun murn
Drunk, aboriginal man	Kuupkeriit, 'drink bitter'	Tatlup peet, 'drink bitter'	Tatlup peet, 'drink bitter'
Duck weed	Chuurak	Tuurak	Tuurak
Dumb	Yellipkuutcha	Kukunan	Kalkuutnan
Dusk, nightfall	Poroin	Poronn	Mendia
Dwarf, male	Po'olk	Warpeet	Warpeet
Dwarf, female	Polkuurk	Warpeheear	Warpechaar
Dysentery	Tuutiyan	Poor gnanno	Porr gneong
Ear	Wirng buulin	Wirng	Wing
Ear-hole	Wuutchuk wirng buulin	Puukuit wirng	Lirpa
Earth	Cha	Maering	Maering
Earth nut	Puewann	Puewann	Pam
Earthquake	Muurmuur ajaa	Puurn puurn maeering, 'heave ground'	Tuuntuunba, 'heave ground'
East	Pupkuumup neowee, 'rising sun'	Pupkuupeetch tirng, 'rising sun'	Kunbeetch gnunnung, 'rising sun'
Eat	Chakna g'no	Tukka wan	Tukkeen
Echo	Gnang'guyuuk, 'sound'	Gnawuurn nuung, 'sound'	Wung a, 'hearing'
Eclipse	*No name*	*No name*	*No name*
Eel basket	Puutchakuurn	Gnarraban	Karkart

English.	Chaap wuurong (broad lip).	Kuurn kopan noot (small lip).	Peek whurrong (kelp lip).
Eel-hole in swamp	Yarnduuk	Narring neung	Narring neung
Eel spear	Tulakneetch	Kuyuut	Kueott
Egg of bird, generally	Mirk kuuk	Ming hnuung	Ming'hneung
Egg of ant	Deengapp	Karpeetch	Mee'hneung
Egg of emu, first laid egg		Purtæ wuuchuup	
Egg of lizard	Wartæbuuk mirk, 'little egg'	Kuurnu mirnk, 'little egg'	Mee'hneung
Egg of snake	Mikkækuurk, 'female egg'	Mikkæheaar, 'female egg'	Mikkit
Egg mound of brush turkey	Gullernnung	Gullernnung	*Not known*
Elbow	Ballu chin	Tulling	Tulling
Elderberry tree, indigenous			
Emetic made of leeches	Puloitch	Puluut	Pilunk
Empty	Kaluppa	Kallup kallup	Kallup kallup
Emu trap	Putaya	Nirræ tupan	Pallart nunna
Enemy	Taart	Kunnang	Kunnang
Entrails, generally	Yuul yuul	Yuul yuul	Kulomeetch
Entrails of opossum	Turong billæ	Parrin tukuung	Pariin tukuung
Entrails of sea snail	Murnduuk	Murnnung	Murnuung
Eperculum of sea snail	Leeagneuk, or Yakerwokk	Tunga neung	Tæær gnamatt
Evening	Knuunkuul gnuchang	Puron kuurteean	Puron kuurtin
Evening star, Venus	Paapee neowee, 'mother of the sun'	Wung'uul, 'twinkle'	Karuung kitnaeetcha, 'twinkle'
Ever	Chuurp chuurp kuutcha	Læenann	Kinnan ba
Everlasting plant	Tapue	Tapuin	Tapuin
Evil spirit	Muuruup	Miuruup	Tambuur
Excrement of man and beast	Kuunong unn	Kuunong	Kuunong
Excrement pit	Tapkuurt	Kuurnang'guurt	Puuit
Excrescence of tree	Chimchim	Timp timp	Puuroin
Eye	Mirnk in uurat	Mirng	Mink
Eye, pupil	Cherk in uurat	Tirng anniu, 'sun mine'	Tirt
Eyebrow	Tanyuuk mirnk	Taruuk mirng	Taruuk mink
Eyelash	Knarrat mirnk, 'hair eye'	Knarrat mirng, 'hair eye'	Gnarrat mink, 'hair eye'
Eyelid, upper	Wart mirnk	Wart mirng	Muurn meenung, 'sky lid'
Eyelid, lower	Wurot mirnk	Wart mirng	Muurn meenung, 'sky lid'
Eye, one-eyed person	Kæp mirr, 'one eye'	Kiiap mirng, 'one eye'	Kiiap mirng, 'one eye'

English.	Chaap wuurong (broad lip).	Kuurn kopan noot (small lip).	Peek whuurong (kelp lip).
Eye, white of ...	Tuurt mirnk ...	Tuurt mirng ...	Tarndeetch mink
Eyesight ...	Teeirn ...	Tirt mirng ...	Mink
Fable, or story ...	Keeyark keeh keeh ...	Koæ koæ ...	Koitpa koæ koæ
Face ...	Mirnk ba kiya'gnuurak	Mirng ba kapuung hnatnæn, 'eyes and nose mine'	Mirng ba kapuung hnatnæn, 'eyes and nose mine'
Faint ...	Pobo muurop ...	Paba gnullatt ...	Paba gnullatt
Fall down ...	Puitkan ...	Yarndapuurtee an ...	Yarnda wuurtin
Family ...	Puupuup kaleek ...	Tukuæ ...	Gnarrakituun
Fang of snake ...	Wirnduuk ...	Wirnuung ...	Wirnuung
Fairy rings formed by grubs	Wullpeyuuk, 'burnt'	Paawetuung, 'burnt'	Muurtpetuung, 'burnt'
Fairy stones ...	Kerm kerm ...	Kiiriit ...	Kiiriit
Far... ...	Puuree o ...	Puuree ...	Puuree
Far, a long distance	Tærær-ær-ær ...	Dee-dee-dee ...	Pirrpuuree
Far-seeing ...	Nakak puuree o ...	Nakeen puuree ...	Puuree
Farewell ...	Wuwuwe ...	Wuwu ...	Wuwuuk
Fast ...	Pirpuurn ...	Marrat marra ran ...	Wiitpeen wirrakan
Fat	Pipuluuk ...	Pipuul ...	Pipuul
Fat of large grub ...	Puurtuluuk ...	Buulortong ...	Buulortong
Fear ...	Pamban ...	Kuunin ban ...	Kuunim ba
Feast ...	Chukkælang ...	Tukkæann ...	Tukkin
Feather ...	Narrak neuk ...	Kurotnnong ...	Yuurnong
Feather ornaments ...	Warwal ...	Warwal ...	Warwal
Feet, carrying deceased children's feet in basket custom ...	Paalk ...	Wandæk ...	Wandæk
Female ...	Only specific ...	Only specific	Only specific
Fence ...	Nalopbun ...	Nalopbun ...	Nalopbun
Fern ...	Muulaa ...	Makkiitch ...	Mukkiin
Fern root, edible ...	Muulaa ...	Murkiin ...	Murkiin
Fern tree ...	Wonon tulong ...	Wuurn wuurn tulong	Kurok Mukkiin, 'grandmother of ferns'
Ferruginous conglomerate	Knurk warran ...	Korwharrann ...	Korwharrann
Few ...	Kartuur ...	Ka'artpan ...	Pang'nunna

English.	Chaap wuurong (broad lip).	Kuurn kopan noot (small lip).	Peek whuurong (kelp lip).
Fight	Tukkcherrang	Partpan	Partpakall
Fight between two chiefs	Puuleitcha gnerrneetch	Puuleitcha wung'itt	Puuleitcha wungyitt
Fin of fish	Muumuuk	Yutang	Tærong
Finger, general term	Mun'ya	Wurt marrang	Marrang nan
Finger, forefinger	Yulaheulop terr, 'spear point'	Yulaheulop tiyeeer, 'spear point'	Yulaheulop tæeær, 'spear point'
Finger, second finger	Tukkaeyuuk kuurnwilla, 'hit snake'	Parteetung kurrang at, 'hit snake'	
Finger, third	Kep kirtæ, 'behind the long one'	Kullarheear kirting, 'behind the long one'	Kullar heear Bukkar kullar heear, 'behind the long one'
Finger, fourth	Kirting eea gnuurak, 'smallest'	Kirting, 'smallest'	Wiinyaheear, 'smallest'
Fire...	Wee	Ween	Ween
Fire, to produce by friction	Kuyonn niitch	Kuyonn kuyonn	Kuyonn kuyonn
Fire, firesticks for producing fire	Pukkup	Pukkup	Pukkup
Fire, to kindle fire	Wirka gno wee, 'make fire'	Kandawan ween, 'make fire'	Piitchawan weena, 'make fire'
Fish, generally	No name or term	No term	No term
Fish, salt-water	Yarrar	Yarrar	Yarrar
Fish, fresh-water	Yuuchuuk	Kuunamuung, 'excrement of large fish'	
Fishing rod	Ballaeparrip	Ballaeparrip	Pirnmarii
Fishing hook and line	Not known	Not known	Puin buin
Fishing with spear and torch	Pundalung o punyart	Pundawan kueeang	Not known
Fist	Mitpukk	Wart marrang	Yappin
Flash man	Chummæ gnuurna muurnin	Gnuurna murnin	Milpah
Flash woman	Chummæ gnuurna muurnin kuurk	Yuurba gnuurna muurninyaar	Mirmiitch
Flesh for food	Ping yin	Tuurap muttnin	Mirmatcha
Flesh, human	Beng guuk	Tuurap neung	Tuuramp muttal
Flesh, ceremony of eating human flesh	Kerwanno chinning	Kerwawanden	Muttal
Flesh of whale, fresh	Banggok	Tuurap neung	Kerwawandæn
Flesh of whale, putrid	Gneepar	Muuruukin	
Flint	Pæeetch	Paat	Muung
Flirt, or coquette	Tantan kuunælap	Tan tan kuuknæheear	

English.	Chaap wuurong (broad lip).	Kuurn kopan noot (small lip).	Peek whuurong (kelp lip).
Float on water	Neurka	Yaawan	Muppuurtin
Flock of birds	Larbargirrar yaawir	Wuurtbæ dærang muttal	Gnarrakitting muttal
Flood	Murtæ kutchink	Kariitchall	Kuuluun pariitch
Flower	*Only specific*	*Only specific*	*Only specific*
Flower of eucalyptus tree	Korr	Korr	Korr
Flower of blackwood tree	Kuulang muutang	Kuulang muutang	Kuulang muutang
Flower of acacia	Kuulang kurrang	Kuulang kurrang	Kuulang kurrang
Fog, or mist	Wuuort	Waart	Waart
Fog from the sea	Kuumaar kuumaar	Kuumaar kuumaar	Kuumaar kuumaar
Fomentation of breast	Kom	Wop	Wop
Fomentation of sore, or pain	Wopkuurna	Wop	Wopkuurnin
Food, generally	Pangkuurn	Tuuluurt	Tuuluurt
Foot	Chinnang	Tinnang	Tinnang
Foot, sole of foot	Pille chinnang, 'young foot'	Tukuuk tinnang, 'young foot'	Tukuuk tinnang, 'young foot'
Footprint of man or beast	Chinna junnak	Tinnang jeean	Poptinnang
Football	Min'gorm	Man'guurt	Yuumkuurt
Fop, or senseless fellow	Marrinæ kuulæ	Marrinæ marr	Wæneu
For	King in	Deen g'no	
Forehead	Kinnæ	Mittint	Mittint
Forest	Kulpakuuro	Yarroæ	Wuro wuruuk
Forget-me-not, sweet-scented	Poang kuurk	Meechap	Meechap
Forget-me-not, red	Gnarra wuurong, 'hair lip'	Gnarat wurong, 'hair lip'	Gnarat wurong, 'hair lip'
Forgiveness	Tukam an	Wirræchan	Nuumbabe
Fresh	Tulkuuk bang	Gnuuteung turap	Gnuuchuung
Fresh water	Telkæ kutchin	Gnuutch'gnan pareetch	Gnuutch pareetch
Frequently	Parba kutchæ g'nuurnang	Parba puriitch kuukna no	Parba puriitch kuurtin no
Friend	Kupa g'num, 'sit down'	Taart taart bulang an, 'sit down'	Kupang al, 'sit down'
Fright	Pamban	Kuunin ban	Kuunim ba
From	Wo'gnareen	Wokaknin	Mungnoro wattano
Frost	Wartpuwuuk kepping	Pariit beem, 'white head'	Waalart
Full	Turark kiian	Karrawæa no	Karraweepu
Fun	Kulngælang	Kulngeetch	Kulngeen
Funeral	Gnippa' gnu	Muurokan	Muurokukan

English.	Chaap wuurong (broad lip).	Kuurn kopan noot (small lip).	Peek whuurong (kelp lip).
Funeral pile	Carbowee	Carbowing	Carbowing
Fungus, mushroom	Peekuurn	Peekuurn	Peekuurn
Fungus, phosphorescent	Kilarn	Kilarn	Puluurt
Fungus, poisonous	Murtkourwe	Murtkapping	Puluurt
Fungus, tree fungus, edible	Puluutch wirmbuul, 'ear wax'	Buuloth wirng, 'ear wax'	Buulot wirng, 'ear wax'
Fungus, underground, edible	Boee wan	Boee wan	
Futurity	Gnam gnampeng kuundeetch	Wuulae whuule kittawunda	Wuulae whuule kittawunda
Gall	Meenguuk	Tittuung	Tittuung
Gallop, like a horse	Pirrpa	Karkuuran	Wirrakan pinnang kuupamin
Gather	Tumbukka	Tambukkæ	Kirnaa
Gentleman	Puunjiliya	Puunjilkerang	Puunjilkerang
Gentleman, young	Wurteepee puunjiliya muunya	Kiuurnai puunjilkerang	Kuurn punjilkeerang
Geranium, native	Kullum kulkeetch	Kawuurn kallumbarrant	Kawuurn kallumbarrant
Get	Miutchak	Maneen	Gnaart
Girl, young	Buurni buurni	Pariit pariit	
Girl, before entering womanhood	Weearkuumeetch kuurk	Marramarrabuul	Marramarrabuul
Girl, betrothed, and visiting her intended husband's relations			
Give	Tannat yanballup kuurk	Kuumagnat yanburtaheear	Kuumagnat yanburtaheear
Glass, volcanic	Wokagee (g hard)	Wokakin	Yu gnaama
Gloaming light in the west	Wurokiin	Wurokiin	Wurokiin
Glow	Kulleitch, 'evening light'	Kullatt, 'evening light'	Kullatt, 'evening light'
Glutton	Pittayang uureen	Tirrera'gnan	Wallawar
Go	Murt gneeang, 'big mouth'	Meeheaar gnuulang, 'big mouth'	Tung'an, 'teeth'
God, or good spirit	Yanango	Yan	Puurpa gnin
	Mam yungrakk	Pirnmeheeal, but the affix Peep ghnatnæn, 'Father ours,' is generally added	Peep ghnatnæn, 'Father ours'
Good	Chulkuuk	Gnuuteung	Gnuuteung
Good-bye	Wuwu wæ	Wu wu	Wuwuuk
Good-night	Kuumpeenyang o	Yuween	Yuween
Gossip, female	Yueetcha kuurk	Yeetkueet mæring heean	Milling e chaar

English.	Chaap wuurong (broad lip).	Kuurn kopan noot (small lip).	Peek whuurong (kelp lip).
Gossip, male ...	Gnuyang bilapp ...	Kulngeetch ...	Kulngin
Grass, general term ...	Chuuchu gom ...	Muul muul ...	Puutong
Grass, for catching game with noose ...		Witt tæn ...	
Grass, kangaroo grass ...	Wuuloitch ...	Wuulot ...	Wuulot
Grass, quaking grass ...	Not known ...	Not known ...	Not known
Grass, rib grass, large ...	Kokæ binnang, 'grandmother of small grass'	Korak binnang, 'grandmother of small grass'	Korak binnang, 'grandmother of small grass'
Grass, rib grass, small ...	Wurtepee binnang, 'small grass'	Kuurna binnang, 'small grass'	Kuurna binnang, 'small grass'
Grass, silver grass ...	Korn ...	Kawuurn ...	Karn
Grass, tussock grass ...	Kuinyok ...	Parræt ...	Parræt
Grass tree ...	Kawee ...	Bukkup ...	Yallander
Grave, burial place ...	Chaa ...	Muurang ...	Po'otch
Gravelly ground ...	Wartæ pillæ ...	Tirt kaari ...	Tirritkull
Gray ...	Tararneetch ...	Narpepee ...	Napkuyeetch
Grease for hair and body	Warrapillæ ...	Willapeeako ...	Willa pingnin
Green ...	Tanattæ gnor. ...	Kuumakuurn knorr ...	Kuumakarrak
Green stone for making celts ...	Kaa puunjill ...	Pirn buunjil ...	Pirn buunjil
Grin ...	Ponpondilam...	Ponpondeean ...	Puunda tung an
Grind ...	Yurondak ...	Waatæ wakko ...	Wattoya
Grinding stone, native ...	Yuron yuron...	Warwhatuur ...	Warwhatuur
Groan ...	Allerwa ...	Gnallerwan ...	Gnarnda
Ground ...	Chaa ...	Mæring ...	Mæring
Growl of wild dog ...	Gnærwonga ...	Gnærwenanong ...	Gnærwenanong
Growth of tree for bucket	Kuumbuuk ...	Gnuppineung ...	Gnuppineung
Grub hook ...	Tirn ...	Purrin ...	Tachnum
Guest ...	Tulkuuk kuulæ, 'good friend'	Gnuuteuk maar, 'good friend'	Nakukan woumkurre, 'good friend'
Guilty ...	Gnuyang billang ...	Kalng kapeeang in ...	Kalng kapeeng in
Gully ...	Wameet chaæ, 'rolling ground'	Wameen mæering, 'rolling ground'	Wameetch mæering, 'rolling ground'
Gum used for cement ...	Tuuliin ...	Kuunang'guuk, 'excrement of grub'	Pekuuk, 'excrement of grub'
Gum used for cement, from Geelong ...	Leel ...	Barrecherang ...	Barrecherang

English.	Chaap wuurong (broad lip).	Kuurn kopan noot (small lip).	Peek whuurong (kelp lip).
Gum, acacia, edible	Tuulin	Karang	Karrang
Gum, keno	Chuutch	To'ott	To'ott
Gum tree, white	Yulong	Wuurott	Wuurott
Gum tree, red	Peeal	Peeank	Ta'art
Gums of jaws	Leeayung uurat	Wartung ang	Kareitch
Gun or musket	Puung puung ghe awæær, 'strike meat'	Puurnbiee muttal, 'strike meat'	Peall
Gurgle, like a stream	Wakuung aa	Wakæpan	Wantirna
Gurgle, throat	Luuroitpa	Luuroitpan	Wuurkirta
Habitation, general term	Laar	Wuurn	Wuurn
Habitation, large family	Martuuk laar, 'big habitation'	Leembeek	Peep wuurn, 'father of habitations'
Habitation, small	Watchepee laar, 'small habitation'	Kuurna wuurn, 'small habitation'	Kuurna wuurn, 'small habitation'
Habitation, temporary	Yullma kæra	Pareenpeen, 'young habitation'	Pareenyeen, 'young habitation'
Habitation for bachelors	Watchepee laar, 'small habitation'	Kuurna wuurn, 'small habitation'	Kuurna wuurn, 'small habitation'
Hail	Piitkæra	Naark	Nææk
Hailstorm	Piitkæra	Pattærang	Nææk
Hair	Knarrank	Gnarrat	Gnarrat
Hair, black	Wokin knarrank	Meeng gnarrat	Meen gnarrat
Hair, red	Kuurkuurn murneetch	Tirraeetch	Leepeetch
Hair, white	Peerin puulort	Kotong	Korpaa
Hair-pin	Kirndeenjukk	Kirndeen	Kirndeen
Halo, lunar	Parpa larneuk wullin kna, 'build for rain'	Mung'geann nok miianga, 'build for rain'	Wuurnong, 'its house'
Halo, solar	Watpallang weeneuk neow'wee, 'burning the wood in the sun'	Parwhardanuung weenuung tirng aa, 'burning the wood in the sun'	Wuurnong, 'its house'
Hand	Mun'yank	Marrang	Marrank
Hand, man's right	Yuulp	Tumbitt	Tumbitt
Hand, woman's right	Yuulp kuurk	Tumbitt heear	Tumbitt heear
Hand, man's left	Warram	Warram	Gneerik gneerik
Hand, woman's left	Warram kuurk	Warram heear	Gneerik gneeræar

English.	Chaap wuurong (broad lip).	Kuurn kopan noot (small lip).	Peek whuurong (kelp lip).
Hand, palm of	Pillim munya, 'young hand'	Tukuuk marrang, 'young hand'	Tukuuk marrank, 'young hand'
Hand, back of	Wurt Munya ..	Wurt marrang	Wurt marrank
Handsome	Tulkuuk	Gnuuteung	Gnuuteung
Handsome man	Tulkœ kulœ	Gnuuteung maar	Gnuuteung maar
Hang, to hang up anything	Pentuung natt	Mappapo	Muppu'gna
Hang, to hang a man	Katnelelang	Kankardeann	Kantnateen
Happy	Tulkiyan	Mirman o	Gnuutchpuurteen
Hard	Tittit	Pineitch	Pineitch
Hat	Gnopur porp, 'cover head'	Gnopur beem, 'cover head'	Tuparrim, 'cover head'
Hate, or hatred	Kuutkuut amban	Gnumœ tubunn o	Gnull kuruuk
Have, this mine	Keewinna gnik, 'this mine'	Teen an, 'this mine'	Natuuk ghnatt, 'this mine'
He	Keela	Teelaree	Teein
Head	Puurk puurk	Beem	Pimmeung
Head, forehead	Kinnœ	Mittint	Mittint
Healthy	Tulku wan, 'good am I'	Weetpuurgnunnong, 'goodam I'	Gnuuteung
Hear, to listen	Gneearnakk	Wung an	Wang a
Heart	Wuuchuupin	Lee'hnan	Lee'hnan
Heartburn	Walpa wuuchuupek, 'burn heart'	Baawan leehnan, 'burn heart'	Baawa leehnan, 'burn heart'
Heat, general	Wullbung ing	Bowaa an	Powaa
Heat of fire	Winba gneenk	Wuurondung'an	Tirrin nung an
Heaven	Maungguurk	Muurnœneung	Muurnœneung
Heel	Muum tinna, 'bottom of foot'	Mum tinnang, 'bottom of foot'	Purrn
Hell	Yaayang, 'no good'	Ummekulleen, 'no good'	Ummeecharra, 'no good'
Her	Keelaa	Teetnee	Teein
Here	King gnan	Deen gniitch	Deen gniitch
Herself	Gneuin	Gnu ghnatt be	Gnu ghnatt be
High	Keeyuga	Kunnœ	Kunnœ
High water, or tide	Gnunja	Gnundun	Knunda
Hill, general term	Puurpok	Warn baleen, or pim neung, 'head'	Pim neung, 'head'
Hill, mountain	Pan'yuul	Ka'ank, or ling'gill pimneung, 'high head'	Ling'gill pimneung, 'high head'
Hill, small	Wurteepee kank, 'small hill'	Kuurna kank, 'small hill'	Mulobit pimneung, 'low head'
Hill covered with trees	Yuulong	Kank wuurot	Gnitta
Him	Keela	Teetnee	Teen

English.	Chaap wuurong (broad lip).	Kuurn kopan noot (small lip).	Peek whuurong (kelp lip).
Himself	Gneuquar	Gnu ghnatt be	Gnu ghnatt be
Hip	Tun'yuuk	Tarrom	Taarom
His	Keeka	Teek'gnat	Nuuknatbee
Hiss	Chuunta	Tuukinjan	Yeekuunjan
Hiss of snake	Chuurndiameen	Tuukinjun ang	Yeekuunjan
Hit	Wirre puurna gneen	Purtpeeyung an	Purtaa
Hoar-frost	Kipping	Walatt	Walatt
Hobbledehoy	Kitneetch	Kutnæt	Kutnæt
Hold, or keep	Muuchak	Mannakæ	Manna
Hole in trees	Mir	Gnarring	Walarr
Honesty	Chullkunk	Gnuuteung	Gnuuteung
Honey	Honey	Honey	Honey
Honeysuckle tree, banksia	Wuurak	Weeriitch	Weeriitch
Hook, grub-hook	Tæærn	Parrin	Parrin
Hope	Yaweean tulkuuchan	Watniitch wuutch puurnan	Mannakueaa nuung
Horn	Kuparuuk	Kuperong	Gnuperong
Host	Kuupang	Puunjil purtpa hneuunduuk, 'owner of place'	Puunjil purtpa hneunduuk, 'owner of place'
Horror, expression of	Ko-o-o	Ko-o-o	Ko-o-o
Hot atmosphere	Kuurkart	Kalongsh	Kalonsh
Hot wind	Wirn mallie	Parakii	Lachlaar kuurn
House	Tukktukk g'nuurnduuk, 'made by blows'	Bardba g'nuurnduuk, 'made by blows'	Bardba g'nuurnduuk, 'made by blows'
Howl	Luurpa	Luurpann	Kurndaa
Hummock of sand	Kowarndeet neuk	Kowarndeet neung	Torn
Hungry	Pung'uu munging gnenguu	Partupung an g'nulang aa	Kulpirno
Hunt	K'nummang	K'nummang	Puupuukan
Hunting bag of skin	Omneneuk	G'nuurnecheann	Gnuurnecheann
Hunting bag of rushes	Palk	Pinnik	Pirkuul
Hurt	Tameelang	Parrandeean o	Kuunkano
Husband	K'nannachee	K'nannapuurn	G'nanap
I	Winekk	G'natuuk	G'natuuk
Ice	Yawaar	Wallart	Wallart
Immoral man	Yuurnælalang	Yuurnanuung	Yuurnanuung

English.	Chaap wuurong (broad lip).	Kuurn kopan noot (small lip).	Peek whurong (kelp lip).
Immoral woman	Pirpaa wituurruuk ...	Karkor neegh heear...	Karkor neegh heear
In, or into ...	Kleenja kuumbuurnga ...	Tinne yuwannæ ...	Tinne
Infant, new-born	Gnillam ...	Kuumakillæ ...	Gnillam
Infant, till named	Puupuup kalink	Tuukuæ, or puupuup	Tuukuæ, or puupuup
Infusion of bark	Pirm pirm ...	Pirm pirm	Pirm pirm
Innocence ...	Chulkuuk ...	Gnuuteung	Gnuuteung
Insane person ...	Gnarkuumbeetch	Gnarkuumbeetch	Gnarkuumbeetch
Insects ...	*Only specific*	*Only specific*	*Only specific*
Insects, very small	Gneunduwan...		
Instep of foot	Wart chinang, ' upper foot '	Wart tinang, ' upper foot '	Wart tinang, ' upper foot '
Ironbark tree	Puloitch ...	Puulot ...	Puumartuuk
Island ...	Mullin ...	Mullin ...	Mullin
It ...	Ka ...	Ann ...	Teein
Itch ...	Bank bank ...	Wirrit nætch	Wirrit nætch
Itchy ...	Baba gnilang ...	Wirritneeanan	Wirrit
Itself ...	Nuok ...	G'nuunat be	Nuunbee
Jaw ...	Muurakin, ' my eater '	Tukkarnk knanin, ' my eater '	Wirn annin, ' my eater '
Jealousy, on man's part	Tuurong muum ...	Muuroin muum ...	Puurtam been
Jealousy, on woman's part	Tuurong muum kuurk ...	Muuroin muum heear	Puurtam been heear
Jester ...	Kulng gheelung ...	Kulng gheean ...	Kuln gin
Joints of bones, generally	Milpeelang ...	Milpeean ...	Milpen
Joint of shoulder	Kookok ...	Ko'hneung	Kokok
Joint of elbow	Palluut yung'ark ...	Talliin ...	Talliin
Joint of wrist	Tartkuurt kurrok kurrok	Kunnaguurt	Kiiyuuk kiiyuuk
Joint of hip ...	Tan'yuuk ya'gnuurak ...	Taruuk ...	Taruuk
Joint of knee ...	Korrondok ...	Korronong	Puroin
Joint of ankle	Polok ...	Polong ...	Po'ol
Joke, or fun ...	Kulng gheelung ...	Kulng gheean	Kulng gin
Joy... ...	Chulkuuk ...	Gnuuteung	Gnuuteung
Jump ...	Chuult kærenn ...	Kupam ...	Pupkupamin
Kangaroo apple	*Not indigenous, and no name*	*Not indigenous, and no name* ...	*Not indigenous, and no name*
Keepsake of children's bones ...	Tæet tæet ...	Wiin wiin... ...	Wiin wiin

English.	Chaap wuurong (broad lip).	Kuurn kopan noot (small lip).	Peek whuurong (kelp lip).
Keepsake of hair	Gnaar puulak	Gnaarat tunnang	Gnaarat tunnang
Kelp, or broad-leafed sea-weed	*No name*	Peek, or peekœæ	Peek, or peekœæ
Kick	Karrak	Kurruwan...	Kurrwaa
Kicker of football	Kuurmukk	Kupakæ	Mumma
Kidney	Marpin	Kuurap	Mumma
Kidney fat	Marpuuk	Kuurap neung	Kuurap
Kill	Puung an	Miwann o	Kuurap gnattung
Kind	Chulkuuk	Gnuuteung	Purrta
Kiss	Chechakae	Totakin	Mutoe mutoe
Knee	Patchin yin	Paariin	Wuuta
Knee-cap	Koronn yuwarrak	Kuuron	Paariin
Knife, iron	Kulpuurn kulpuurn yowwær, 'cut flesh'	Mumbuurt mumbuurt muttal, 'cut cut flesh'	Kuuron neung
			Niitch
Knife, reed knife for cutting skins	Taark	Chaark	Chaark
Knife, made of shell, for cutting hair or flesh	Nang'gœr	Timbonn	Timbonn
Knife, made of flint, for skin marking and cutting up human bodies	Wuurokwil	Wuurokiin	Wuurokiin
Knife, made of grass tree, for skinning animals	Tateewutchu	Taark	Tæk
Knob stick	Warranuuk yuuloa, 'deformity'	Warrannuung wurotnat, 'deformity'	Wirrhneung
Knob stick, plaything	Ueetch ueetch	Ueetch ueetch	Ueetch ueetch
Knot on string	Kartnawuurnak	Mukunaku	Mukuunma
Know, to know	Cha'gnan	Tiiamanno	Tiiamanno
Knuckle	Wart mun'ya...	Wart marrang	Wart marrang
Korrobora	Yapingna	Karweann...	Karween
Lady, married	Lædæ kuurk	Lædæ g'naar	Puunjilkærang yaar
Lady, single	Wurtepee lædæ	Kuurna lædæ	Puunjilkærang yaar
Ladies' pockets, plant	Pueorok	Pueorok	Puyurok

English.	Chaap wuurong (broad lip).	Kuurn kopan noot (small lip).	Peek whuurong (kelp lip).
Lagoon	Chukkil	Ya'ang	Ya'ang
Lake	Yambaar	Turnapung	Killink
Lame, generally	Wære wærip	Waamp	Gnæn g'næn cheepa
Language	Challæ	Talliin	Taaliin
Large	Martuuk	Meheaaruung	Leenkil
Laugh	Wæk	Weiikan	Weiika
Lava	Tintæen	Kuulor	Kuulor
Laving water into mouth custom	Wiwi kuuyang	Kurtee kurteetch	Kurtee kurteetch
Lazy	Yattchang	Yuung kuunan	Gnummæ turamp
Leaf	Kæraneuk	Tærineung, or tærang	Tærang
Leave	Winnakatcha win	Wanna kunna meen..	Wanna gna
Leave off	Winnakak	Wanna ake	Wanna awan
Leave behind	Gna gna gnuutcha wang, 'closed are my ears'	Gnuutarbunna wirng, 'closed are my ears'	Gnuutarbunna wing, 'closed are my ears'
Left-handed man	Warram	Warram	Nirreen nirree
Left-handed woman	Warram kuurk	Warram heear	Nirreen nirreear
Leg	Only specific in parts	Only specific	Only specific
Leg, right	Yuulpeea gnuurak	Tumbit gnatnæn	Tumbit gnatnæn
Leg, left	Warram gneea gnuurak	Warram gnatnæn	Warram gnatnæn
Leg, thigh	Karrip pekk	Karrip	Karrip
Leg, lower	Kuurn muurk	Kuppuul	Kuppuul
Liangle	Ee angwill	Marwhang	Marwhang
Lichen	Tartuuk	Turtartuung	Kuntart
Lift	Wiewak	Kærank gnako	Nulpa
Light, daylight	Pærpa	Neenann	Wurtpa
Lightning	Changuuk	Martuung	Pillætuung
Lightning, forked	Millar kuuk, 'double'	Millerk millerk kupa manuung, 'come down double'	Pillætuung
Lightning, sheet	Charræma	Yarwan	
Lily, water lily	Bukuruum	Piitkuruup	
Limestone	Tiroyapp	Wirran	Tiiandeetch marri
Lip, upper	Wart wuuro	Wart wuurong	Whuurong
Lip, lower	Wuuro	Wuurong	Whuurong
Listen	Gneerna knutt chineen	Wang'an	Wang'a'nin

English.	Chaap wuurong (broad lip).	Kuurn kopan noot (small lip).	Peek whuurong (kelp lip).
Listening, with ear on the ground	Terpee watuung	Puutuurteen	Tukuyuung
Litter, of young animals	Puupuæ kuurnuum	Tukuæ tukuæ	Kuuneii
Little	Watchepuuk	Kuurnong	Puundin
Live	Muuruundiann	Puundeean	Poatong
Liver	Poatchak	Poat	Poatong
Lock of hair, keepsake	Gnaar puulak	Gnaarat tunnang	Gnaarat tunnang
Log	Kaalk	Yuurak	Nulla'hneung
Log, hollow	Mæer	Wallarr	Wallarr
Long or tall	Chu warrng	Wuuruumbit	Wuuruumbit
Long, very long log of wood	Charng	Wuuruumbit kannak	Wuuruumbit kannak
Long time ago	Mulla meea	Wuulekito	Mulli yitto
Look or observe	Gnaakak	Gnaake	Gnaakawarr
Lose	Ipiya	Yangdee an	Yangdeen
Lose the way	Pung pung killa o	Bung bung eearn o	Yangkeepa
Loud	Weering ii gnuureen, 'ears, mine!'	Weering a amin, 'ears, mine!', oh	Pinnang kueein
Love	Cherring dubugneen	Keean dubugnan	Keean dubugnan
Low	Nær	Kullæworr	Kuulkuurt
Low tide	Gneearka	Gneeremun	Palarna
Lungs	Chiichiruuk	Tiiwir yætch	Tæwuyit
Mad, insanity	Gnarkuumbeetch	Gnarkuumbeetch	Gnarkuumbeetch
Mad, with rage	Pirna wuchuup, 'come heart'	Wattan lee'hneung, 'come heart'	Wattan lee'hneung, 'come heart'
Maggoty meat	Peeek	Tætoæ	
Maid or maiden	Weearkuurnat kuurk	Marramarrabuul	Marramarrabuul
Maid, old	Puungoitch chan'gork	Puunoitch teean	Puunoitch teean
Majellanic cloud, large	Karn kuutchuun, 'male gigantic crane'	Karn kuuron, 'male gigantic crane'	Karn kuuron, 'male gigantic crane'
Majellanic cloud, small	Baapeekuutchuun, 'femalegigantic crane'	Gnærang kuuron, gigantic crane' 'female	Gnærang kuuron, 'female gigantic crane'
Make	Marpak	Muyuban	Muyuba
Make war	Challæ charrong gna o	Keetbawan	Purtpakan
Malarious smile	Kuumar kuumar	Kuunæturong	Wupkuya

xxiv

English.	Chaap wuurong (broad lip).	Kuurn kopan noot (small lip).	Peek whuurong (kelp lip).
Male	Mam kuurnuum	Peepkuurn	Peepkuurn
Mallee scrub	Punaetuuk	Maleen	Punaetuuk
Man, white race	Knummakeek	Knummateetch	Gnammateetch
Man, white	Knummakeek	Knummateetch	Gnammateetch
Man, old white	Knummakeek	Knummateetch	Gnuulank
Man, young white	Kuulkuurt kuulkuurn, 'young man'	Gnuin gnuitch mar, 'young man'	Warran warran
Man, aboriginal race	Kuulae	Maar	Maar
Man, aboriginal, old	Martee kuulae	Knarram knarram	Gnuulank
Man, aboriginal, young	Kuulkuul kuulkuurn	Gnuin gnuitch mar, 'very good man'	Warran warran
Man, wild black	Yuul yuul	Yuul yuul	Yuul yuul
Manhood, ceremony	Katneetch	Katnitt	Tapmit wuurong
Manna, exudes from trees	Buumbuul	Buumbuul	Puumbuul
Manna, produced by cicada	Buumbuul	Buumbuul	Puumbuul
Many, a crowd	Larbargirrar larbargirrar	Wuurt ba daerang, wuurt ba daerang	Gnarra kituung
Markings on rugs	Karrapak	Karrapoko	Karrapaa
Marriage, general term	Wuucharrenat	Wupan, 'given'	Yu gnumeen ban
Marriage ceremony	Wuuk charrang iitch	Wopo wan, 'give me'	Yu gnumma
Marriage by betrothal	Karrim karrim kuuruuk	Karrim karrim gnarr	Karrit meecharr
Marriage, by stealing a woman and compulsion	Pirmillang, 'stealing'	Korron gneean, 'stealing'	Mannumeen, 'stealing'
Marriage of widow	Nupkuutyang, 'twice married'	Puntaeteyan puundak, 'twice married'	Purokan, 'twice married'
Marriage, by woman taking forcible possession of man			
Marriage by elopement	Nupkuutyang	Puntaeteyan	Punkaetaen
Marriage of woman against her will, by order of chief	Yuurtmelang bula	Yuurtme andarr	Yuurtmeenda
Married couple, new	Wokilang	Wokatneean	Wokaen
Marriage feast	Tunyatt muchaelang	Kuunmart korteyen	Kuunmart korteyen
Marrying cousin	Chukkaelaeng o Kokwilguurk	Tukkeaanann Kuurukeear	Tukkawan gnuuluup Kuurukeear

English.	Chaap wuurong (broad lip).	Kuurn kopan noot (small lip).	Peek whuurong (kelp lip).
Marrying niece	Yatt'yang wingbuul	Gnammæ wæng	Gnammæ wæng
Marrow	Cheecheyuuk	Buyuum	Buyuum
Marrow-bones	Cheecheyuuk	Tætætuung	Tætæt
Marsh	Chukkil	Yaang	Yang
Marsh mallow	Gnurritch	Gnuurat	Muulong kuulirn
Mask made of kangaroo pouch	Tirn maaruuk	Pirn maaruuk	Pirn maaruuk
Mat of plaited grass	Peeep	Yillirn	Yillirn
Matter from wound	Puutchon	Keeraark	Potonn
Me	Winekk	Gnatook	Natuuk
Meal of food	Chukkilanang'no	Takkeeawan	Tukkinwann
Meal of friendship	Chukkælang	Takkee	Tukkee
Medicinal plants	Only specific	Only specific	Only specific
Medicine	No term	No term	No term
Medicine stone	Kamgam	Kareitch	Kareitch
Meeting, an ordinary one	Piyaar	Kuyuurn	Kuyuurn
Meeting, great	Munn'ya	Marrang	Marrang
Meeting married woman on path	Puunyar	Parrom	Yarrueetch
Memory	Gnulla g'nittælang wirmbulek, 'not shut ear'	Panguiitch gnuurtaban wirng, 'not shut ear'	Pang gnuurtin wing aa, 'not shut ear'
Message stick	Karrapiitch wee	Kaarat pittin ween	Kaarat pittin ween
Messenger	Wækerr	Wækerr	Weehnirr
Messenger, death messenger	Wækerr	Wækerr	Weehnirr
Meteor	Mirrnp pillæ, 'deformity'	Gnumme waar, 'deformity'	Gniirram puuloin
Midwife	Gneein	Gneein	Gneein
Mignonette, native	Boang gork, 'bad smell'	Wombeecheear, 'bad smell'	Wombecheear, 'bad smell'
Mildew	Takkilup lamlam	Mulluurn	Mnllurn
Milk	Chirkuum	Gnarmiin neong	Gneeang hmiin
Milk of sow thistle	Kuumbuurk	Nullæ nullæchong	Gnuppa neung
Milky way	Baarnk, 'big river'	Baarnk, 'big river'	Tarrdeen chunuurn, 'big river'
Millstone, or mortar	Yuron diitch	Watæ wanuut	Wattæ wan
Mine, or my own	Winnan akk	Gnatuuk gnat	Naatuuk gnatt

English.	Chaap wuurong (broad lip).	Kuurn kopan noot (small lip).	Peek whuurong (kelp lip).
Mirage on mountains	Woppelong unyok wuulun'gna, 'rising for rain'	Wertpeeunyok miunga, 'rising for rain'	Tampmeen mireen miiunger, 'rising for rain'
Mirage on plains	Kareer kareera	Kareer kareera	*Not known*
Mist	Wuort, or wartepeen kuureen	Waart, or kuureen	Kuureen
Miserable	Yetchung beng'gek, 'tremble flesh mine'	Yuunkuunan tuurap an, 'tremble flesh mine'	Nummæ kuurtæn, 'tremble flesh mine'
Mole on skin	Pupperkup	Puppuk kuyeetch	Puppuk kuyeetch
Month	Kiapp warteep tanyuuk, 'one small moon'	Kiappa kuurntaruung, 'one small moon'	Kiappa yaheear, 'one small moon'
Moon	Tanyuuk	Kuurntarung	Yaheear
Moon, full	Mirtæ tanyuuk, 'full moon'	Meheearong kuurntaruung, 'full moon'	Yaheear
Moon, new	Tanyuuk neuk, 'young moon'	Taaruuk nuung, 'young moon'	Tukuæ taaru, 'young moon'
Moonblind	Yappi yang'in	Yappa ennin	Yartæ antnin
Moonlight	Yappama gnuureen tanyuuk, 'shine moon'	Yappapaaghnatnæn kuurdaruuk, 'shine moon'	Yappa ghnatnæn taaru, 'shine moon'
More	Yaa neuk	Wannan nong	Yuuko
Morning	Pirna an neowee, 'come to me, sun'	Wattung an tirng, 'come to me, sun'	Wartparra gnunnung, 'come sun'
Morning star, 'Jupiter'	Tukkeeyuuk neowee gna, 'strike sun it'	Burtit tung tirng, 'strike the sun'	Purtætuung gnunnung gnat, 'strike sun it'
Moss or lichen	Gnarrang neeja	Gniiratt mæren	Wing kuuromp
Mould on food	Kamp kamp	Mullom	Mullonn
Mound, native mound	Pok yu	Pook	Puulwuurn
Mourning for adult	Kuutchelang o peeko	Kuteeanan marmda gna	Merre
Mourning for child	Gnullar watcheep	Pangkuparnk	Gniincharp
Moustache	Muunyuur cher	Bo worrong	Bo worrong
Mouth	Gnang	Gnuulang	Gnuulang
Mud	Peek	Pupall	Yuum
Murder	Taakin yuulmu	Purti yuung	Purti yuung
Murmur	Gninnæ wan, 'vexed me'	Laachlarp an, 'vexed me'	Laachlarp an, 'vexed me'
Murnong root	Pun'yin	Muurang	Keerang
Murnong root, cooked	Taluum	Yuwatch	Yuwatch
Muscle	Pochæ tutchukk	Poat whork	Poroitch
Mushroom, edible	Peekuurn	Peekuurn	Peekuurn

English.	Chaap wuurong (broad lip).	Kuurn kopan noot (small lip).	Peek whuurong (kelp lip).
Mushroom, poisonous ...	Murtkourwe ...	Murtkapirng ...	Puluurt
Mussel, meat of ...	Chaluup ...	Timbonn ...	Timbonn
Mustard, wild plant ...	Puyuruuk ...	Puyuruuk ...	Poroyuuk
Nails of fingers ...	Liritt munya...	Pirring marrang	Pirrin marrank
Nails of toes ...	Liritt chinna ...	Pirring dinnang	Pirrin tinnang
Name ...	Knarre gneuk ...	Leeneung ...	Leehnuung
Names, ceremony of ex-changing men's names	Knyarre knakk ...	Leen'gnann ...	Leen'gnann
Names, ceremony of ex-changing women's names			
Naming children ...	Knyarre kuurk ...	Leenyarbiin	Leenyarbiin
	Taaku minyarra, 'strike a name'	Purtung parrang o ling, 'strike a name', ...	Purtung ba ling, 'strike a name'
Navel ...	Warro ...	Peekuurt ...	Peetch
Nævus marks...	Koorp pang'uliit chinning	Moorpmoork piknunnot	Muurpee unnot
Near ...	Wallu yu ...	Walokat ...	Waluung
Near-sighted ...	Warnmirk ...	Warnkilmirng ...	Warnkilmeeng
Neck ...	Kuurndin ...	Kart ...	Kart
Necklace of kangaroo teeth ...	Marn marn ...	Marn marn ...	Michmitt
Necklace of porcupine quills ...	Yuulo neuk ...	Mirnmirtuung ...	Mirnmirtuung
Necklace of reeds ...	Charkuun ...	Tarkuun ...	Taekuurn
Nest of bird ...	Larneuk, 'habitation'	Wuurnong, 'habitation'	Wuurnong, 'habitation'
Nest of brush turkey, or lowan ...	Gullern'nung, 'lip or ridge'	Gullern'nung, 'lip or ridge'	Gullern'nung, 'lip or ridge'
Nest of powerful owl ...	Karram karram, 'open nest'	Kulk kulk...	*Unknown*
Nest of ant ...	Larneuk, 'habitation'	Wuurnong, 'habitation'	Wuurnong, 'habitation'
Net for hair ...	Warrak puup, 'net head'	Kuurrer beem, 'net head'	Kuurrer, 'net'
Net for catching eels ...	Puuniakuurt ...	Knarrapiin ...	Kart kart
Net, long drag net for fishing ...	Kalwill ...	Moall ...	Moall
Nettle ...	Mullukk ...	Mullukk ...	Mullukk
Never ...	Tuurp tuurp kutcha	Kiheeareet nan	Pang at

English.	Chaap wuurong (broad lip).	Kuurn kopan noot (small lip).	Peek whuurong (kelp lip).
New	Chulkuuk	Gnuuteung	Gnuuteung
Nickname for men	Wuurakk kætch	Kuuloin	Kuuloin
Nickname for women	Wuurakee kuurk	Kuuloit gneear	Kuuloit gneear
Night	Poroin	Porronn	Puuron kuurtin
Night, sleeping time	Kuumbee an, 'sleep me'	Yu wakk, 'sleeping time'	Yu waak, 'sleeping time'
Nightmare	Kæratcha neen murupa, 'pressing sleep me'	Wanjangan murupa, 'log pressing sleep me'	Wanjangan muurpa, 'log pressing sleep me'
No	Gnulla wotch	Bang at	Peng at
Noise	Wuung'garuuk	Wuung'garuung	Wandee ee wee
None	Gnulla wotch	Bang at	Peng at
North	Pilmallæ, 'hot wind'	Parrakii, 'hot wind'	Laahlaar kuurn, 'hot wind'
Noose, fibre for catching birds		Witt tæn	
Noose-stick for catching birds			
Nose	Parrem	Patkiyang	Patkiyang
Nose-borer, made of bone	Ka	Kapuung	Kapuung
Nostril	Yullo	Willang	Willang
Notch in tree for toe	Wallar ka	Wallar kapuung	Tuurnuut
Nurse	Wulluum	Kiuulon	Penk
Nutgall on trees	Gnaæern	Kneeirnduuk	Marnda gnin
	Puimballip	Puimballip	Wuurtnong karrihnat
Of	No term	No term	No term
Off	Yan gna	Yanan	Yanan
Old	Pruung kuiitch	Wuulæ wrulætch	Puutnuitch
On	Yuropakk	Mittako	Mittako
One-eyed	Kiiap mirnk or kæp mirr	Kiap mirng	Kiappa mink
Orchis	Hinnæhinitch, 'bat-faced'	Hinnæhinitch, 'bat-faced'	Hinnæhinitch, 'bat-faced'
Orion, constellation	Kuppikuurk	Kuppiheear	Tambuura
Ornament, general term	Marpælang	Muyupeean	Muyupin
Ornament for head of chief, made of swan's feathers	Tariitch	Kunnuk wirrin	Taratt
Ornament for head, made of cockatoo's crest feathers	Muung'an muung'an	Muung'an muung'an	Taratt

English.	Chaap wuurong (broad lip).	Kuurn kopan noot (small lip).	Peek whuurong (kelp lip).
Ornament for head, a band of plaited bark	Marak kulla	Marak kulliin	Muuloteen peem
Ornament, reed necklace	Charkuun	Tarkuun	Takuurn
Ornament, kangaroo teeth necklace	Marn marn	Marn marn	Mirlmirt
Ornament for loins of women, made of emu-neck feathers	Chilbarne	Tirrbarrin	Tirrbareen
Ornament for loins of men, strips of opossum skin	Parrang geetch	Parrang geetch	Parrang geetch
Ornament for upper arm, rope of ring-tail opossum skin	Kunkuntutchuk	Mille wuuk	Mille wuuk
Ornament for wrist of women, band of ring-tail opossum skin	Kunkuntutchuk kuurk	Morrom	Morrom
Ornament of emu-tail feathers, representing a tail, used by men while dancing	Chorrong	Tuuring	Tireen
Ornament, bunches of leaves round ankles while dancing	Kirraka	Kirrambirm	Kirrambirm
Ornament, nose reed	Taang taang	Moreen	Tuurnuut
Orphan, male	Palliin	Parrapeetch	Kokeetch
Orphan, female	Palliin guurk	Parappeheear	Kokæheear
Our	Winna gna luuk	Gnok gnok	Gnaatu'hnat
Oven, for cooking	Tulluun	Yuwiitch	Marii
Over	Wilkak	Wilkake	Kunuunuung
Overtake	Gnunna chung'een	Gnunna tung an	Gnunnataa
Pacify	Knuul knuul nieææ	Gnuul gnuul nakæ	Gnuul gnuul
Paddle or oar	Tak tak gnunnak, 'strike, water'	Purt purt mærtiitch, 'strike, strike water'	Purt purt mærtiitch, 'strike, strike water'

English.	Chaap wuurong (broad lip).	Kuurn kopan noot (small lip).	Peek whuurong (kelp lip).
Pain	Tum milaa an ...	Muurpeeanno ...	Wuuruunda
Paint ...	Karmelung ...	Karmeean... ...	Karma
Paint, black ...	Kolorn nillerwutt	Mooit purmeeyarko ...	Meeinju wertiin
Paint, white ...	Pæk	Martang	Martang
Paint, red ...	Waapp	Wilapp	Wilapp
Pair, a pair of anything	Puuliit ...	Puuliitcha ...	Puuliitcha
Palaver or conference ...	Kulpuumup kuliitch	Pullip pullip kullat	Palleen kuukna kallatt
Parry	Pirngognakk ...	Watpee gnun o	Yarnda wuurna
Past	Nurawilang ...	Nuurawee an	Wuluba
Path, footpath or track ...	Parring	Ta'an	Ta'an
Peep of day ...	Kulleitch ...	Kullatt ...	Kullatt
Periwinkle ...	Gnummat ...	Gnummat... ...	Gnummat
Perspiration ...	Wuruman ...	Wirre kuupanu	Wirreeopa
Penny royal, native ...	Poang guurk, ' bad smell '	Wombeheearmuurtparakk, ' bad smell '	Wapkuyeetch, ' bad smell '
Pierce	Bukkuurna ...	Bukkæra nuung	Pakeepa
Pin, bone pin... ...	Kee'een˙ ...	Keeneen ...	Keeneen
Pin, for pegging out skins	Tuptup karra... ...	Warnwhardorr ...	Warnwharndorr
Pin, bone pin for picking out thorns	Ke'een	Ke'een	Ke'een
Pin, for fastening clothing	Gnarræng gnarræng	Gniith gniith ...	Beeju beeju
Pith of rush ...	Pot pot	Pot pot	Pot pot
Pity	Tuukam an, ' sorry am I '	Wirrechann ...	Weepo wing gno gno
Plain or flat country ...	Waapung knaraar ...	Waark	Wææwhekk
Planet	Chachee neowee, ' sister of sun '	Kaaki tirng, ' sister of sun '	Mink gill, ' eye ours '
Plant	Only specific ...	Only specific ...	Only specific
Play or diversion ...	Wuyam cherrang gno ...	Kulmba wan ...	Mellim bukkal
Play of the eagle ...	Warromillang ...	Warroneean ...	Warroneean
Pleasant or pleasure ...	Tulkuuk ...	Mirman	Mirma
Pleasant to smell ...	Tulkuuk butang	Kuuchuung narroban	Weitchpirna
Pleasant to taste ...	Puyuurwilapp ...	Pueeuurweetch ...	Pueeuurweetch
Pleiades or seven stars ...	Kutchakarkuurk, ' flock of cockatoos '	Kuurokeheaar, ' flock of cocka-toos '	
Pluck or courage ...	Tititwuuchuup ...	Pinukilik ...	Likkætuung
Pointers, constellation ...	Chuulirm, ' magpie larks '	Tuulirmp, ' magpie larks '	Tuulirmp, ' magpie larks '

xxxi

English.	Chaap wuurong (broad lip).	Kuurn kopan noot (small lip).	Peek whurrong (kelp lip).
Pole, carried by woman	Charng	Wuurombit kannak	Wuurombit kannak
Pole, carried before chiefess	Marœnœ kunnœ	Marœne kunnuk	Marœne kunnuk
Pole-bearer	Tarriitch	Tarratt	Tarratt
Pole ceremony	Marœnœ ja	Marœne mirring	Marœne mirring
Pond or waterhole	Yarrum	Killink	Muuluupit killink
Porcupine spikes	Yuulo neuk	Willineung	Willineung
Pouch for baby on mother's back	Nuurn nuurn	Gnuurn gnuurn	Gnuurn gnuurn
Pouch of quadrupeds generally	Piinjuuk	Panuung	Panuung
Pouch of native cat or dasyure		Gnarniitch neung	Panuung
Pouch of pelican	Kuurmbuuk	Karp karp neung	Moaluung
Pour	Karm karm mok	Towirrdan	Kankna
Prickly box	Kagna gna	Kuro karann	Petek
Prickly bushes	Kuukee karann	Karann	Karann
Proud flesh	Karann	Turam	Turam
Puke	Paang	Karnan	Karn ma
Pull	Karma	Winakkœ	Wirrenchaa
Pulse	Tirndak	Tumtumban, 'beat, beat'	Tuumtuumbaa, 'beat, beat'
Punk	Chuumchuumbaa, 'beat, beat'	Nuunkœn	Nuunken
Push	Puurnkuyœ kalk	Yuurndœakœ	Yuurnda
Quarrel	Yuurnkœaka	Keetbandaa	Kœbukkall
Queen or chiefess	Challecharrang	Wung'ee'heaar, 'listen to woman'	Wung'ee'heear, 'listen to woman'
Queen of the Pleiades	Gnœaarnœetch kuurk, 'listen woman'	Gneeang'gar	Gneeang'gar
Quench fire	Wirpill	Tiingeenakee	Milkeen aa
Quench thirst	Puut kuurnak	Wuyupan karnt, 'longing throat'	Kuurn aa
Quick	Wneetpa kuurndeek, 'longing throat'	Marratt marraran	Wœtkuurtin
Rain	Pirpuurn	Miiyang	Maayang
Rainbow	Walaa	Tarn tarn paarot	Tuurann
Raise, to lift	Tœrakœa guurk	Kœrang gnak o	Kœra gna
Rasp, indigenous fruit	Wiwak	Barring guut	Barring guut
	Barring guutch		

English.	Chaap wuurong (broad lip).	Kuurn kopan noot (small lip).	Peek whuurong (kelp lip).
Rasp, made of lava	Tintæn	Kuulor	Kuulor
Rattle	Teerar a gnak	Kirk kirk gnakæ	Tærrakirta
Rays of sun	Puung a ruuk neowee g'na, 'rushes sun its'	Weearmeetch, 'rushes'	Puung'ortuung munnanatt, 'rushes'
Reckon, to count	Gnuurtak	Gnuurtakæ	Tuurtaa
Red	Pit pit tarneetch	Tirraeetch	Lepeetch
Reed	Kærk	Taark	Tærk
Reed-pipe, for sucking water	Chuup chuup	Gnaluum	Gnaluum
Reflection of bush fire in sky	Tærapekuurk, 'flickering'	Yanmeeheaar, 'flickering'	Yanmeechaar, 'flickering'
Regent	Yaapihineokk	Warnpu warnu	Warn wung yitt
Relationship	Kænginbaa winnanik	Kaandeetch gnatuuknatt	Kiiambaa gnatuhatt
Respect	Chulkuuk	Gnuuteung	Wang'un gnuuteung
Revenge	Pirrpirp pirp	Mallækætæ yiin	Tuuknateetch nin
Rib	Lun'yin	Yeeyeer	Yeeyeer
Right, or correct	Tulkuuk	Gnuuteung	Gnuuteung
Ring for nose	Taang taang	Tuurnot	Muuren
Rise up	Piitkaa	Mirtann	Mirtaako
River	Baar	Baarnk	Warroneung
Rivulet, or burn	Peerbæær	Turtpa karapp	Turtuung
Roast or broil flesh	Wampeeya yowwir	Paawurko muttal	Muurtpoko muttal gnan
Rocks, large	Yuronn yuronn	Yak kot	Yuuluurn
Rocks, jagged, on sea-shore	Koroitch koroitch	Morra morra meetch	Morra morra meetch
Roguery	Pirmilang, 'stealing'	Kuuronee an, 'theif him'	Manumeetch, 'taker'
Root of tree or plant	Wuyuurk	Warann	Wueok
Rope, matrimonial rope	Wartko	Wartko	Wartko
Rope for tying corpse	Bowiitch	Parret	Parret
Rope for strangling people	Maronn maronn	Kuutchuul kuutchuul	Kuutchuul kuutchuul
Rotten	Puungguitch	Puurnoitch	Puurnoitch
Rough	Chimp chimp mok	Kuuruutch kuurruutch	Wuin wuinbeetch
Round	Murnkuum	Murnkuurt	Ynumkuurt
Rug, man's kangaroo skin	Dallang	Wianjereetch	Kiiapirn
Rug, opossum rug, large	Willakuurn	Baaluun	Baalunn

English.	Chaap wuurong (broad lip).	Kuurn kopan noot (small lip).	Peek whuurong (kelp lip).
Rug, opossum rug, small	Tuulu mannæ	Tulluukuut mannæn	Knærret
Run	Pirpaa	Karkurann	Wirrakan
Run to me	Pirpeeka	Wattenakæ	Wirrakan nin
Run away	Yuun millang	Yuun meea ko	Kuuninbaa
Rush, large	Pot pot	Pot pot	Pot pot
Rush, basket rush	Puung'ort	Weearmeetch	Puung'ort
Rush, brown	Punng'injaar	Pung'injaar	Pung'injaar
Rush for eel-traps	Mork	Mork	Morkort
Rush, jagged	Tarr	Tarr	Tarr
S.	*No sound*	*No sound*	*No sound*
Salt	Kiriitch	Lapeetch	Lapeetch
Salutation, or greeting	Gna keenatt, 'here you are'	Gna tanwarr, 'here you are'	Gna tanwarr, 'here you are'
Sand	Kolak	Kuulak	Kuulak
Sap of tree	Kondok	Konong	Konong
Scabby	Bunk bunk	Wirreeneetch	Wirreeneetch
Scales of snake	Paapmok	Yarraneung	Yarraneung
Scorpio constellation	Kumcherap, 'crowded'	Kummin bieetch, 'crowded'	Gnirpeen pieetch, 'crowded'
Scratch	Pung pung gnillan	Weereetneann	Tuurnang in
Scratch on tree	Wiretna	Wirraeranno	Marraneung
Scream	Karndaa	Karndann	Karndaa
Scrub	Minmin	Yerroæ	Wuuro wuuruuk
Sea	Waarre	Waare	Mirteetch
Seaweed	Peekoæ	Peekoæ	Peekoæ
Sea sand	Kolak	Kuulak	Kuulak
Sedge, with edible root	Puurteetch	Puurteetch	
See	Nakelang	Nakeen	Nakeen
Seeds, generally	Torrong	Tirremuut	Poramuuk
Seed or cone of she-oak	Torrong guuk	Tirreemuut	Poramuuk
Seed or cone of banksia	Buundaruuk	Buundarong	Warwarong
Seed of native cherry tree	Muumee palatt	Palatt	Palatt
Seed of common acacia	Puupee tuulin	Kuulan karrank	Kundart
Seed of blackwood tree	Puurpeetch chimukk	Kuulan mutan	Kundart
Seed of gum trees, generally	Koreok	Koar	Korrert

English.	Chaap wuurong (broad lip).	Kuurn kopan noot (small lip).	Peek whuurong (kelp lip).
Seed of box tree	Koreok ...	Koar ...	Kulanuung
Seed of privet	Puurpee karann ...	Beem karann ...	Kulanuung
Sew	Teengak ...	Kurpin ...	Kurpa
Shadow	Gnaak ...	Gnaakuur ...	Wo'ol
Shake	Chuun chuun buung ak	Warng warng geen ...	Tuun tuun ba
Shake hands ...	Muutcha at tutt chukk, 'take the hand'	Manan marrang, 'take the hand'	Manna marrang, 'take the hand'
Sharp	Gnariitch ...	Arrimbirt ...	Linming
Sharp, or quick of hearing	Tulkuuk wirng buuleen, 'good ear'	Gnuuteung wirng, 'good ear'	Gnuutchkill wing, 'good ear'
Sharpen, to sharpen	Yurondak ...	Watæwakuur ...	Watuya
Sharping stone	Yuron yuron...	Warwhatorr ...	Warwhatorr
She	Keela ...	Teelaree ...	Teelang
She-oak tree ...	Kuuluurt ...	Gneering ...	Gneering
Shells, generally	Chitchewaruuk ...	Tirrewarrong ...	Pakkaneung
Shell of cuttlefish	Pæet ...	Pæet ...	Pæet
Shell of crab ...	Gnummakok, 'boat mine'	Tuurongneung, 'boat mine'	Tuurongneung, 'boat mine'
Shell of crayfish	Gnummakok, 'boat mine'	Tuurongneung, 'boat mine'	Tuurongneung, 'boat mine'
Shell of mutton-fish	Cherruuk ...	Tærre warrong ...	Tærre warrong
Shell of large whelk	Gnummakok, 'boat mine'	Tuurongneung, 'boat mine'	Wilwill
Shell of mussel	Chaluup ...	Timbonn ...	Tallop
Shell, eperculum of whelk	Leean neuk gnumatcha, 'teeth of whelk'	Tannaneung gnumma hnatt, 'teeth of whelk' ...	Tannaneung gnumma hnatt, 'teeth of whelk'
Shell of sea-snail, used as a spoon ...	Mæng hmæt ...	Maing hmæt ...	Mæng hmæt
Shield for warding off spears ...	Puural ...	Kæram ...	Puural
Shield for warding off blows ...	Muumkalk ...	Malkar ...	Mulkar
Shield of bushes for stalking game	Teengit jang ...	Kurpit mart ...	Kurpit mart
Ship	Gnunnak, 'bark'	Torong, 'bark'	Torong, 'bark'
Short	Muulop ...	Muulopit ...	Muulopit
Shore, seashore	Tirr kutchin ...	Tirr pareetch	Tirr pareetch
Shoulder ...	Bukkureeak knureeak ...	Kok ...	Kok
Shoulder blade	Nunnjir wart...	Minjær wart ...	Minjær wart

English.	Chaap wuurong (broad lip).	Kuurn kopan noot (small lip).	Peek whuurong (kelp lip).
Shout	Karndakk	Karndam	Kowææ
Shrub, or bush	Poroitcholl	Piitpurong	Piitpurong
Sick, or sickness	Weekuuchang	Gnullerwan	Wuulor wa
Side	Kulkik lun'ying	Yeeyeer	Gninhnan
Side, right	Yuulpin	Tumbit gno	Tumbit gno
Side, left	Warramin	Warram gno	Warram gno
Sigh, 'oh dear me'	Yuunkan gnang guae yat	Yangdano gnawn gnan	Tirt annin, 'eye mine'
Sight	Mirn nuuk, 'eye mine'	Tirng annin, 'sun mine'	Popirta
Signal smoke	Wurræ	Karwhin	Kalkuurtnan
Silence	Tittarik	Kort kort	Puuruutch
Sinew, general term	Knarram	Puuruutch	Murheearong puuruutch, 'big sinew'
Sinew, Achilles	Murtæ knarram, 'big sinew'	Meeheearong puuruutch, 'big sinew'	
Sinew of kangaroo tail	Knarram	Puuruutch	Puuruutch
Sing	Yinglang	Laerpean	Laerpeen
Sirius, or Dog-star	Putchupum	Paarupum	Maarupeng
Sit	Puura gno	Kuupann	Kuupa
Sit down	Puurang no	Gneengan	Kuupang in
Skeleton	Kultanyu	Warruun warruun	Gnumeenjaar
Skin of man or beast	Mitchin	Muurn	Mitch
Skin of cicada	Teriinuurnap	Wirrinkuurneetch	Wirrinkuurna
Skin of snake	Meetchuuk	Muurnuung	Muurnong
Skin ornamenting	Karakenik	Karrakeen	Karrapa
Skull, of any kind	Challæpop	Talliin beem	Parin beem
Sky	Marng'guurk	Muurnong	Muurnong
Sleep	Kuumban	Yuwann	Yuwinn
Sleep talking	Ya ya heelan	Yaheear teearno	Yuyuur kinno
Sleep walking	Nimpmeen kuurnang o	Kambirnee an	Kambirneen
Sleepy	Kuumball gnu	Yuwawan	Yuwawan
Sleet	Putkæra	Naark	Næk
Slow	Yatchang kuurneela	Kullang kuurneann	Gnuul gnuul
Small	Watchepuuk	Kuurnong	Kuurnei
Small-pox	Tow warrann	Mirn warrann	Mirn warrann
Smell	Wuucheaa wuurechuuk	Poteen	Potaa
Smell, good smell	Tulkuuk wuureetch	Gnuutchputan gnarrupan	Gnuuteung wapirna

English.	Chaap wuurong (broad lip).	Kuurn kopan noot (small lip).	Peek whuurong (kelp lip).
Smell, bad smell	Wuutchaeaa ...	Wombeetch ...	Wombeetch
Smell, unwholesome	Kuunaeturong ...	Kuunaeturong ...	Wambuuna leehnan
Smell, malarious	Kuumar kuumar ...	Kuunaeturong ...	Wapkuya
Smoke	Puureen ...	To'ong ...	To'ong
Smoke, bad smelling	Wuucheyaa ...	Waperann ...	Wapkuya
Smooth	Biin biin ...	Biin biin ...	Yuruut
Sneeze	Kinnae chan, 'tickling nose'	Cheenea, 'tickling'	Cheenea, 'tickling'
Sniff with nose	Nittaelang kaa'gnak, 'shut the nose'	Gnutae kuppung, 'shut the nose'	Gnutae kuppuung, 'shut the nose'
Snore	Yuurop ma ...	Puuron ban	Yuun kuurang
Snow	Yuun kuyang ...	Yuun kuurang	Wenba
Soar, like an eagle	Warromillang ...	Waroitneean	Tullap
Soft	Ta'ap ...	Tullap ...	Lirpeen
Song, a song	Ying'elang ...	Lirpeean ...	Lirpeen
Song of bird	G'narre pillang ...	Lirpeean ...	
Song of piping-crow, or organ-bird	Kaaruma ...	Kaaruman ...	Gnark kueaa
Sore, a sore	Waerpin ...	Ming ...	Meeng
Sorrow	Pirpa wuuchu bak, 'beating heart'	Kuurkuran lichnan, 'beating heart'	Weerakan lichnan
South	Kuureen, 'drizzly quarter'	Kuureen, 'drizzly quarter'	Kuureen, 'drizzly quarter'
Sound or noise, like thunder	Wuungarok ...	Wuungaruung ...	Wuungaruung
Sound of stone thrown into water	Nulla nulla kok ...		
Sour	Keeawilapp or kiriitch ...	Tapkirtin ...	Tapkirtin
Southern Cross	Kunkun chuuromballank, 'knot or tie'	Keeaweetch or lapeetch ... Kunkun tuuromballank, 'knot or tie' ...	Gnumme chaar
Sorcery stones	Kerm kerm ...	Kaaratch ...	Not known
Spark of fire	Tiller ka ...	Tiller pan ...	Kaaratch
Spawn of frogs and fish	Chaarneuk ...	Tuulortuung ...	Puee puee
Speak	Wuurake ...	Lakkako ...	Tuulortuung
Speak, general term	Taeaer ...	Tiyeaer ...	Myitpan
Spear, smooth-pointed war	Karp ...	Tuulowarn ...	Tiyeaer
Spear, barbed war	Leeawill ...	Tung'ung'gill ...	Tuulawarn
			Tung'ung'gill

English.	Chaap wuurong (broad lip).	Kuurn kopan noot (small lip).	Peek whuurong (kelp lip).
Spear, flint-jagged war	Muuwill	Wuurokigill	Wuurokiin
Spear, kangaroo	Taaer	Narmall	Terr
Spear, best quality	Bundit, 'bite'	Bundit, 'bite'	Bundit, 'bite'
Spear, reed	Chaark	Gnirrin	Terr
Spear, eel	Tuulakneetch	Kuyuut	Kuyuut
Spear with emu feather attached	Witchin	Taaratt	Taaratt
Spear, thrower stick	Kiirek	Gniiruung	Karpong golang
Spectacles	Teaert mirr, 'dazzle eye'	Aetchaet termirn, 'dazzle eye'	Teaert ming, 'dazzle eye'
Spell	Yuucomaa muuruup, 'frightened for devil'	Yuunyuumban muuruup, 'frightened for devil'	Yuumban muuruup, 'frightened for devil'
Spell, rubbish	Woreetch	Wuulon	Wuulon
Spirit, good or great	Mam yungrakk	Pirnmeeheeal	Pringheeal
Spirit, bad male	Muuruup	Muuruup	Tambuur
Spirit, bad female	Gnulla gnulla kuurk	Gnulla gnulla gneear	Gnulla gnulla gneear
Spirit, man's	Gniiyarr	Wirreenk	Wirreenk
Spirit, woman's	Wirree gork	Wirreeyaar	Weeyarr
Spirit or ghost	Muuruupuuk	Muuruup hneung	Muuruup hneung
Spirit in cave on seashore	Not known	Puit chepetch	Puit chepetch
Spirit of beast	None	None	None
Spirituous liquor	Ballin kork, 'motherless girl'	Kokke heear, 'motherless girl'	Lapeetch, 'pungent water'
Spittle	Kowwarr	Tuulort	Tuulort
Sponge	Gnuunkee	Gnuunkee	Gnuunkee
Spoon formed of shell	Tarre warrong	Tarre warrong	Tarre warrong
Sporran	Piian'geaetch	Piian'geaetch	Piian'geaetch
Spring of water	Kuulan nuuk	Pupkupan pareetch, 'coming out water'	
Spring of the year	Bukkar yak eelang nor, 'summer coming'	Bukkar ya eeawan, 'summer coming'	Bukkar ya eeawan, 'summer coming'
Spur on wing of lapwing	Yuloœ yuuk	Willanyuung	Willanyuung
Spur on wing of powerful owl	Leeawiluuk	Meenim mahamneung	Willanyuung
Spur of platypus	Yuloœ yuuk	Willanyuung	Willanyuung
Squaring skins for rugs	Tulgorakk	Tuuloin kuurtakœ	Tuuloin kuurtakœ
Squeak	Kagga wuudchan	Kawuurdeean	

English.	Chaap wuurong (broad lip).	Kuurn kopan noot (small lip).	Peek whuurong (kelp lip).
Squint ...	Chuunkee mirnk, 'squint eye'	Muurngottitch mirng, 'squint eye'	Wartu wirteen mink, 'squint eye'
Stage in tree for corpse	Kalk	Barrangkuurt	Barrangkuurt
Stalking game	Kærambung o	Tæran bowann	Tæra buurtna
Stalking the feather	Witchim	Tarratt	Tarratt
Stand	Charrekan	Kardan	Kardan
Stars, generally	Chachee neowee, 'sisters of the sun'	Kaakii tirng, 'sisters of the sun'	Mink gill, 'eye ours'
Stars, small ...	Chachee neowee, 'sisters of the sun'	Narweetch mæring, 'star earth'	Peepeetchee kupen, 'crowded'
Start ...	Pung'yin gnan, 'frightened me'	Pardopum me an o, 'frightened me'	Pardopum meeno, 'frightened me'
Steal or stealing	Pirmelang	Yuupeann...	Mannumeetch
Steamboat ...	Preen preen nuurnup, 'smoke along'	Tongtong pirndeheear, 'smoke along'	Torong
Steep, steep hill	Knæær	Kullee wuur	Kuul kuurt
Stem of tree or plant	Tutcha kuuk	Wuurtneung	Wuurtneung
Sticks for beating time	Tirn tirn	Popok	Popok
Sting ...	Kuurnaneeng	Kuurang an, 'bite me'	Murpa
Stinking ...	Wuutchaeaa	Wumban	Wuumbeetch
Stomach ...	Pæling ink	Tuuku	Tuuku
Stomach ache	Gneuro ang æ	Koroit gna gnan	Koroit gna gnan
Stone ...	Laa'a	Marrii	Marrii
Stones, applied hot to pain spot ...	Tueetch pakk yakuutch	Paawat kueakuut	Paawat kueakuut
Stones, for curing toothache ...	Kerm kerm	Kaaratch	Kaaratch
Stones, for sorcery ...	Kerm kerm	Kaaratch	Kaaratch
Stones for celts ...	Laa...	Marrii	Marrii
Stones, for basket-making	Parpu gna	Paapirano	Paapirano
Stones, for grinding celts	Yuron yuron	Warwhatuur	Warwhatuur
Stoop ...	Wuumælang	Yurotan	Yurotan
Stooping custom of mothers-in-law ...	Gneealuun guurk	Naluun	Naluunyar
Storm, which destroys blossoms ...	Borran borran kulan chimmuk	Borran borran kula muutang	Borran borran kuula muutang

English.	Chaap wuurrong (broad lip).	Kuurn kopan noot (small lip).	Peek whurrong (kelp lip).
Storm, which blows young magpies out of their nests ...	Kang'ælap kang'ælap kææræ	Towitt towæk keerre	Towitt towæk keerre
Stormy day ...	Muun muurt ...	Pulla peetch	Pulla peetch
Storm, hurricane ...	Puundaa yirneen	Puundeen knuurnduka	Puundeen knuurnduka
Stringy-bark tree ...	Warng ar ...	Kuurang ...	Mariin
Strike ...	Wirræ puurnan	Pitpirneen	Purta
Strip off clothes ...	Baardak ...	Nirrremakæ	Nirrremin
Strip bark off tree ...	Kuulpuurn ak	Kuulpæraakæ	Waarpa
Stripes of paint on body when dancing ...	Kuutchelang ...	Kuuteean ...	Kuuteean
Strong ...	Tirt tirt bang...	Peenituuram	Pineitch
Stump of tree... ...	Tuulo ...	Tuulokuut	Tuulokuut
Sugar ...	Sugar ...	Sugar ...	Sugar
Sulky ...	Pirna wuchupuuk, 'come heart'	Wattan leehneung, 'come heart'	Wattan leehnan, 'come heart'
Summer ...	Kartii ...	Kaluun, or peep kaluun, 'father of heat' ...	Peep kaluun, 'father of heat'
Summons to attend meeting ...	Mutchapilkuurk	Marrapeear ...	Marrapeear
Sun ...	Neowee ...	Tirng ...	Gnunnung
Sundew ...	Kullum kulkeetch	Kullum barran	Kullum barran
Sunrise ...	Pirna an neowee, 'come me sun'	Wattung an tirng, 'come me sun' ...	Kumba gnunnung, 'come sun'
Sunset ...	Mirma neowee, 'go down sun'	Ki kan tirng, 'go down sun'	Kaapa gnuunang, 'go down sun'
Sunshine ...	Kuulpuung a ...	Kolpegnan	Yarnda buuna
Sunstroke ...	Tukka neowee gno, 'hit sun me'	Pawan beem an tirng gnan, 'burn head sun mine'	Paawa peemneung nunnang gna, 'burn head sun mine'
Supernatural ...	Poitka gnarnerk, 'hair on end'	Mirtun gnarrarnun, 'hair on end'	Parmæn pæmun, 'hair on end'
Swamp ...	Chukkil ...	Yaang ...	Yaang
Sweet ...	Puuyurwilapp	Puyuurweetch	Puyuurweetch
Sweetheart, male ...	Korweetch ...	Pinning gar	Pinningnan
Sweetheart, female ...	Korweetch kuurk	Pinning gar yarr	Pinning
Swelling ...	Karring gna ...	Karretan ...	Waawaa
Swim ...	Neukaa ...	Yaween ...	Yandaa
Swoop of eagle, upwards ...	Warromelang	Warromeann	Kaapa

xl

English.	Chaap wuurong (broad lip).	Kuurn kopan noot (small lip).	Peek whuurong (kelp lip).
Swoop of eagle, downwards	Kutchæwarragna	Kiitpannoman	Kaapa
Tail of quadruped	Pirrkuurk	Wirraneung	Wirraneung
Tail of bird	Pirrkuurk	Kuulortong	Kuulortong
Tail of fish	Pilarnduuk	Pilarnuung	Pilarneung
Tail of platipus	Pilarnduuk	Pilarnuung	Pilarnuung
Take	Muutchak	Mannakæ	Wumba
Take this	Muutchaka	Mannakæ	Wumba
Talk	Wuurakæ	Lakkawan...	Lukkiin
Tame	Tulkuchang	Gnuul gnuul uutnann	Gnuul gnuul
Taste	Teurwa	Puyuurweetch	Tukku
Taste, good	Puyuurwilap wuurong	Gnuuteung puyuurweetch	Gnuuteung puyuurweetch
Taste, bad	Wuæ wuæ worre	Wapkuyee moot	Wapkuyee moot
Tear	Kutcha mirnk, 'water eye'	Pareetch mirng, 'water eye'	Pareetch mink, 'water eye'
Teats of animals	Kuuruum, or ko'om, 'human'	Nuppang	Nuppang
Teeth generally	Leea	Tung'ang	Tung'ang
Teeth, upper	Porb leea	Beem tung'ang, 'head teeth'	Beem tung'ang 'head teeth'
Teeth, front	Wuuro leea gnek, 'lip teeth'	Wuurong tung'ang, 'lip teeth'	Wuurong tung'ang, 'lip teeth'
Teeth, back	Wirng dak, 'ear teeth'	Wirng gnan, 'ear teeth'	Wirn gnan, 'ear teeth'
Teeth, eye	Taak yung'art, 'eye teeth'	Mirng gnatnin, 'eye teeth'	Mirn munmin, 'eye teeth'
Teeth, children's first	Tang'atuuk leea	Kuuminung tung'ang	Kuuminung tungung
Teeth, children's second	Karrinjorrok	Karraneuk kuuruung	Wiinyiyarr
Teeth, wisdom	No name	No name	No name
Temples	Teunpuutch teunpuutch, 'beat beat'	Lupæ lupirt, 'beat, beat'	Teunpuurtteunpuurt, 'beat, beat'
Tender	Kulkuyubang	Kulkuutch	Wiin
Terror	Pamban	Kuuin ban	Kuuninba
That or this	Kee'eek	Dikgnat	Nonbee
Thaw	Yannkiya	Yanan	Puurpa
There	King ga	Mukæ	Mung'æ
They	Keng gnuuk	Tineæ	Nuyu
Thigh	Kareep	Karip	Kareep
Thin	Nulla bepuul	Warruundeetch	Warruundeetch
Think, I think	Merring gekk	Gnaaki	Nukiin
Thirsty	Kuukna gnæn	Kuuknan	Kuurtnan

English.	Chaap wuurong (broad lip).	Kuurn kopan noot (small lip).	Peek whuurong (kelp lip).
Thistle, imported thistle	Punpun dillup, 'prick, prick'	Punpun deetch, 'prick, prick'	Punpun deetch, 'prick prick'
Thistle, sow thistle	Tallark	Tullark	Tullark
Thistle, marsh thistle	Chulluk chulluk	Tullark wireetjar, 'mate of thistle'	Tullark wireetjar, 'mate of thistle'
Thorn	Kukee karann	Karann	Pundang
Thread, made of sinew	K'narram	Puuruutch	Puuruutch
Thread, made of fur	Tulang	Wung'ar	Weerang an
Threaten	Gnuul gnuul wuutyœ	Gnuul gnuulo nakœ	Gnuul gnuul tin'yœœn
Throat	Yan yan gnuurak	Yan	Tullark
Through	Pukkumaa	Pukkeepann	Pukkeepa
Throw	Yuungak	Yarndeen	Yarnda
Throw a boomerang	Chireemukk	Kaarta bukku	Kaarta bung'een
Throw a spear	Yuun'gak	Yarndakee	Yarnda
Thrust with a spear	Punda	Pundun o	Pundun o
Thumb	Baap mun'ya, 'mother of fingers'	Gneerang marrang, 'mother of fingers'	Gneerank marrank, 'mother of fingers'
Thunder	Murndaar	Murndall	Murndall
Thunder cloud	Tarrachee murndaar	Tarrat murndall	Tarrat murndall
Tide	Gnunjaa, 'rising'	Gnundun, 'rising'	Kuttepaa, 'rising'
Tippet of rushes for toothache	Puung'ort	Weearmeetch	Ma'al
Tired	Tirt kuugna	Part puung'ang	Waawo'gna
Titree	Pallawar	Puunong	Puunuung
To-day	Gneunjall	Kalo	Kalo
Toes, generally	Chinna	Tinnang	Tinnang
Toe, large	Paap chinna, 'mother of toes'	Kneerang tinnang, 'mother of toes'	Kneerang tinnang, 'mother of toes'
To-morrow	Pirp pirp pirp	Mallang eebœ	Tuungna teetch
Tongue	Chalœœ	Talliin	Tulliin
Tooth, for rubbing children's gums	Kunne neuk	Kunnuk neung	Kunnuk neung
Toothache	Kœœm	Karratch	Karratch
Torch, for night fishing	Yapuurœlap	Yappeheear	Merk
Torch, for night walking	Yapp	Yapp	Yapp
Touch	Chinbukk	Tinbukk	Tuumba
Tough	We'er we'er	We'erkuyeetch	Piniitch
Towsie head of hair	Laarb	Wuurn beem	Wotkil beem

English.	Chaap wuurong (broad lip).	Kuurn kopan noot (small lip).	Peek whuurong (kelp lip).
Tracker, native	Kappang o tinning, 'follow foot'	Wuurongkuurtan, 'follow track'	Wuurongkuurtann, 'follow track'
Trail of man	Poop chinna, 'print foot'	Poorp tinnang, 'print foot'	Poorp tinnang, 'print foot'
Trail of lizzard	Pirpa muurndarnk, 'running lizzard'	Karkuuran muunee, running lizzard	Tarnuung muulin at, 'running lizzard'
Trail of snake	Parring'guuk kuurnwilla	Tarnuung kuurang at, 'running snake'	Tarnuung kuurang at, 'running snake'
Travel or travelling	Yan'gna, 'go'	Yannan, 'go'	Puurpa, 'go'
Trees, generally	Yuulong	Wuurot	Wuurot
Tremble	Muumuur an	Puurng puurnga wan	Yarremee kuutah
Tribe, tribes of aborigines generally			
Trough for holding water	Kuule	Maar	Maar
Trysting place	Gnannak	Torong	Torong
Tuff or tuffa	Trending gnaraen	Taenda haenan	Taendo hinnan
Tumble down	Turtee match	Tarra lok	Tarra lok
Tusk of quadruped	Pueet ka	Yarnda puurteeann	Yarndaa wuurtin
Twilight in morning	Wirnduuk	Wirnuung	Wirnuung
Twilight in evening	Kuumba kullitch, 'sleep twilight'	Yuwan kullatt, 'sleep twilight'	Yuwan kullatt, 'sleep twilight'
Twin children	Wueetpa kullitch, 'dusk'	Wuuyupeet kullatt, 'dusk'	Wuyupaa kullatt, 'dusk'
Twinkle	Teenjerapp	Kurpim biyeetch	Kurpim biyeetch
	Muurmuuraa kulkuuk	Wung'uul	Minkill
Udder of quadruped	Chaekorm	Gnarmiin	Gnarmiin
Ugly	Wokae mirng, 'black eye'	Meen mirng, 'black eye'	Gnumeenjar
Umbilical cord	Wirowok	Peekort	Peechuung
Umbilical cord custom	Warro	Peekuurt	Peetch
Undee	Kenneuneuk	Kang'gaenuung	Waeneunuung
Unkind	Yatchang	Gnummee gulleen	Gnummee jaar
Until	King'an	Deenbee	Kullo
Up	Keeyuga	Kunnae	Kunnu
Urine	Chirrop	Kaeirn	Kaeirn
Us	Pareea	Baar gnatnaen	Gnarrakit wanuung
Valley	Knaeer	Kully kully wuur	Murtong
Vein	Pirpa kuurk, 'running blood'	Karkurann kuureek, 'running blood'	Weerakan kerrik, 'running blood'

English.	Chaap wuurong (broad lip).	Kuurn kopan noot (small lip).	Peek whuurong (kelp lip).
Vegetables	*Only specific*	*Only specific*	*Only specific*
Venus, planet	Paapee neowee, 'mother of the sun'	Wung'uul, 'twinkle'	Marhearrong, 'large'
Vengeance	Pirnawuuchuup	Warrakilæk	Watta le'hnan
Venom of snake	Barring guyuuk	Barring guutong	Barring guutong
Vex	Pinna wuutchubak	Watann lihnann	Watta lihnann
Village, native	Munn'yah	Marrang	Gnarrakituung wuurng
Violet, small indigenous	Neeak neeak mirnk, 'seeing eye'	Nachnachmikk, 'seeing eye'	Nachnachmikk, 'seeing eye'
Virgin	Weearkuurneetch kuurk	Marramarrabuul or keearn	Marramarrabuul or keearn
Volcano, active	Walpa kuulor, 'burning hill'	Baawan kuulor, 'burning hill'	*No name*
Vomit	Kartna	Karnann	Kartna
Waist	Nalukæk	Aluurk	Aluuk
Walk	Yan gnang o	Yanna wan	Puurpuukall
Wand, for noosing birds	Parræm	Putkiyang	Putkiyang
Warm	Wulpung æn	Paawan	Paawan
Wart	Chim chim mok	Timp timp	Timp timp
Wash	Karwilang	Puroneeann	Gnormæng
Water	Kutchin	Pareetch	Pareetch
Water, fresh	Telkæ kutchin, 'good water'	Gnuutchgnan pareetch, 'good water'	Gnuuteung pareetch, 'good water'
Water, salt	Piinbal	Mirteetch	Mirteetch
Water, foul or muddy	Puppal	Puppal or yuurm	Yuurm
Waterhole	Yarrum	Killink, 'sound of stone dropped into water'	Killink, 'sound of stone dropped into water'
Wave	Piinbaal	Wuupareitch	Wopuut tuutnæn
We...	Pareea gnurak	Baar gnatnæn	Gnarrakit wanuung
Weak	Bo'olk	Warpee	Wanuupa
Weapon, general term	Pulk pulk	Muut muut chuul	Muut muut chuul
Weapons, bundle of	Kæp kulleen	Kiap kulluung	Kiap kulling
Web of spider	Larnuuk mun'yak kareek, 'house of spider'	Wuurnong marrakukk gnat, 'house of spider'	Pirrii hmeung, 'their net'
Wedding	Knuuluurpee	Knuuluurp	Gnuuluurp
Weed, water weed	Piik kuuruuk	Piik kuuruuk	Piik kuuruuk
Weed in lagoons and swamps	Churak	Tuurak	Tuurak

English.	Chaap wuurong (broad lip).	Kuurn kopan noot (small lip).	Peek whuurong (kelp lip).
Weep	Yeereeyaa	Luung an	Weepa
Well, healthy	Tulku wan, 'good am I'	Gnuuteung niit, 'good am I'	Gnuuteung, 'good'
Well, native well	Chuung ang o, 'to dig'	Tuunda wan, 'to dig'	Kunnung, 'to dig'
Well, exclamation	Neaa a	Yaa	Yaa
West	Mirmupp neowee, 'go down sun'	Kiitmeet tirng, 'go down sun'	Kameetgnunnang, 'go down sun'
What	Neaa	Nunn aa	Gnunna
When	Winjaa	Uunda	Uunda
Which	Ween'yatuuk	Wuundaræcha nuung	Wuundaræcha nuung
Whine, like a dog	Gnilman	Gneeneetan	Gnin hnitta
Whisker	Knunnyæ	Gnarriin	Gnarriin
Whisper	Teert charring gna gno, 'speak in my ear'	Tirtpan an, 'speak in my ear'	Tirtpan, 'speak in my ear'
Whistle, to	Chae kuurna	Tirng kærann	Wuinja
Whistle, by holding the lower lip	Taekuuna	Tækerann	Teewirna
Whistle or cry of snake	Tukkælang kuurnwil	Purteeann kuurang	Kurnda
White	Turrarnupp	Gnupkuyeetch	Tarndeetch
Who, whose, whom	Winyaar	Gnaara	Gnarra
Wicked man	Pirm pirm ætch	Korrang korrang ætch	Manno manno mætch
Wicked woman	Pirm pirm millakork	Korrang korrang ætchaar	Manno manno mætchaar
Widow	Puunjak	Puundak	Puundak
Widower	Puunjall tanyuuk	Nakeecheruuk	Nakeecharro
Wife, general term	Muttchumee	Mullin'gar	Mullang
Wife, first	Karre nupkuurk, 'reared together'	Karræmakeear, 'reared together'	Karræmakeear, 'reared together'
Wife, second, and following	Paakunekuurk	Weehneear	Weehneear
Wild	Pirna wunchuup	Warrakeek læk	Warrakeek læk
Wild aboriginal	Yuul yuul	Yuul yuul	Yuul yuul
Wind, general term	Mot mot	Muurnduuk	Gnuurnduuk
Wind, north	Pirmmallæ, 'hot wind'	Barrakii, 'hot wind'	Barrakii, 'hot wind'
Wind, south	Kuureen, 'fog or misty wind'	Kuureen, 'fog or misty wind'	Kuureen, 'fog or misty wind'
Wind, west	Kuumar kuumar, 'cold wind'	Kuumar kuumar, 'cold wind'	Kuumar kuumar, 'cold wind'
Wind, east	Laplap kurtii, 'warm wind'	Laplap kuurn, 'warm wind'	Laplap kuurn, 'warm wind'
Wind, whirlwind	Weeyuung weeyuung guur	Weeyuung weeyuung guur	Weeyuung weeyuung guur
Wind, strong	Gnaarachaak	Uunduuk	Uunduuk

English.	Chaap wuurong (broad lip).	Kuurn kopan noot (small lip).	Peek whuurong (kelp lip).
Wing of bird	Tutchaktuuk	Warritnong	Wirritnong
Wink	Nimpmar	Millaepan	Millaepa
Winter	Moatt moatt, 'cold'	Gnuurnduuk, 'cold'	Gnuurnduuk, 'cold'
Wish	Yaaweeann	Watniitch	Wannae ka
Witch	Yunggi yapp, 'solitary'	Kuin'gnatyambateetch, 'solitary'	Yambateetch, 'solitary'
Within	Keeyuga	Likkae nuung	Likkae nuung
Without	Cholkuurna	Yeekuwan	Teekuurnaeko
Woman, white	Knamakeek kuurk	Knamataeheear	Gnamataecharr
Woman, white, old	Kalla kalla kuurk	Kukuwitch	Gnullang yaar
Woman, white, young	Yarkuurnap kuurk	Marramarrabuul	Marramarrabuul
Woman, aboriginal	Beng beng go...	Tannumbor	Tannumbor
Woman, aboriginal, old	Gnalla gnalla kuurk	Kukuwitch	Gnullang yaar
Woman, aboriginal, young	Weearwuurnup kuurk	Marramarrabuul	Marramarrabuul
Woman, aboriginal, single	Tulkuuk kuulae kuurk	Knuighwhaar tannumbor	Knuutch tannumbor
Woman, young and betrothed	Charn kork	Keearn	Keearn
Woman, aboriginal, married	Gnanaetch wilkuurk	Gnanna puurkeear	Gnanna puurkeear
Woman, aboriginal, married and childless	Kukuya	Kuurokutann	Bang att tukuae
Woman, aboriginal, near confinement	Gnarram	Moaegorm	Moaegorm
Woman, aboriginal, unchaste	Kyn kuurk	Keeandeetch	
Wood or timber for fuel	Wee	Ween	Wee
Wound	Waerpek	Meeng	Meeng
Wounded	Chut kuurnae nut	Muttae tanno	Meeng
Wraith, man's	Muuruup pakk	Muuruup man	Muuruup man
Wraith, woman's	Muuruup kuurakk	Muuruup yernan	Muuruup yernan
Wraith, child's	*None*	*None*	*None*
Wrestle	Partuum cherrang	Bartuuniyeeban	Yarnda
Wrestler, champion wrestler	Wartwaer	Warkill	Warkill
Wrestling, game of	Partuum partuum	Bartuunum	Bartuunum
Wrist	Kayuuk kayuuk gnuurak	Kayuuk kayuuk	Kayuuk kayuuk

English.	Chaap wuurong (broad lip).	Kuurn kopan noot (small lip).	Peek whuurong (kelp lip).
Wrong	Porm porm jaa	Gnummee kuunan	Gnummee kuunan ...
Yawn ...	Churrnan ...	Tarna no ...	Tarna gnin
Yell	Karndaa ...	Karndann...	Karnda
Yelp, like dog	Luupa ...	Luupan ...	Paaya
Yellow ...	Puundar ...	Puundar ...	Puundar
Yes ...	Ko	Ko ...	Ko
Yesterday ...	Challie yu ...	Gnangkatt ...	Gnangkatt
You	Wininn ...	Gnutook ...	Gnuutuuk
Young	Watcheepuuk ...	Kuurnong...	Kuurneii
Yourself ...	Winnang nek ...	Gnatook gnat ...	Nuutuuk
Zodiacal light ...	Pittil weetchuwa, 'rain coming' ...	Pattin amano, 'rain coming' ...	Miya amanok, 'rain coming'

QUADRUPEDS.

English.	Chaap wuurong (broad lip).	Kuurn kopan noot (small lip).	Peek whuurong (kelp lip).
Animal ...	*Only specific* ...	*Only specific* ...	*Only specific*
Bandicoot, brown	Bo'o	Karroæ	Karroæ
Bandicoot, banded	Wateun	Warron	Warron
Bat, common ...	Hinnæhinnitch	Hinnæhinnitch	Hinnæhinnitch
Bat, vampire or flying fox	Wutpa chureep	Wurt pattereep	*Unknown*
Bear, or sloth	Wirngbuul	Wirn'gill ...	Wirn'gill
Bear, young, one on mother's back	Kuurangdat kuurk	Kuurangdat neung ...	
Bull ...	Buul	Buul	Buul
Bullock, worker	Muutchelup ka'at	Wumbeetch barran'guurt, 'bringer of dray' ...	Wam wum barran'guurt, 'bringer of dray'
Cat, domestic...	Puus	Puus	Puus
Cattle ...	Chang birk, 'long horns'	Wuromkilwerang, 'long horns'	Wuurangkil, 'long horns'
Cow, milch ...	Kowuutch	Kowuutch...	Kowuutch
Dasyure, black and spotted native cat ...	Work	Wuulok ...	Meen
Dasyure, brown and spotted native cat	Porgormuum	Kuppung ...	Kuppung
Dasyure, tiger-cat	Neumarng	Wuumeniitch	Wuumeniitch
Dog, domestic	Kuurnuumek...	Kaal	Kall
Dog, wild ...	Wilter	Burnang	Purnang
Dog, wild female	Bab wilter	Kneeriin heaar burnang	Gneeriin heear
Dog, Barrukills dog	Karlok	Kullong ...	Kaarlo

xlviii

English.	Chaap wuurong (broad lip).	Kuurn kopan noot (small lip).	Peek whuurong (kelp lip).
Foal	Watchepee gump gump, 'young horse'	Neeghnit, 'its cry'	Tuukuyuung neeghnit nat, 'young of horse'
Horse	Gump gump	Gump gump, or neeghnit, 'itscry'	Neeghnit, 'its cry'
Jerboa, or bilboa	Yaakar	Yaakar	Yaakar
Kangaroo, general name	Kuuræ	Kuuriin	Kuuriin
Kangaroo, old male	Murtæ kuuræ, 'big kangaroo'	Meheaarong kuuriin, 'big kangaroo'	Leenkil kuuriin
Kangaroo, young male	Wurtepee kuuræ	Kuurn kuuriin	Gnalan'gir
Kangaroo, flying doe	Merrin'gar	Marenn	Marenn
Kangaroo, red	Kæmun'gor	Puunporn	Kæmun'gor
Kangaroo, brush	Kalarn	Kalarn	Kalarn
Kangaroo, wallaby	Peere	Peeree, or berra	Berra
Kangaroo, joey	Puupuuwuuk	Tuukue yuung kuuriin gnat, 'young one kangaroo this'	Kuurndeen kuuriin gnat
Kangaroo rat	Potchuuk	Paruuk	Paruuk
Kangaroo mouse	Paruut	Kuurna muttal, 'small meat'	Gnuupiin
Opossum, common	Willæ	Kuuramuuk	Kuuramuuk
Opossum, old male	Pittin yannee	Kalpinnang	Kalpinnang
Opossum, old female	Parpoork	Yuulondiitch	Yuulondiitch
Opossum, young, in pouch	Kokok	Kuuro hneung	Kuuro hneung
Opossum, ringtail	Pun'ya	Weearn, 'its cry'	Weearn, 'its cry'
Platypus	Mirwil, or mirpeeal	Allertil	Torron'gil
Porcupine, ant-eater	Yuluwill	Willang gnilak	Wilang'gil
Rat, British rat	Paruutch	Paruut	*Not known*
Rat, rabbit-rat	Kinngnor	Kinngnor	Kinngnor
Rat, water-rat	Pirppaeer	Muuruung	Muuruung
Sheep	Tchekcha, 'feed on the ground'	Tachmæring, 'feed on the ground'	Tachmæring, 'feed on the ground'
Squirrel	*Only specific*	*Only specific*	*Only specific*

English.	Chaap wuurong (broad lip).	Kuurn kopan noot (small lip).	Peek whuurong (kelp lip).
Squirrel, large flying ...	Poroll ...	Wieeteetch, 'its cry' ...	Waeateetch, 'its cry'
Squirrel, small flying ...	Tuan ...	Tuugan	Tuukan
Squirrel, feather-tailed ...	Gniin guutch ...	Gnundiit	Gnundeetch
Swine	Peepig ...	Tuurn maering, 'turn ground' ...	Tuurn maering, 'turn ground'
Wombat	Meeam ...	Meeam	Meeam

BIRDS.

English.	Chaap wuurong (broad lip).	Kuurn kopan noot (small lip).	Peek whuurong (kelp lip).
Bird, general term	Yowwir	Muttal, 'meat' ...	Muttal, 'meat'
Avoset ...	Akarn akarn ...	Akarn akarn ...	
Bittern	Karwor ...	Buulan	Puulan
Bower or satin-bird	Loreetch ...	Loreetch ...	Lorotch
Brush turkey, or lowan	Laahwin ...	Laahwin ...	Laahwin
Bunting, large	Chilpinjir, 'sing for summer'.	Tirptirp kulluun, 'sing for summer'	Taedæ
Bunting, small	Chirpkærnmirnk, 'bright eye'	Eelpieetch, 'bright eye'	Tuurtuum mireen, 'bright eye'
Bustard, or wild turkey	Taariwill ...	Barrim barrim	Barrim barrim
Cock, domestic fowl	Kuurn kuurn kullat, 'call for daylight'	Kuurn kuurn kullat, 'call for daylight'	Kuurn kuurn kullat, 'call for daylight'
Cockatoo, common	Chimupp ...	Gniyuuk ...	Gniyuuk
Cockatoo, banksian	Wirann ...	Wilann, or kappatch ...	Wilann
Cockatoo, black with red feathers in tail	Bonbonturong, 'eater of she-oak cones' ...	Bonbontæremot, 'eater of she-oak cones'	Bonbonpuuramuuk, 'eater of she-oak cones'
Cockatoo, long-billed	Kutchukka ...	Kuurakeetch ...	Kuurukeetch
Coot ...	Kibuul ...	Kuii ...	Kowæ
Cormorant, large	Yuungar ...	Wallongkarang ...	Yuunkar
Cormorant, small	Tærebilleguurk, 'white breast' ...	Gnupkuee miheear, 'white breast'	Gnupkuumaheear, 'white breast'
Crane, native companion	Kuutchon ...	Kuront, 'its cry' ...	Kuront, 'its cry'
Creeper, white-throated		Tirn tirn ...	
Crow, common	Wæee, 'its cry' ...	Waa, 'its cry' ...	Waa, 'its cry'

English.	Chaap wuurong (broad lip).	Kuurn kopan noot (small lip).	Peek whuurong (kelp lip).
Crow, with white eye	Tirrtu	Tirrtu	Tirtkuurt
Curlew	Kuuriwirp, 'its cry'	Wirruuk, 'its cry'	Wirruuk, 'its cry'
Duck	Only specific	Only specific	Only specific
Duck, grey duck or drake	Gnarre	Tuurbarnk	Tuurbang
Duck, mountain or shel-drake			
Duck, musk duck	Pitchan'gor	Kuuroe kuuroe, 'its cry'	Pitchangkuur
Duck, teal	Gnunyawil	Ptureepart	Warraweetch
Duck, wood duck	Pirnder	Pirnæer	Kirt kirt
Duck, widgeon	Peeup peeup, 'its cry'	Gnaawok	Gnakurang
Duck, speckled duck	Wirrinourt	Wirrinourt	Pirndaeer
	Barræmakuurk	Parræmat keear	Parræmat keear
Eagle	Pirrpil	Kneeangar	Gneeangar
Egret, or white heron	Gnummakeek yowwer, 'white man's meat'	Gnummateetch muttal, 'white man's meat'	Pukkin'geear, 'white man's meat'
Emu	Kowwirr	Kappring, or barringmall	Kapping
Flycatcher, white-fronted		Murn murn gnuurat	
Gannet	Bukkuurrum, 'dive into water'	Bukkuurruum, 'dive into water'	Wirtnuk
Goose	Only specific	Only specific	Only specific
Goose, grey	Kurral	Buudergil	Kiirall
Goose, tree goose	Gnaak gnaak, 'its cry'	Gnarowar	Paatuum
Grebe, great-crested	Kæeern	Parrin	Parrin
Grebe, small dobchick	Kuurmkuurmeetch	Kuurmkuurmitt	Kuurmkuurmitt
Gull, large	Tarook	Taarook	Kokok
Gull, small	Tarook	Taarook	Kokok
Hawk	Only specific	Only specific	Only specific
Hawk, kestrel, large	Charrak	Tarrakukk, 'its cry'	Tarrakekk, 'its cry'
Hawk, kestrel, small	Kuyong kuyong, 'its cry'	Kuyong kuyong, 'its cry'	Mæmit
Hawk, falcon	Warrall	Mariibar	Mirræpa
Hawk, swamp	Chuurk	Pirrween, 'its cry'	Pæween, 'its cry'
Hawk, white	Buukannæ	Linyarr	Linyarr

English.	Chaap wuurong (broad lip).	Kuurn kopan noot (small lip).	Peek whuurong (kelp lip).
Hawk, kite	Chukkchukk bo'ang, 'eater of carrion'	Tætcha wuumbeetch, 'eater of carrion'	Tikkok
Hawk, black-shouldered kite	Millamarr	Warn warneetch yakerr	*Not known*
Hen, domestic	Kuurn kuurn kulleitch, 'call for daylight'	Kuurn kuurn kulleitch, 'call for daylight'	Kuurn kuurn kulleitch, 'call for daylight'
Heron, common	Kuukup wuuchu	Kuukup	Gnarrapiin
Heron, white-necked	Kuukæbang'gar, 'old basket'	Bangkar, 'old basket'	Yuheup kuyuurn, 'old basket'
Heron, nankeen or night heron	Kuukæ kalwar, 'grandmother of herons'	Koro kalwar, 'grandmother of herons'	Kalwar
Ibis	Kuum kuum bulu kuurk, 'relation of another'	Wirram guæ	Tirrim guæ
Jay	Muunyukill	Muunyukill	Muunyukill
Kingfisher, sacred	Bunbun yuchuuk, 'catch fish'	Banban kuunamang, 'catch fish'	Tuuran
Lapwing, large	Pirrit pirrit, 'its cry'	Petereet, 'its cry'	Pateratt, 'its cry'
Lapwing, small	Munjarra kuurk, 'relative of another'	Mundaratt	*Not known*
Lark, or pipit, native	Tirteen charuuk	Warwharkeet	Tirpurtii
Laughing jackass, large	Kuurnk kuurnk, 'its cry'	Kuunit	Kuunit
Laughing jackass, small	Kaan billaguurk	Karntuluung	Pirrim pirrim
Lyre bird	Buuln buuln, 'its cry'	Buuln buuln, 'its cry'	*Not known*
Magpie, or organ-bird	Kuurruuk, 'its cry'	Kirræa, 'its cry'	Kirræa, 'its cry'
Magpie, black	Killirn, 'its cry'	Gillin gillin, 'its cry'	Killirn, 'its cry'
Magpie lark	Chirmp chirmp, 'its cry'	Tuulirmp, 'its cry'	Tuulip, 'its cry'
Minah, or soldier-bird	Pirndeen	Puutch	Poatch
Osprey	Wo'ok	Wo'ok	Pareetch pareetch kounterbuul, 'cut cut whale'
Owl	*Only specific*	*Only specific*	*Only specific*
Owl, common	Warroma will	Wirmall	Wirmall

English.	Chaap wuurong (broad lip).	Kuurn kopan noot (small lip).	Peek whuurong (kelp lip).
Owl, barn or screetch	Bokanng	Kannamiraetar	Weemall
Owl, fern or goatsucker	Yeratta kuurk, 'woman's owl'	Yeearatta heear, 'woman's owl'	Yeratta heear, 'woman's owl'
Owl, kuurku	Peepniyaa	Markupar	Kookok, 'its cry'
Owl, little	Muulnup	Mumkiit	Mumkiit
Owl, powerful	Yuuitch pilap	Yuuitch peetch	Yuuitch peen
Parraqueet	*Only specific*	*Only specific*	*Only specific*
Parraqueet, blue mountain	Kulling'arr, or naenett	Kallang'ii	Kalling'ii
Parraqueet, crested	Yatchukee yowirr	Wang wilann	Wang wilann
Parraqueet, crimson-fronted	Yuukap	Yuukuitch	Yuukuitch
Parraqueet, grass	Gnaeno'gnor	Laenokuur	Pirndaerakk
Parraqueet, swamp	Yuulu yuulo uurakk	Yuulu yuulo weeriitch	Pirndaerakk
Parraqueet, lorry	Porkill	Naluuk marrang, 'stringy bark parraqueet'	Naluuk marrang, 'stringy bark parraqueet'
Parraqueet, leek	Kueetch kueetch, 'its cry'	Waertorrong	Waertorrong
Parraqueet, rose hill	Muuluumbaer	Kueetch kueetch, 'its cry'	Kueetch kueetch, 'its cry'
Parraqueet, shell	*Only specific*	Muuluumbaer	Muuluumbaer
Parrot	Mirrann	*Only specific*	*Only specific*
Parrot, gang gang	Waertuuk tuurong	Merann	Mirrann
Parrot, king lory	Putchang al	Waertuurong	Waertuurong
Pelican	Ta'app	Kartpaerapp	Kartpaerup
Pigeon, bronzewing	Chapallin kuurk, 'related to another'	Kuuree, 'its cry'	Kuura, 'its cry'
Pigeon, small	Uuraeep	Chapallin heear, 'related to another'	Kirrae buunong
Pigeon, crested		Wareeek	*Not known*
Quail, large	Puuron'gii	Arinn	Keechullart
Quail, small	Yuugib	Arrokii	Peepeep, 'its cry'
Quail, painted	Nib nib	Kuunaemit	Kuunamilan
Reed fauvette, or sedge-bird	Kuulin kruulin chark, 'hidden in the reeds'	Kuulin kruulin tark, 'hidden in the reeds'	Taeak
Robin, with white spot on brow	Chimp kirk	Timmon	Chump kaeen

English.	Chaap wuurong (broad lip).	Kuurn kopan noot (small lip).	Peek whuurong (kelp lip).
Robin, with white spot before eyes...	Pilp gnuuneeart	Murn murn gnuuratt	Kombeem, 'cover head'
Robin, yellow-breasted	...	Puuluun buitch	...
Robin, grey	Chaluunwœr ...	Taluundeaar	Temkirn
Sandpiper, large	Dipeet dipeet, 'its cry'	Dipeet dipeet, 'its cry'	Dipeet dipeet, 'its cry'
Sandpiper, small	Pirrtuup	Pirtuup	Pirtuup
Seapie, or oyster-catcher	Gnaakurn gnaakurn, 'look out'	Gnaakurn gnakurn, 'look out'	Peepeek, 'its cry'
Shepherd's companion, or black fantail flycatcher	Cherrup cherrup	Prien prien, 'its cry'	Præn pæn, 'its cry'
Shrike	Yaya kuula	Yaya kuula	Wirrawill kurakk
Snipe, large	Chimkalk	Tirmpkall	Tashuiitch
Snipe, painted	Puulokor	Puulokor	Puulokor
Spoonbill	Kuuke kuunawar, 'grandmother of swan'	Kuuruuk kuunawar, 'grand-mother of swan'	Puurn whuurong, 'spoon mouth'
Summer bird, black-faced		Wirng ...	
Swan	Kuunawarr	Kuunawarr	Kuunawarr
Swallow, common	Weewheetch, 'its cry'	Weewheetch, 'its cry'	Weewheetch, 'its cry'
Swallow, bottle nest	Yuulowil kuurk	Willan keear	Purndætæœa
Swallow, wood martin	La'arp	La'arp	Piruung piruung
Swallow, sand martin	Not known	Pæntuurong	Pæntuurong
Swift, or black martin	Wirnchaller	Martæær	Mirrærbaaar
Tern, or sea swallow	Taarook	Taarook	Kokok
Thrush	Wuurbaruuk	Wuurbaruuk	Wing
Titmouse	Wirtuuk	Pirtuup	Tirteyarr
Titmouse, frontal shrike tit		Waawelann	
Wagtail, flycatcher	Yellpillup	Yellhelpeetch	Timptimp
Water-hen	Kuyapuul	Kuii	Kuæ
Wattle-bird	Kannee yuulong, 'peck at tree'	Kanakk wuurot, 'peck at tree'	Yungkulk
Whip-bird	Not known	Not known...	Not known
Wren, emu-tailed	Tirnwitt	Wreenwitt	Wirringwitt
Wren, blue-headed	Cheecheer, 'its cry'	Tæreæær, 'its cry'	Purpurteetch

English.	Chaap wuurong (broad lip).	Kuurn kopan noot (small lip).	Peek whuurong (kelp lip).
Wren, slate-coloured *	Teupeetch teupeetch	Mirnam mirnam	Tee'cheetch, 'its cry'
Wren, yellow-rumped		Gnarriin beeal	
Wren, firetail	Woreewill kuurk	Yuloinkeear	Pundit tii
Wryneck	Tirn tirn, 'its cry'	Tirn tirn, 'its cry'	Tirtæheaar

* The wren which builds a false nest on the top of the true one.

It will be seen that, in the case of the crane, crow, curlew, duck (mountain and wood); goose (large and small), kestrel hawk, swamp hawk, lapwing, laughing jackass, lyre-bird, magpie, black and lark magpie, native companion, owl, parraqueet, pigeon, quail, sandpiper, sea-pie, shepherd's companion, swallow, blue-headed and slate-coloured wren, wryneck, the foal, horse, ring-tail opossum, and flying squirrel, the native names have been applied to the various animals in imitation of the peculiar sounds they utter; the only exception being that, in the case of the horse (which is not indigenous), the epithet *gump gump* is used to signify the sound which is produced by the impact of its hoof upon the sward in the bush. I have called attention to this fact, because it seems to lend some countenance to the onomatopoetic theory of the origin of speech; or, in other words, to the highly plausible assumption that the latter, like writing, was suggested by the instinct of imitation. I am aware that this is ridiculed by no less distinguished an authority than Professor Max Müller as the "bow-wow" theory; but I think the facts are against him.

REPTILES.

English.	Chaap wuurong (broad lip).		Kuurn kopan noot (small lip).		Peek whuurong (kelp lip).
Reptile	Only specific ...	...	Only specific	...	Only specific
Bunyeep	Puneep	...	Torrong	...	Torrong
Frog, large green	Wo'ork, 'good-night,' 'its cry'	...	Teearmp, 'good-night'	...	Work, 'good-night,' 'its cry'
Frog, small green	Wærwær, 'its cry'	...	Wærwær, 'its cry'	...	Karra knitt
Frog, small black	Tom tom, 'its cry'	...	Wirrang kupeetch	...	Karra knitt
Frog, burrowing frog	Wokok, 'its cry'	...	Wokok, 'its cry'	...	Wokok, 'its cry'
Frog, long-legged	Wirwirr, 'its cry'	...	Wirwirr, 'its cry'	...	Wirwirr, 'its cry'
Frog, toad ...	Puuputtyuuk, 'its cry'	...	Kukuleen	...	Po'wit, 'its cry'
Iguana, large... ...	Wallap	...	Wallap	...	Walapp
Iguana, lazy, with blue tongue	Yuurkuurn	...	Yuurok	...	Yuuruuk
Lizzard, general term	Muurndarnk	...	Muunee	...	Mullin
Lizzard, frilled	Wirræneurn	...	Wirræneurn	...	Wirræneurn
Lizzard, prickly	Wirrakuutch	...	Wirrakuurt	...	Wirrakuut
Lizzard, middle size	Muurndarnk	...	Muunee	...	Tuurk
Lizzard, black-headed	Tuurkpuurn	...	Tuupuurn	...	Tuupuurn
Lizzard, smallest size	Turuuchall	...	Tuuruuchall	...	Yinning
Snake, general term	Kuurnwill	...	Kuurang	...	Kuurang
Snake,* banded	Kuurnwill	...	Kuurang	...	Kuurang

* Venomous.

English.	Chaap wuurong (broad lip).	Kuurn kopan noot (small lip).	Peek whuurong (kelp lip).
Snake, black ...	Wuin wuin ...	Mowang ...	Mowenk
Snake,* black, with white cheeks ...	Wuin wuin gnaluuk ...	Yuyuuk gnaluuk ...	Mowenk
Snake, boa ...	Chalam ...	Kirtuuk ...	Wiruuk
Snake, short-tailed ...	Gnullin gnullin ...	Gnullin gnullin ...	Gnullin gnullin
Snake,* tiger-snake ...	Kuurnwill ...	Kuurang ...	Kuurang
Snake, green—newly skinned— ...	Paamok ...	Yarrineung ...	Paatneung, or paameen
Snake, fawn-coloured ...	Wuin wuin ...	Mirng gnaaluuk, 'sharp eye' ...	Kirrae kirrae kuuneetch, 'blood colour'
Tadpole ...	Yeem ...	Koroe ...	Koroe
Tortoise ...	Tuukuurwill, 'turn mud'	Tuurong'gil, 'turn mud'	Tuurong'gil, 'turn mud'

* Venomous.

FISHES AND CRUSTACEA.

English.	Chaap wuurong (broad lip).	Kuurn kopan noot (small lip).	Peek whuurong (kelp lip).
Fish, saltwater, general term	Yarrar	Yarrar	Yarrar
Fish, freshwater, general term	Mo'om	Kuunamuung ...	Pirnmarii
Blackfish, freshwater ...	Chuulin	Yerræ chaar ...	Yerræ chaar
Clamshell fish ...	*No name*	Yuyuuk	Yuyuuk
Crab, saltwater ...	Kalweetch	Kalweetch ...	Kalweetch
Crab, freshwater ...	Yaapeetch	Weechang	Yapeetch
Crawfish	Yarram	Yarram	Yarram
Cuttlefish, or octopus ...	Paar munya, ' many hands '	Karrat marrang, ' many hands '	Karrat marrank, ' many hands '
Eel, freshwater ...	Puunyart	Kuyang	Kuyang
Eel, lamprey	*Not known*	Kuyang dakk ...	Kuyang dakk
Little fish in fresh water	Tuurt kuurt	Tuurt kuurt ...	Tuurt kuurt
Little fish in fresh water	Yuchuuk	Kuunamuung ...	Pirnmarrii
Mussel, freshwater ...	Challuup	Timbonn	Timbonn
Mussel, saltwater ...	Mæhmæt	Mæhmæt	Mæhmæt
Mutton-fish, large ...	Tullik	Tullik	Tullik
Mutton-fish, small ...	Munjir	Wiichurong ...	Munjir
Periwinkle	Gnumatt	Gnumatt	Gnumatt

English.	Chaap wuurong (broad lip).	Kuurn kopan noot (small lip).	Peek whuurong (kelp lip).
Seal	Kuurn muurn	Kuurn muurn	Kuurn muurn
Shark	Tallang irræ ...	Talling irring	Gnuwang
Shrimp	Yapeetch ...	Weechang...	Mitaaen
Sting ray	Kunnæ wilkuurk	Kannak ee aar, ' stick in '	Mirmæ, ' playful '
Trout, colonial ...	Yerrar ...	Yerrar ...	Yerrar
Whale	Kounterbuul ...	Kounterbuul	Kounterbuul

INSECTS.

English.	Chaap wuurong (broad lip).	Kuurn kopan noot (small lip).	Peek whuurong (kelp lip).
Insects, small ...	Gneun gneunduwan ...	Kuunumining ...	Kuunumining
Ant	*Only specific* ...	*Only specific* ...	*Only specific*
Ant, bright blue and solitary ...	Tirrewitchin ...	Tirrewirrin ...	Kurokuumal
Ant, bull-dog... ...	Wuluukii ...	Kuumal ...	Kuumal
Ant, jumping ant ...	Pirk pirk, 'jump jump'	Pirk pirk, 'jump jump'	Mirtann, 'jump'
Ant, sugar ant ...	Teulong'or ...	Tuulorngor ...	Parrakup
Ant, white ant ...	Kulkeetch ...	Parann ...	Parann
Ant, small, with strong smell	Gneeko ...	Kaetuuk ...	Kaetuuk
Ant which builds large nest like a chimney ...	Pirtor ...	Pirtor ...	Pirtor
Bee, honey-bee ...	*No name* ...	*No name* ...	*No name*
Bee, native ...	Moronn ...	Moronn ...	Moronn
Beetle, general name ...	Teunkeep ...	Teunkeep ...	Teunkeep
Beetle, burying beetle ...	Taerae witchin ...	Taerae waeenn ...	Taerae waeenn
Beetle, jumping beetle ...	Chuurteen ...	Gnuurteen ...	Gnuurteen
Beetle, water beetle ...	Paapee challuup ...	Kneerang timbonn, 'mother of mussels' ...	Kneerang timbonn, 'mother of mussels'
Butterfly, all kinds ...	Ballumbar ...	Ballumbii ...	Pallumbii
Caterpillar	Kukil	Kapkap pulla	Karratch
Caterpillar, hairy ...	Tirn'gibap beng, 'rough skin' ...	Kerpeetch tuurap, 'rough skin' ...	Mulkar
Centipede	Teering bang'arrak, 'many hands'	Tirring bang'arrak, 'many hands'	Puundar maarrank, 'many hands'

English.	Chaap wuurong (broad lip).	Kuurn kopan noot (small lip).	Peek whuurong (kelp lip).
Chrysalis, or pupa	Puuronbeetch	Puuronbeetch	Puuronbeetch
Cicada, large green	Kalgall	Tarrakuurt	Tarrakuurt
Cicada, small green	Kalgall	Tarrakuurt	Tinmir kuurt
Cicada, large black	Kalgall	Muundorong	Peekan
Cicada, small black	Kalgall	Muundorong	Tinmir kuurt
Cricket	Tarrondal	Tarrondal	Taruundal
Earwig	Kuurtuuk kuurtuuk wuurmbuul, 'enter ear'	Kuurtue kuurtue wirng, 'enter ear'	Kuttal kuttal wing, 'enter ear'
Flea, not indigenous	Flea	Flea	Leetch
Fluke	Not known	Not known	Not known
Fly	Only specific	Only specific	Only specific
Fly, blowfly	Pitchik	Wuurol	Wuurol
Fly, cleg or March fly	Muuron	Muurol	Keppekuee
Fly, large March fly	Maam	Maam	
Fly, dragon fly, bee-eater	Muur muur aa, 'tremble'	Puurn puurn meetch, 'tremble'	Puurot wirng, 'tremble ear'
Fly, dragon fly, common	Nalukanna kuuraee, 'nose like kangaroo'	Alukapuung kuuriin, 'nose like kangaroo'	Alukapuung kuuriin, 'nose like kangaroo'
Fly, hornet	Kuuke wuul wuul, 'grandmother of mason fly'	Kuurruuk aa wuurol, 'grandmother of mason fly'	Kuurruuk wuurol, 'grandmother of mason fly'
Fly, house fly	Minnik	Minnik	Minnik
Fly, mason fly	Wuul wuul	Wuurol wuurol	Wuurol wuurol
Fly, mantis	Kaernduuk peep gniya gnaa, 'digger of grubs for the fern owl'	Parraenong kuupartakil gnat, 'digger of grubs for the fern owl'	Markopakk
Fly, causing blight in the eye	Nimpninp kork, 'sting the eye'	Meenmindor, 'sting the eye'	Puundin mink, 'sting the eye'
Grasshopper	Gneear gneear	Gneear gneear	Gneear gneear
Grub in acacia tree	Gnaluun gnuum tuuliin	Gnaluun muum karrank, 'large abdomen'	Gnaluun muum karrank, 'large abdomen'
Grub in blackwood tree	Muutchangar	Muutechuuk	Muutichuuk
Grub in banksia tree	Puutchuum	Pirn weeriitch	Poronn
Grub in eucalyptus tree	Puuron	Kaawuuk	Gnulluert

English.	Chaap wuurong (broad lip).	Kuurn kopan noot (small lip).	Peek whuurong (kelp lip).
Grub, very large, in eucalyptus tree	Muurkarm	Minnæmuuk	Minnæmuuk
Grub which forms fairy rings	Pitchoitch	Pitott	Tachnum
Leech, common	Chuulong	Tuulong	Tuulong
Leech, yellow	Challeep mun'girr	Tuuleen barnk	Tuuleen barnk
Louse, black	Muunyu	Paruum	Baruum
Louse, white, imported	No name	No name	No name
Louse on snake and lizards	Muunyu	Paruum	Baruum
Maggot	Bitchik	Tirtue	Tirtue
Mosquito	Muurukar	Kirk kirk	Martwharngill, 'singing'
Moth, largest size	Nullamuum tuullin, 'moth of acacia tree'	Nullamuum karrank, 'moth of acacia tree'	Nullamuum karrank, 'moth of acacia tree'
Moth, death's-head	Puuroitch wirrembuul, 'dark ear'	Puurot wirng, 'dark ear'	Puurot wirng, 'dark ear'
Piper, with sting	Kuuke barran, 'mother of pipers'	Gnærang barran, 'mother of pipers'	Kuuruuk kuunal, 'mother of pipers'
Scorpion	Wirann	Wirumm	Pirrpee
Snail	Chuulim gnun'ger	Tuuleen barnk	Tillæ koromp
Spider, general term	Wupkueaa pueetmuuk, 'bad smell'	Pueet pueet palatt, 'bad smell'	Poin poin
Spider, tarantula	Muurnakureek	Murrakukk	Poin poin
Spider, goes into ear	Kuurta kuurta kuurk, 'enter the ear'	Kuurta kuurta wirng, 'enter the ear'	Tetett muung
Soldier bug, red	Nimpor	Nimpor	Nimpuul
Tick on native animals	Muun'yu	Baruum	Paruum
Wood louse or slater	No name, as it was imported	Not known	Not known
Worm, earth worm	Cho'or	Ko'ork	Kuuk
Worm in animals	Kuulaer	Kuuloæ yong	Kuuloæ yong
Worm, glow worm	Lanjerr	Landeetch	Ween muliin, 'fire lizzard'

RELATIONSHIPS.

RELATIONSHIPS IN THE CHAAP WUURONG LANGUAGE.

Male speaking.	I call.	Meaning.	Calls Me.	Meaning.
My great grandfather by father's side	Chuang chuang kuukuurnæ	Great grandfather	Kuukuurnæ	Great grandson
„ great grandfather by mother's side	Kuukuurn kuurre	Great grandfather	Kuukuurnæ	Great grandson
„ great grandmother by father's side	Gnyarre kuurre	Great grandmother	Gnummæ	Great grandson
„ great grandmother by mother's side	Chuang chuang kukæ	Great grandmother	Chuang chuang kuurk	Great grandson
„ grandfather by father's side	Kuukuurnæ	Grandfather	Kuukuurnæ	Grandson
„ grandfather by mother's side	Gnummæ	Grandfather	Gnummæ	Grandson
„ grandmother by father's side	Meemee	Grandmother	Meemee...	Grandson
„ grandmother by mother's side	Kuurruk	Grandmother	Koke	Grandson
„ father	Maamee	Father	Watcheepee	Son
„ step-father	Yaanitmam	Other father	Karrim karrim	Step-son
„ father-in-law	Niitchang gnaa'yak	Father-in-law	Niitchang niitch	Son-in-law
„ mother	Baabee	Mother	Puupue	Son
„ step-mother	Yaa'gnik bab	Other mother	Yaa'gnik puupuup	Step-son
„ mother-in-law	Naluunkuurræ	Mother-in-law	Naluunjee	Son-in-law
„ father's brother, single or married	Yaanitmam	Other father	Yaanatwutcheep	Nephew
„ father's eldest sister, single	Wardii wardiitch	Old aunt	Paapee gneakk	Nephew
„ father's eldest sister, married	Naluukæ	Aunt	Watcheepee	Nephew
„ father's other sisters, single or married	Naluukæ	Aunt	Watcheepee	Nephew
„ mother's eldest brother, single	Churnbap	Uncle	Nunnung nup	Nephew
„ mother's eldest brother, married	Meemim guurk	Married uncle	Nunnung nup	Nephew
„ mother's other brothers, single	Churnbap	Uncle	Nunnug nup	Nephew
„ mother's other brothers, married	Meemim gnurk	Uncle	Nunnung nup	Nephew
„ mother's eldest sister, single	Bap kuuruuk	Aunt	Bap kuuruukæ	Child

Male speaking.	I call.	Meaning.	Calls Me.	Meaning.
My mother's eldest sister, married	Yaagnek bab	Other mother	Yaagnek puupuup	Other son
,, mother's other sisters, single	Muung kuuræ	Aunt	Nunmung nup	Nephew
,, mother's other sisters, married	Yaagnek bab	Other mother	Puupu ekk	Nephew
,, father's eldest brother's son, single	Waawæ	Cousin	Kuutæ	Cousin
,, father's eldest brother's son, married	Wardii kuuræ	Cousin, married	Kuutæ	Cousin
,, father's eldest brother's son, married, and with a family	Wardii kuuræ	Cousin, with family	Kuutæ	Cousin
,, father's youngest brother's son, single	Watcheepek	Cousin	Watchipp	Cousin
,, father's youngest brother's son, married	Wardii kuurk	Cousin, married	Kuutæ	Cousin
,, father's youngest brother's son, married, and with a family	Wardii kuuræ	Cousin, with family	Kuutæ	Cousin
,, father's brother's daughter, single or married	Chaachee	Cousin	Kuutæ	Cousin
,, father's sister's sons, single or married	Chaawillæ	Cousin	Chaawillæ	Cousin
,, father's sister's daughters, single or married	Yuurpee kuuræ	Cousin	Chaawillæ	Cousin
,, mother's brother's sons, single or married	Yuurpeetch	Cousin	Chaawillæ	Cousin
,, mother's brother's daughters, single or married	Yuurpee kuurk	Cousin, feminine	Chaawillæ	Cousin
,, mother's sister's sons, single or married	Waawæ	Cousin	Kuutæ	Cousin
,, mother's sister's daughters, single or married	Chaache	Sister	Kuutæ	Cousin
,, mother's eldest sister's youngest daughter, single or married	Kuutæ	Cousin, feminine	Waawæ	Cousin
,, brother	Waawæ	Brother	Kuutæ	Brother
,, brother, single, if older than me	Wardiiche	Brother	Kuutæ	Brother
,, brother, married, if older than me	Wardiikuuræ	Brother, married	Kuutæ	Brother
,, brother, single, if younger than me	Wardiiche	Brother	Kuutæ	Brother
,, brother, married, if younger than me	Wardiikuuræ	Brother, married	Kuutæ	Brother
,, youngest brother, single or married	Kuutæ	Youngest brother	Kuutæ	Brother
,, step-brother, eldest	Yaa'gnak waa	Other brother	Kuutæ	Brother
,, step-brother, youngest	Yaa'gnak kuut	Other brother	Kuutæ	Brother

Male speaking.	I call.	Meaning.	Calls Me.	Meaning.
My sister	Chaache	Sister	Waawæ ...	Brother
,, sister, youngest ...	Kuutuuk	Young sister	Waawæ ...	Brother
,, step-sister ...	Yuuwanik chaatch	Other sister	Yaanik kot	Step-brother
,, step-sister, youngest	Yuuwanik kuntuuk	Other sister	Waawæ ...	Step-brother
,, brother's wife ...	Mutchuum ...	Sister-in-law	Korweetch	Brother-in-law
,, youngest brother's wife	Kuurwekuurk	Sister-in-law	Korweetch	Brother-in-law
,, sister's husband ...	Kuurwee ...	Brother-in-law	Korweetch	Brother-in-law
,, brother's son ...	Watchepee...	Son ...	Yaanik mam	Other father
,, brother's son's wife	Mæt kuurk	Niece ...	Metchee ...	Uncle
,, brother's daughter	Men'gap ...	Daughter	Yaanik mam	Other father
,, sister's son ...	Gnunna nup	Nephew...	If I am married— Churnbup. If I am single— Nummii	Uncle
,, sister's son's wife	Karrinjek ...	Niece ...	Karrinjæ	Uncle
,, sister's daughters	Chinna pung'æ	Niece ...	Churmbap	Uncle
,, sister's daughter's husband	Naluunjek ...	Nephew...	Naluun ...	Uncle
,, wife	Muttchumee	Wife ...	Nunechee	Husband
,, wife's grandfather ...	Gnum mee ...	Grandfather	Gnum gnum	Grandson
,, wife's grandfather's brother	Yuwaa'gnik na'wan	Grandfather	Gnummee	Grandson
,, wife's grandfather's sister...	Yaa'gnak mutchuum...	Other grandmother	Aawan ...	Grandchild
,, wife's grandmother ...	Mutchuum ...	Grandmother	Gnum mekk	Grandson
,, wife's grandmother's brother	Gnum mee ...	Grandfather	Gnum gnum	Grandson
,, wife's grandmother's sister	Yaa'gnak mutchuum...	Grandmother	Gnum mekk	Grandson
,, wife's father	Nitchang niitch	Father-in-law	Nitchang niiyæ	Son-in-law
,, wife's father's brother	Yaa'gnak nitchang niitch	Other father-in-law	Nitchang niiyæ	Son-in-law
,, wife's father's sister	Muung go ...	Aunt ...	Nunna nap	Nephew
,, wife's mother ...	Naluunkuurræ	Mother-in-law	Naluunjæ	Son-in-law
,, wife's mother's brother	Nalum	Uncle ...	Naluunjæ	Son-in-law
,, wife's mother's sister	Yaa'gnak naluunguurk	Other mother-in-law	Naluunjæ	Other son-in-law
,, wife's brother's son ...	Nunna nup	Nephew...	Churmbap	Uncle
,, wife's brother's daughter ...	Chinna bung'ga	Niece ...	Churmbap	Uncle
,, wife's sister's son ...	Yuuwanek wutcheep...	Other son	If I am single— Yu'waa'gnek mam	Other uncle

Male speaking.		I call.	Meaning.	Calls me.	Meaning.
My wife's sister's son	...	Yuuwanek wutcheep...	Other son	If I am married— Yu'waa'gnek mam ...	Other uncle
,, wife's sister's daughter	...	Yaa'gnek munggup ...	Other daughter	Yaagnek mam ...	Other father
,, son ...	...	Wutcheep ...	Son	Maamee...	Father
,, eldest son	...	Wutcheep ...	Eldest son	Maamee...	Father
,, second son	...	Bukkar kullart wut-cheep ...	Middle son	Maamee...	Father
,, youngest son	...	Puutkueea korm	Last stick	Maamee...	Father
,, daughter	...	Meng'gapp ...	Daughter	Maamee...	Father
,, eldest daughter	...	Meng'gapp ...	Eldest daughter	Maamee...	Father
,, second daughter	...	Bukkar kuurmdeetch...	Middle daughter	Maamee...	Father
,, youngest daughter	...	Puutkueea korm	Last breast	Maamee...	Father
,, son's wife	...	Mætkuurk ...	Daughter-in-law	Metchæ ...	Father-in-law
,, son's son	...	Kuukuurnæ	Grandson	Kuukuurn	Grandfather
,, son's daughter	...	Kuukuurn korakk	Granddaughter	Kuukuurnæ	Grandfather
,, daughter's husband	...	Gniitchang niitch	Son-in-law	Gniitchang niitch...	Father-in-law
,, daughter's son	...	Gnummæ ...	Grandson	Gnummæ	Grandfather
,, daughter's daughter	...	Gnumkuurk	Granddaughter	Gnummæ	Grandfather

Female speaking.	I call.	Meaning.	Calls me.	Meaning.
My great grandfather, by father's side ...	Kuukuurn ...	Great grandfather	Kuukuurn kuurk...	Great grand-daughter
„ great grandfather, by mother's side...	Kuukuurnæ	Great grandfather	Num kuurk ...	Great grand-daughter
„ grandfather, by father's side	Kuukuurn ...	Grandfather	Kuukuurn kuurk...	Granddaughter
„ grandfather, by mother's side	Gnummæ	Grandfather	Num kuurk	Granddaughter
„ grandmother, by father's side	Meemee	Grandmother	Yarræ kuurk	Granddaughter
„ grandmother, by mother's side	Kokæ	Grandmother	Koke ...	Granddaughter
„ father ...	Maamee	Father	Meng'gep	Daughter
„ step-father	Yaanitmam	Other father	Yaagnek men'gep...	Other daughter
„ father-in-law	Metchekk	Father-in-law, 'small stick'	Miitkuurk	Daughter-in-law
„ mother	Paapæ	Mother ...	Popoæ ...	Daughter
„ step-mother	Yaagnik bab	Other mother	Yaagnik puupuup...	Other child
„ mother-in-law	Karrinjee	Mother-in-law	Karrinjee	Daughter-in-law
„ father's brother, single	Watchip	Not a father	Meng'gap	Daughter-in-law
„ father's brother, married	Yaa'gnik mam	Other father	Yaagnik meng'gap	Other daughter
„ father's eldest sister, single	Paapæ gnek	Old aunt	Paapæ nee	Niece
„ father's eldest sister, married	Nulluuk ...	Aunt ...	Meng'gep	Niece
„ father's other sisters	Nulluuk ...	Aunt ...	Meng'gep	Niece
„ mother's brother, single	Churmbup	Uncle ...	Chinnapung kuurræ	Niece
„ mother's brother, married...	Meemim kuura	Uncle ...	Meemim kuuræ ...	Niece
„ mother's eldest sister, single, if older than my mother ...	Bap kuurongjæ	Oldest aunt	Bap kuurong kuurk	Niece
„ mother's eldest sister, married	Yaagnek bab	Other mother	Yaa'gnik puupuup	Child
„ mother's other sister, single	Muung kuurræ	Aunt ...	Chinnapung ...	Niece
„ mother's other sister, married	Yaagnik bab	Other mother	Yaagnik puupuup...	Child
„ father's brother's son, single	Waawik	Cousin ...	Kuutuuk	Cousin
„ father's brother's son, married	Wardiitch kuurk	Cousin, married	Kuutuuk	Cousin
„ father's brother's son, married, and with a family	Wardii kuurk	Cousin, with family	Kuutuuk ...	Cousin
„ father's youngest brother's son, single	Waawee ...	Cousin ...	Kuutuuk ...	Cousin
„ father's youngest brother's son, married	Wardii yee...	Cousin, married	Kuutuuk ...	Cousin
„ father's youngest brother's son, married, and with a family ...	Wardii kuurk	Cousin, with family	Kuutuuk	Cousin

Female speaking.	I call.	Meaning.	Calls me.	Meaning.
My father's brother's daughters, single and married	Chaachæ	Cousin	Kuutuuk	Cousin
,, father's sister's husband	Churm bap	Uncle	Chinnapung	Niece
,, father's sister's son	Chaawilæ	Cousin	Chaawil kuure	Cousin, feminine
,, father's sister's daughter	Yuurpee kuurk	Cousin	Chaawil knure	Cousin, feminine
,, mother's brother's wife	Karrinjæ	Aunt	Karrin	Niece
,, mother's brother's son	Chow'will	Cousin	Chow'will kuurk	Cousin, feminine
,, mother's brother's daughter	Chow'will kuurk	Cousin, feminine	Chow'will kuurk	Cousin, feminine
,, mother's sister's son	Kuutæ	Cousin	Kuuto akk	Cousin
,, mother's sister's daughter	Chaachæ	Cousin	Kuutuuk	Cousin
,, mother's sister's youngest daughter	Kuutuuk	Young cousin	Chaachæ	Cousin
,, brother	Waawek	Brother	Kuutuuk	Sister
,, brother, married, if older than me	Waawæ	Brother	Kuutuuk	Sister
,, brother, married, and with a family	Wardii kuurk	Brother, married	Kuutuuk	Sister
,, youngest brother, single or married	Kuutæ	Brother	Chaachæ	Sister
,, sister	Chaachæ	Sister	Kuutuuk	Sister
,, eldest sister, single	Kullart kuurk	Eldest sister	Kotoæ	Sister
,, eldest sister, married	Chaachæ	Sister	Kotoæ	Sister
,, second sister, single or married	Bukkar kullart kuurk	Middle sister	Kotoæ	Sister
,, third sister, single or married	Bukkar kullart wuuro knurk	Middle lip		
,, youngest sister, single or married	Puutknutch kuurm	'Pock shakings'	Kotoæ	Sister
,, step-brother	Yaa'gnak waa	Other brother	Chaachæ	Sister
,, step-sister, if older than me	Chaachæ	Sister	Yaanak kuutuuk	Other sister
,, step-sister, if younger than me	Kuutuuk	Younger step-sister	Kuutuuk	Other sister
,, brother's son, single or married	Watchip	Son	Chaachæ	Sister
,, brother's daughter, single or married	Meng'gapp	Niece	Gnulluuk	Aunt
,, brother's daughter, single or married	Meng'gapp	Niece	Gnulluuk—if I am single ... Gnallunkæ—if I am married	Aunt / Other mother
,, sister's son, single	Gnunna gnupp	Nephew	Bapap—if I am single...	Aunt
,, sister's son, single	Gnunna gnupp	Nephew	Yaagnek—if I am married	Aunt
,, sister's daughter, single	Muung kuurae	Niece	Yuwanek bab	Other mother

Female speaking.	I call.	Meaning.	Calls me.	Meaning.
My sister's daughter, married ...	Yuwanik puupuup	Other daughter	Yuwanek bab	Other mother
,, husband	Gnunneetch chek	Husband	Muttchuum	Wife
,, husband's grandfather	Gnumme	Grandfather	Gnumkuurk	Granddaughter
,, husband's grandfather's brother	Yaagneknum	Grandfather	Gnumkuurk	Granddaughter
,, husband's grandfather's sister	Kuukek	Grandmother	Kuukek...	Granddaughter
,, husband's grandmother, by father's side	Gnerrekuurk	Grandmother	Gnerrekuuræ	Granddaughter
,, husband's grandmother, by mother's side	Kuuke	Grandmother	Gnerrekuurk	Granddaughter
,, husband's grandmother's brother	Gnumme	Grandfather	Gnumkuure	Granddaughter
,, husband's grandmother's sister	Yaagnekmeem	Other grandmother	Meem	Granddaughter
,, husband's father	Metchikk	Father-in-law	Metkuuræe	Daughter-in-law
,, husband's father's brother	Metchikk	Father-in-law	Metkuuræe	Daughter-in-law
,, husband's father's sister, single	Muung kuurre	Aunt	Chinnapung	Niece
,, husband's father's sister, married	Yaagnekbab	Other mother	Yaa'gnek puupuup	Other child
,, husband's mother	Karrinjee	Mother-in-law	Karrin	Daughter-in-law
,, husband's mother's brother	Karrinjee	Uncle	Karrin	Niece
,, husband's mother's sister	Karrinjee	Aunt	Karrin	Niece
,, husband's brother	Korweetch	Brother-in-law	Korrwee kuurk	Sister-in-law
,, husband's brother's son	Nunnanup	Nephew	Yaa'gnak bab	Other mother
,, husband's brother's daughter	Chinnapung	Niece	Yaa'gnak bab	Other aunt
,, husband's sister	Kumuutchae	Sister-in-law	Kumuutchae	Sister-in-law
,, husband's sister's son	Watchip	Nephew	Nulluuk	Aunt
,, husband's sister's daughter	Meng'gap	Niece	Nulluuk	Aunt
,, son ...	Watchip	Son	Baabee	Mother
,, eldest son	Puupuæ	Eldest son	Baabee	Mother
,, youngest son	Puutkueet koom	Youngest son	Baabee	Mother
,, daughter	Meng'gap	Daughter	Baabee	Mother
,, eldest daughter	Gnarrum gnarrum kuuræ puupuup	Eldest daughter	Baabee	Mother
,, youngest daughter	Puutkuee koom	Youngest daughter	Baabee	Mother
,, son's wife	Karrinjee	Daughter-in-law	Karrin	Mother-in-law
,, son's son	Gnum mek...	Grandson	Meemee...	Grandmother
,, son's daughter	Gnarre kuurak	Granddaughter	Meemee...	Grandmother
,, daughter's husband	Nalluunjek...	Son-in-law	Nalluun guurk	Mother-in-law
,, daughter's son ...	Kuukek	Grandson	Kuukæ	Grandmother
,, daughter's daughter	Kuukæ	Granddaughter	Kuukæ	Grandmother

RELATIONSHIPS IN THE KUURN KOPAN NOOT LANGUAGE.

Male speaking.	I call.	Meaning.	Calls me.	Meaning.
My great grandfather, by father's side	Wurowuromitt kuukuur	Long long grandfather	Wurowuromitt kuukuur	Long long grandson
„ great grandfather, by mother's side	Wurowuromitt gnapuurn	Long long grandfather	Wurowuromitt kuuruuk	Long long grandson
„ great grandmother, by father's side	Wurowuromitt leenyaar	Long long grandmother	Wurowuromitt leenyaar	Long long grandson
„ great grandmother, by mother's side	Wurowuromitt kuuruuk	Long long grandmother	Wurowuromitt kuuruuk	Long long grandson
„ grandfather, by father's side	Kuukuurn	Grandfather	Kuukuurn	Grandson
„ grandfather, by mother's side	G'napuurn	Grandfather	Gnapuurn	Grandson
„ grandmother, by father's side	Leenyaar	Grandmother	Mullatt	Grandson
„ grandmother, by mother's side	Kuuruuk	Grandmother	Kuuruuk	Grandson
„ father	Peep, or peepii	Father	Kuuparng	Son
„ step-father	Wanman peep	Other father	Karrim karrim	Step-son
„ father-in-law	Naluung'garr	Father-in-law	Naluunggar	Son-in-law
„ mother	Kneerang	Mother	Kuuparng	Son
„ step-mother	Wanman gneerang	Other mother	Kuuparng	Step-son
„ mother-in-law	Naluunyaar	Mother-in-law	Naluun	Son-in-law
„ father's brother, single or married	Wanman peep	Other father	Kuuparng	Nephew
„ father's eldest sister, single	Kullart nan peep	Old aunt	Kullart peep	Nephew
„ father's eldest sister, married	Leembiin	Aunt	Kuuparng	Nephew
„ father's other sisters, single or married	Leembiin	Aunt	Kuuparng	Nephew
„ mother's eldest brother, single	Nummii	Uncle	Warrang att	Nephew
„ mother's eldest brother, married	Meemim	Married uncle	Warrang att	Nephew
„ mother's other brothers, single	Nummii	Uncle	Warrang at	Nephew
„ mother's other brothers, married	Meemim	Uncle	Warrang at	Nephew
„ mother's eldest sister, single	Bap kuuruuk	Aunt	Tukue	Child
„ mother's eldest sister, married	Waanuung kneerang	Other mother	Tukue	Other son

Male speaking.	I call.	Meaning.	Calls me.	Meaning.
My mother's other sisters, single	Baapap	Aunt	Nummii	Nephew
,, mother's other sisters, married	Waanuung kneerang	Other mother	Tukuæ	Other son
,, father's eldest brother's son, single	Wardii	Cousin	Kokong	Cousin
,, father's eldest brother's son, married	Wardiitch	Cousin, married	Kokong	Cousin
,, father's eldest brother's son, married, and with a family	Wardiheear	Cousin, with family	Kokong	Cousin
,, father's youngest brother's son, single	Kokong	Cousin	Wardii	Cousin
,, father's youngest brother's son, married	Wardiitch	Cousin, married	Kokong	Cousin
,, father's youngest brother's son, married, and with a family	Wardiheear	Cousin, with family	Kokong	Cousin
,, father's brother's daughters, single and married	Kaakii	Cousin	Kokong	Cousin
,, father's sister's sons, single and married	Towill	Cousin	Towill	Cousin
,, father's sister's daughters, single and married	Towill heear	Cousin, feminine	Towill	Cousin
,, mother's brother's sons, single and married	Towill	Cousin	Towill	Cousin
,, mother's brother's daughters, single and married	Towill heear	Cousin, feminine	Towill	Cousin
,, mother's sister's sons, single and married	Koko	Cousin	Wardii	Cousin
,, mother's sister's daughters, single and married	Kaakii	Sister	Kokong	Cousin
,, mother's eldest sister's youngest daughter, single and married	Koko heear	Cousin, feminine	Wardii	Cousin
,, brother	Wardii	Brother	Koko	Brother
,, brother, single, if older than me	Wardiitch	Elder brother	Koko	Brother
,, brother, married, if older than me	Wardiiheear	Brother, feminine	Koko	Brother
,, brother, single, if younger than me	Wardiitch	Brother	Koko	Brother
,, brother, married, if younger than me	Wardiiheear	Brother, feminine	Koko	Brother
,, brother, youngest, single or married	Koko	Youngest brother	Koko	Brother
,, step-brother, eldest	Wannang wardii	Other brother	Wannang koko	Other brother
,, step-brother, youngest	Wannang koko	Other brother	Wannang wardii	Other brother

Male speaking.	I call.	Meaning.	Calls me.	Meaning.
My sister ...	Kaakii ...	Sister ...	Wardii ...	Brother
,, sister, youngest ...	Koko heear	Young sister	Wardii ...	Brother
,, step-sister ...	Wannang kaakii	Other sister	Wardii ...	Step-brother
,, step-sister, youngest	Wannang koko heear		Wardii ...	Step-brother
,, brothers' wives ...	Mullatt ...	Sisters-in-law	Korweetch	Brother-in-law
,, youngest brother's wife	Pinning'gar'yarr	Sister-in-law	Pinning'gar	Brother-in-law
,, sister's husband...	Pinning'gar	Brother-in-law	Pinning'gar	Brother-in-law
,, brother's son ...	Kuuparng ...	Son ...	Wannang peep	Other father
,, brother's son's wife ...	Tukuae kunna heear	Sister-in-law, or 'child's long stick of a woman'		
,, brother's daughters ...	Gnaart ...	Daughter	Pinning'gar	Brother-in-law
,, sister's sons ...	Warrang at	Nephew...	Wannang peep	Other father
			If I am married— Meemim	
			If I am single— Gnummii	
,, sister's son's wife ...	Karrin ...	Niece ...	Karrin ...	Uncle
,, sister's daughters ...	Warrang a heear	Niece ...	Karrin ...	Uncle
,, sister's daughter's husband	Naluung nuung	Nephew...	Naluung	Uncle
,, wife	Mullung'gar	Wife ...	Nannabuurn	Husband
,, wife's grandfather ...	Naapuurn ...	Grandfather	Naapuurn	Grandson
,, wife's grandfather's brother	Wannang naapurn	Other grandfather	Naapuurn	Grandson
,, wife's grandfather's sister	Waanuung mullatt	Other grandmother	Mullatt...	Grandchild
,, wife's grandmother ...	Mullatt ...	Grandmother	Nannapuurn	Grandson
,, wife's grandmother's brother	Naapuurn ...	Grandfather	Naapuurn	Grandson
,, wife's grandmother's sister	Waanuung mullatt	Other grandmother	Naapuurn	Grandson
,, wife's father ...	Naluung'gar	Father-in-law	Naluung'gar	Son-in-law
,, wife's father's brother	Waanuung naluunkar	Other father-in-law	Naluung'gar	Son-in-law
,, wife's father's sister	Baapap ...	Aunt ...	Bapkuuruuk	Nephew
,, wife's mother ...	Naluunyaar	Mother-in-law	Naluun...	Son-in-law
,, wife's mother's brother	Naluun ...	Uncle ...	Naluun...	Son-in-law
,, wife's mother's sister	Wannan naluunyaar...	Other mother-in-law	Naluunjæ	Other son-in-law
,, wife's brother's son ...	Warrang at	Nephew...	Nummii	Uncle
,, wife's brother's daughter ...	Warrang a heear	Niece ...	Nummii	Uncle

Male speaking.	I call.	Meaning.	Calls me.	Meaning.
My wife's sister's son ...	Wannan kuuparng ...	Other son	Meemim—if I am married ...	Uncle
" wife's sister's son ...	Wannan kuuparng ...	Other son	Wannan peep—if I am single ...	Other father
" wife's sister's daughter ...	Waanung gnaart ...	Other daughter	Wannan peep ...	Other father
" son ...	Kuuparng ...	Son ...	Peepii ...	Father
" eldest son ...	Kullart ...	Eldest son	Peepii ...	Father
" second son ...	Bukkar kullart ...	Middle son	Peepii ...	Father
" youngest son ...	Wiinyatt kunnak ...	Last stick	Peepii ...	Father
" daughter ...	Gnarn ...	Daughter	Peepii ...	Father
" eldest daughter ...	Kullart heear gnart ...	Eldest daughter	Peepii ...	Father
" second daughter...	Bukkar gnart ...	Middle daughter	Peepii ...	Father
" youngest daughter ...	Tiinjeen gnuppang ...	Last breast	Peepii ...	Father
" son's wife ...	Tukuæ kunnaheear ...	Daughter-in-law, 'small stick'	Tukuæ kunnuk, 'small stick' ...	Father-in-law
" son's son ...	Kuukuurn ...	Grandson	Kuukuurn ...	Grandfather
" son's daughter ...	Kuukuurn heear	Granddaughter	Kuukuurn ...	Grandfather
" daughter's husband ...	Naluunkar ...	Son-in-law	Naluunkar ...	Father-in-law
" daughter's son ...	Naapuurn ...	Grandson	Naapuurn ...	Grandfather
" daughter's daughter ...	Napheear ...	Granddaughter	Naapuurn ...	Grandfather

Female speaking.	I call.	Meaning.	Calls me.	Meaning.
My great grandfather, by father's side ...	Wurowuromit kuukuur	Great grandfather	Kuukuurgna ...	Great grand-daughter
„ great grandfather, by mother's side...	Wurowuromit gnapuur	Great grandfather	Wurowuromit gna-puur ...	Great grand-daughter
„ great grandmother, by father's side ...	Wurowuromit leehnaar	Great grandmother	Wurowuromit leeh-naar	Great grand-daughter
„ great grandmother, by mother's side	Wurowuromit kuuruuk	Great grandmother	Wurowuromit kuu-ruuk ...	Great grand-daughter
„ grandfather, by father's side	Kuukuurn ...	Grandfather	Kuukuurn heear ...	Granddaughter
„ grandfather, by mother's side	Naapuurn ...	Grandfather	Naapuurn ...	Granddaughter
„ grandmother, by father's side	Leenyarr ...	Grandmother	Leenyarr ...	Granddaughter
„ grandmother, by mother's side	Kuuruukii ...	Grandmother	Kuuruuheear ...	Granddaughter
„ father ...	Peep, or peepii	Father ...	Gnaart ...	Daughter
„ step-father	Wannan peep	Other father	Karrim karrim neear	Other daughter
„ father-in-law	Tukue kunnukk	Father-in-law	Tukue kunnaheear, 'small stick' ...	Daughter-in-law
„ mother	Kneerang ...	Mother ...	Gnaart ...	Daughter
„ step-mother	Wannang kneerang	Other mother	Wannan tukue	Other child
„ mother-in-law	Karrin ...	Mother-in-law	Karrin ...	Daughter-in-law
„ father's brother, single	Kuuparr ...	Uncle ...	Gnaart ...	Niece
„ father's brother, married	Wannan peep	Other father	Wannan gnaart	Other daughter
„ father's eldest sister, single	Kullart nan peep	Old aunt	Kullart nan peep ...	Niece
„ father's eldest sister, married	Leembiin ...	Aunt ...	Gnaart ...	Niece
„ father's other sisters	Leembiin ...	Aunt ...	Gnaart ...	Niece
„ mother's brother, single ...	Nummii ...	Uncle ...	Wairrang a heear	Niece
„ mother's brother, married...	Meemim ...	Uncle ...	Wairrang a heear	Niece
„ mother's eldest sister, single, if older than my mother ...	Bap kuuruuk	Oldest mother	Bap kuurruuk heear	Niece
„ mother's eldest sister, married	Waanuung kneerang...	Other mother	Tukue ...	Child
„ mother's other sisters, single	Baapap ...	Aunt ...	Baapap ...	Niece
„ mother's other sisters, married	Waamung kneerang...	Other mother	Tukue ...	Child
„ father's brother's son, single	Wardii ...	Cousin ...	Kokoheear ...	Cousin
„ father's brother's son, married	Wardiitch ...	Cousin, married	Kokoheear ...	Cousin
„ father's brother's son, married, and with a family ...	Wardiiheear	Cousin, with family	Kokoheear ...	Cousin

Female speaking.	I call.	Meaning.	Calls me.	Meaning.
My father's brother's daughter, single or married	Kaakii	Cousin	Kokoheear	Cousin
,, father's sister's husband	Gnummii	Uncle	Warrang a heear	Niece
,, father's sister's son	Towill	Cousin	Kokoheear	Cousin
,, father's sister's daughter	Towill heear	Cousin, feminine	Towill heear	Cousin
,, mother's brother's wife	Karrin	Aunt	Karrin	Niece
,, mother's brother's son	Towill	Cousin	Towill heear	Cousin
,, mother's brother's daughter	Towill heear	Cousin, feminine	Towill heear	Cousin
,, mother's sister's son	Koko	Cousin	Koko heear	Cousin
,, mother's sister's daughter	Kaakii	Cousin	Koko heear	Cousin
,, mother's sister's youngest daughter	Baapap	Youngest cousin	Baapap	Cousin
,, brother	Wardii	Brother...	Koko heear	Sister
,, brother, married, if younger than me	Koko	Brother...	Kaakii	Sister
,, brother, married, and with a family	Wardiiheear	Brother...	Koko heear	Sister
,, youngest brother, single or married	Kokong	Brother...	Kaakii	Sister
,, sister	Kaakii	Sister	Kaakii	Sister
,, eldest sister, single	Kullart	Eldest sister	Koko heear	Sister
,, eldest sister, married	Kaakii	Sister	Koko heear	Sister
,, second sister, single or married	Bukkar kullart heear	Middle sister	Koko heear	Sister
,, third sister, single or married	Bukkar gnulluuk wuurong heear	Middle lip	Koko heear	Sister
,, youngest sister, single or married	Tienjeetch gnuppang heear	'Pock shakings'	Koko heear	Sister
,, step-brother	Wannang wardii	Other brother	Wannan koko heear	Other sister
,, step-sister, if older than me	Kaakii	Sister	Koko heear	Sister
,, step-sister, if younger than me	Koko heear	Younger sister	Kaakii	Sister
,, brother's son, single or married	Kuuparng	Nephew...	Leembiin	Aunt
,, brother's daughter	Gnaart	Niece...	If I am single—Bapap	Aunt
,, brother's daughter	Gnaart	Daughter	If I am married—Yaagnak bab	Other mother
,, sister's son	Warrang at	Nephew...	If I am single—Leembiin	Aunt
,, sister's son	Warrang at	Son	If I am married—Yaagnak bab	Other mother

Female speaking.	I call.	Meaning.	Calls me.	Meaning.
My sister's daughter, single ...	Baapap ...	Niece ...	Waanang gneerang	Other mother
,, sister's daughter, married...	Wannan tukuæ	Other child ...	Waanang gneerang	Other mother
,, husband	Nannabuurn ...	Husband ...	Mullingar ...	Wife
,, husband's grandfather ...	Kuukuurn ...	Grandfather ...	Kuukuurn heear	Granddaughter
,, husband's grandfather's brothers	Wannan kuukuurn	Grandfathers ...	Kuukuurn heear	Granddaughter
,, husband's grandfather's sisters	Kuuruukii ...	Grandmothers ...	Kuuruu heear	Granddaughter
,, husband's grandmother, by father's side	Leeneaar ...	Grandmother ...	Leeneaar ...	Granddaughter
,, husband's grandmother, by mother's side	Kuuruuk ...	Grandmother ...	Kuuruuk heear ...	Granddaughter
,, husband's grandmother's brother	Naapuurn ...	Grandfather ...	Kuukuurn ...	Grandfather
,, husband's grandmother's sisters	Leeneaar ...	Other grandmothers	Leeneaar ...	Granddaughter
,, husband's father ...	Tukuæ kunnuk ...	Father-in-law	Tukuæ kunna heear, 'child's stick' ...	Daughter-in-law
,, husband's father's brother...	Tukuæ kunnuk ...	Father-in-law	Tukuæ kunna heear, 'child's stick' ...	Daughter-in-law
,, husband's father's sister, single ...	Baapap ...	Aunt ...	Karrin	Niece
,, husband's father's sister, married	Waanung kneerang...	Other mother	Waanuung tukuæ...	Other child
,, husband's mother ...	Karrin	Mother-in-law ...	Karrin	Daughter-in-law
,, husband's mother's brother	Karrin	Uncle ...	Karrin	Niece
,, husband's mother's sister ...	Karrin	Aunt ...	Karrin	Niece
,, husband's brother ...	Pinning'gar ...	Brother-in-law	Pinning'gar yaar ...	Sister-in-law
,, husband's brother's son ...	Warrang'att ...	Nephew... ...	Wannang kneerang	Other mother
,, husband's brother's daughter	Baapap ...	Niece ...	Wannang kneerang	Other mother
,, husband's sister... ...	Kumoitch ...	Sister-in-law ...	Kumoitch ...	Sister-in-law
,, husband's sister's son ...	Kuuparng ...	Nephew... ...	Leembiin ...	Aunt
,, husband's sister's daughter	Gnaart	Niece ...	Leembiin ...	Aunt
,, son	Kuuparng ...	Son ...	Kneerang ...	Mother
,, youngest son ...	Tarntiich naapuurn	Youngest son ...	Kneerang ...	Mother
,, daughter	Gnaart	Daughter ...	Kneerang ...	Mother
,, son's wife	Karrin	Daughter-in-law	Karrin	Mother-in-law
,, son's son	Naapuurn ...	Grandson ...	Leen'yaar ...	Grandmother
,, son's daughter ...	Leen'yaar ...	Granddaughter ...	Leen'yaar ...	Grandmother
,, daughter's husband ...	Naaluun ...	Son-in-law ...	Naaluun yaar ...	Mother-in-law
,, daughter's son	Kuuruuk ...	Grandson ...	Kuuruuk ...	Grandmother
,, daughter's daughter ...	Kuuroheear ...	Granddaughter ...	Kuuruuk ...	Grandmother

NAMES OF PLACES.

———•———

IT is deeply to be regretted that the opportunity for securing the native names of places has, in many districts, gone for ever. In most localities the aborigines are either dead or too young to have learned the names which their fathers gave to the various features of the country; and in those parts where a few old men are still to be met with, the white inhabitants, generally speaking, take no interest in the matter. With a very few worthy exceptions, they have done nothing to ascertain and record even those names which appertain to their own properties. How much more interesting would have been the map of the colony of Victoria had this been attended to at an earlier period of its history.

The following are the native names of some conspicuous places in the Western District, and, as far as could be ascertained, their meanings. It must be noticed that rivers have not the same name from their source to the sea. The majority of Australian streams cease to flow in summer, and are then reduced to a chain of pools or waterholes, all of which, with their intermediate fords, have distinguishing names. The river which connects these waterholes in winter has no name. Every river, however, which forms one continuous stream during both summer and winter has a name which is applied to its whole length. For example, Taylor's River, or Mount Emu Creek, is called " Tarnpirr," " flowing water," from its source in Lake Burrumbeet to its junction with the Hopkins. At the same time, every local reach in these rivers has a distinguishing name.

Aboriginal Name.	Meaning.	Description.
Baaweetch muurn...	Burning skin	Locality of Yangery House, near Tower Hill
Barrat		Mouth of Curdie's River
Bo'ok		Mount Shadwell
Bukkar whuurong	Middle lip	Bank between Lakes Bullen Merri and Gnotuk. A gap in this dividing bank is said to have been made by a bunyip, which lived at one time in Lake Bullen Merri, but, on leaving it, ploughed its way over the bank into Lake Gnotuk, and thence at Gnotuk Junction to Taylor's River, forming a channel across the country
Bukkiin kat	Bone	Large lagoon between Farnham and the sea coast
Bullen meri		Upper lake near Camperdown
Buloin mæring		Surrounding banks of Lake Bullen Merri
Buulok		Lake Boloke
Buunong	Ti-tree	Locality of Koort-koort-nong House
Chærang a bundit...	Twigs of spear tree	River near east side of Cape Otway
Deen maar	This blackfellow here	Julia Percy Island
Deen merri	This stone here	River Moyne, where it enters the lagoon at Rosebrook
Djerinallum	Sea swallow, or tern	Mount Elephant, from flocks of these birds frequenting the marshes in the neighbourhood
Gnaakit gnummat	Sea view	Locality of Yangery village
Gnarnk kolak	Sandy river	Moyne River, from the sea to lagoon
Gnallo kat	Backbone	Waterhole between Farnham estate and the sea coast
Gnarwin	Windy	Island in swamp between Farnham estate and the sea coast
Gnotukk		Lake near Camperdown Cemetery
Gnotukk		Camperdown Public Park
Gnulla milip	Big mouth	Waterhole in Merri River
Gnummi		Site of Glenormiston House
Gnuura buurn buurn	Name of a plant growing there	Neighbourhood of Glenormiston House
Kaakeear wart	Shoulder blade	Waterhole in Spring Creek

Aboriginal Name.	Meaning.	Description.
Kannong	...	Waterhole in Koroit-street, Warrnambool, celebrated as a drinking place for kangaroos
Karm karm ...	Building of stones ...	Point of land below Wuurong House, where the aborigines formed their wuurns of stones
Kart karram ...	Prickly bushes ...	Site of Boodcarra House
Kart wuurot ...	Large gum-trees ...	Lake at foot of Lehuura
Kiirank ...		A greenstone rock in Spring Creek, which supplied stones for tomahawks
Kill ombeetch ...	Yellow scum on the water	Lake Keilambete
Kilwerr		Waterhole below Woodford-bridge
Kirk mæring ...	Place of wild dogs ...	Camperdown Cemetery
Kirrkuur ...	Prickly bushes ...	Site of Goodwood House
Kolak	Sand	Site of Colac
Konda		Swamp to the west of Belfast
Koroitch ...	Nettles ...	Banks of Tower Hill Lake
Kunbeetch kuuramuuk	Opossum jumps from tree to tree	Part of Merri River
Kuul murtuup ...	Oval shape ...	Small crater outside of Mount Rouse
Kuulan		Spring of water in Mortlake
Kuulmittop ...		Crater in Mount Rouse
Kuulokaar ...	Sandy hole ...	Pond in town of Belfast
Kuulor	Lava	Name of Mount Rouse
Kuunong kaal ...	Midden of wild dogs	Dunmore Home Station
Kuurn kuurn muuthang	Little blackwood tree	Remy Hill, near Camperdown
Kuurn naa mullin ...	Little islands ...	Islands on west side of Lady Bay
Kuurnkolak ...	Small sand ...	Lake Colongulac
Kuurnuuk buurnuuk ...		Spring in horse paddock, Larra
Kuuro baruum ...	Grandmother of lice	Outlet of Tower Hill Lake
Kuutoit kill ...	Wild parsley ...	Koroit township
Læeek		Site of Wooriwyrite House
Lærott		Waterhole opposite Woolsthorpe
Lehuura... ...		Northern peak of Mount Leura
Lippuuk... ...	Nose ...	Laverock Bank, near Warrnambool
Lurtpii		Spring on Spring Creek, celebrated for spirits

Aboriginal Name.	Meaning.	Description.
Meenin'guurt	... ...	M'Arthur's Hill, near Camperdown
Meeri	Gang gang parrots	Tidal reach of the Merri River from the sea to the first ford
Minjaar... ...	... ...	Site of Minjah House
Mirch hill ...	... ...	Tower Hill Lake
Mirrmit kirram ...	Short shield	Site of Killarney Village
Mortom	Round	Spring in township of Penshurst, a few yards from the spot first occupied as a home station by the late Mr. John Cox. At this locality the aborigines were first supplied with clothing and food by a government protector
Mum killink ...	Short waterhole ...	Boodcarra Lake
Mumbit kank ...	Short hill ...	Flat-topped hill near the Salt Creek
Murreng yillak ...	Stony ...	Hill behind Cape Otway Lighthouse
Murrheeal ...	...	Scrub between Tower Hill Flat and the Lake
Muum a bareetch ...	Bottom of the water ...	Part of Spring Creek near Mount Rouse
Muum gnamatt ...		Bank on east side of Tower Hill Lake
Parrang kuutcha ...	Name of an edible root found there...	Tower Hill Island
Peetcha mirng ...	Close the eye ...	Waterhole in Spring Creek at Minjah Bridge
Pirtuup ...	Sandpiper ...	High ground in Warrnambool
Pitteen gill ...	Grass tree ...	Site of Dennington Village
Purng gnuum ...	Tadpole ...	Waterhole in Moyne River
Purtit puuloheear...	Hit fat ...	Locality of Farnham House
Puulorn buurn ...	Ferny hole ...	Waterhole in Moyne River, near Rosebrook, famous for fish
Puunong puunong	Ti-tree... ...	Waterhole in Hopkins River, near Framlingham Aboriginal Station
Puupuul ...	...	Spring which forms the commencement of Spring Creek
Puurkaar ...	...	Western Hill, Warrnambool
Puuroyuup ...	...	A gully near Wooriwyrite House, on Taylor's River, where a massacre of aborigines took place on the first occupation of the district
Puutch beem ...	High head ...	Mount Eels
Puuyuupkil ...	Mesembryanthemum, or pig's face	Land at Port Fairy, celebrated for 'pig's face'

Aboriginal Name.	Meaning.	Description.
Taap heear	...	Waterhole in Spring Creek above Minjah Bridge, which the aborigines say was formed by an earthquake
Taa puuk	...	Mount Napier
Taarak	...	Swamp near Larra House
Talla taerang	Cutting grass ...	
Tambuurn tambuurn geear	Twigs of boughs with leaves	
Tarpirr	Young of spotted bandicoot	Hill near Koortkoortnong
	Running water ...	Taylor's River, general name from its source to its junction with the Hopkins
Taeraa mukkar	Sweet root like a parsnip ...	West side of Tower Hill Flat
Terang	Twigs with leaves	Terang Township
Taerii neung	Covered with leaves	Waterhole in River Moyne, above Rosebrook Bridge
Tae rak	...	Lake Condah
Tikkarakil	Gravelly ground...	Valley from Yangery Village to the Merri River
Timbonn	Mussel shell	Timboon Township
Tirmbee whirk	...	Part of Spring Creek below Woolsthorpe
Tirr buunong	Edge of the ti-tree	Tributary of the Hopkins above Tuuram
Torn	...	Sand hummocks to the west of Warrnambool
Torretong	Backbone	First waterhole in Merri River above navigation
Tullin neung	Tongue	High ground below Dennington Bridge
Tung att	Teeth belonging to it	Scoriae about Mount Eels
Tung'ung buunart...	Eels bite the stones	Falls of the Hopkins. Eels collect there in such numbers that they are supposed to eat the stones below the falls
Tuulirn	Red earth	Kilnoorat Cemetery bank
Tuuliurruk	...	Lake three miles to the east of Larra House
Tuunda beean	...	Wannon River Falls
Tuunuunbee heear	Moving moving female	South peak of Mount Leura
Tuuwuul	Hill	The Sisters, two sandhills on the seacoast opposite Tower Hill
Tuuwuul	Hill or mountain	The Grampian Mountains
Tuuram	...	The tidal estuary of the River Hopkins
Waark	Plains ...	Great pastoral plains, having Mount Elephant as a centre
Waaronn	Spotted bandicoot	Hill on West Cloven Hills Estate
Wamkuunitt	Cheek of the laughing jackass	Hill one mile south of Bullen Merri

Aboriginal Name.	Meaning.	Description.
Warrnatts	...	Camperdown Township
Warrnatts	...	Spring in Camperdown Township
Warndaa	...	A boggy gully two or three miles west of Merrang House : the scene of a massacre of aborigines in 1842
Warra gnan	...	Waterhole near the mouth of the River Merri
Wilann	Black cockatoo	Hill at the mouth of Curdie's River
Wirkneung	...	Warrnambool Cemetery
Wirn wirn	Back tooth	Mount Taurus
Wirngill	Bear ...	Clump of ti-tree in the lagoon between Farnham and the seacoast
Wirpneung	Mouth of river	Mouth of River Hopkins
Wirrang	...	Locality of Wooriwyrite Bridge
Wirrang eering	Sheoak bank	Locality of Aringa House, near Belfast
Wirrang'guurt	Point	Point of land to the west of the mouth of the Merri River
Wirring ii	Noise ...	Site of Kilnoorat Church
Wirrwhork	Wrist ...	Waterhole above Wooriwyrite Bridge
Wirt parreetch	Back water	Spring of water on western shore of Lake Gnotuk
Wiyeetch	...	Rivulet near Yangery Village
Wuukuurn	Lazy frog	Darlington Township
Wuuriwuurit	Banksia tree	Locality of Kilnoorat Cemetery
Wuuriwuurit	Banksia tree	Glenormiston old home station
Wuurna weewheetch	Home of the swallow	Point of land on west side of Lake Bullen Merri. To this spot Queen Fanny, 'Bareetch Chuurneen,' was pursued by the white men, who murdered nearly all of her tribe at Puuroyuup, on the banks of Taylor's River, and pursued the remnants of them to Lake Bullen Merri. She had a child with her, and yet, burdened as she was, she swam with it on her back across the lake to a point called Karm Karm, below where Wuurong House now stands, and thus escaped
Wuurom birng yaar	Long waterhole ...	Waterhole in Merri River, at Woodford
Wuurun killing	Long water ...	Waterhole in Spring Creek, opposite Quamby
Wuurong killing	Lip of waterhole	A spring on Mount Fyans Station, where the bunyip lives

Aboriginal Name.		Meaning.	Description.
Wuurong yeering...	...		Waterhole in Spring Creek, at Woolsthorpe Bridge, where the aborigines first saw a bullock
Yaal ...	...	...	Scrub on west side of Tower Hill Flat
Yang kutt	...	Feather-tail flying squirrel...	Locality of Cooronga House
Yatt dinapp	...	Frog's mouth	Large lagoon to the east of Belfast
Yatt mirng	...	White eye	Crater in Tower Hill Island
Yatt mirng	...	White eye	Cave near Mount Rouse ; the birthplace of 'White Lady'
Yoluuk or Aethith	...		Large Island at Port Fairy
Yuumkuurtakk	...		Lagoon three miles west from Minjah House ; the scene of a massacre by white men of many aborigines, chiefly women and children, of the Morpor tribe.

GRAMMAR AND SENTENCES.

THE Native Grammar is very meagre, and will be best understood by an examination of the accompanying illustrative sentences in the 'Kuurn kopan noot' language. In the following illustrations the first line shows the original sentence, the second its translation into the aboriginal language, and the third a literal re-translation into English. It will be observed that, from the poverty of the language, the re-translation often fails to embody the full meaning of the original sentence. Hence, also, it is impossible to account for many discrepancies in the application of words in sentences. It is right, however, to say that, though much trouble was taken, it was found very difficult to make the aborigines understand what was wanted. It is on this account that so many illustrative sentences have been given. From these sentences the reader may form his own conclusions independently of the writer.

ARTICLES.

Sometimes the pronoun 'this,' 'deen,' is employed where in English 'the' would be used; and occasionally the numeral 'one,' 'kiiappa,' is used where in English the indefinite article is employed. But there are no articles, properly speaking.

NOUNS.

Gender is distinguished by 'heear,' 'feminine,' after the specific name, but this affix is only used where we would use the word female. The possessive case is represented by the affix 'gnat,' 'belonging to.' There is no distinction of numbers in nouns. When numbers are intended, the numeral adjectives are used, *e.g.*, spear one, spear two, spear three, &c.

SENTENCES ILLUSTRATIVE OF THE CASES OF NOUNS.

An opossum runs up the tree.

Kan	beewætnan	wuurotæ	kuuramuuk.
Going	up	tree	opossum.

My dog bit the leg of the opossum.

Buundan	pirn'guunong	kuuramuuka	kaal	gnan.
Bit	leg	opossum	dog	mine.

Give the opossum to the dog.

Wuukakæ	kaal	kuuramuuka.
Give	dog	opossum.

Take the opossum from the dog.

Kuuruin	kartakæ	kaal	kuuramuuka.
Take	from	dog	opossum.

The opossum sits on a branch of the tree.

Kannæ	gneengannæ	kuuramuuk	wuurkæ	nuung.
Up	sits	opossum	branch	on.

The opossum has a young one in its pouch.

Kuuramuuk	hnat	tuukuæyuung	paanætnuung.
Opossum	of	young one	pouch its.

The young opossum sits on its mother's back.

Kuurna	kuuramuuk	gnuurn gnuurn	gnætnong	kneerangatong.
Young	opossum	sitting on	back	mother of it.

The young opossum sits on the tree with its mother.

Kannæ	gnæng gannæ	kuurna	kuuramuuk	kneerangænong.
Up	sits	young	opossum	mother its.

The young opossum runs away along with its mother.

Karkuuran	kuurna	kuuramuuk	puulæ	wætnanda	kneeraneung.
Run	young	opossum	two	together	mother its.

Take the young from the opossum.

Mannakæ	kuurahneung	kuuramuuk	gnat.
Take	young one	opossum	belonging to.

ADJECTIVES.

There is no distinction of cases or genders in adjectives. There is no comparative degree, and the superlative is expressed variously. *See* ILLUSTRATIVE SENTENCES.

SENTENCES ILLUSTRATIVE OF THE USES OF ADJECTIVES.

My dog is better than yours.

Yang'æ yang'æ	gnuuteung	kaal	gnan	gnuutook gnat.
Good	good	dog	mine	yours.

This dog is the best.

Kiiappa	deen	gnuuteung	kaal.
One	this	good	dog.

Good, very good.

Gnuuteung	yangæ yangæ	gnuuteung.
Good	very	good.

High, very high.

Kannæ	kannæ	puuræ.
Up	up	far.

That is a very high tree.

Wuurambæt	kannak	deen	wurrot.
Long	stick	this	tree.

Very old.

Wuulæ wuulæ	kuurn.
Very	old.

That is an old man.

Nuunambæ	gnarram gnarram.
That	old man.

That is a very old man.

Nuunambæ	gnallam.
That	old man.

An old opossum rug.

Puurnoitch.
Rotten rug.

PRONOUNS.

I ...	...	...	Gnatook.
My	...	...	Gnan (affixed to noun).
Mine	...	...	Gnatonghatt.
Me	...	...	Gnan (affixed to verb).
We	...	...	Gnatook.
Our	...	...	Gniiyæ (affixed to noun).
Ours	...	...	Gnatook gnat.
Us	...	...	Gniiyæyuung.
You (those)		...	Gnutook, or gnin.
Yours (thine)		...	Gnutook gnat, or gnu (affixed to noun).
You—plural		...	Gnutook gnuutæn.

Yours—plural	...	Gnuutæn.
He—this one	...	Didnæ, or deelaræ.
Him—this one	...	Didnan.
His—belonging to him		Gneung gnatbee, or gneung (affixed to noun).
They—these	...	Didnanæ.
Them—these	...	Didnanæ.
Theirs ...	...	Gnu gnallan gnatbee.
This ...	...	Dææn.
That ...	...	Nuubee.
That one near you	...	Noolambee.
That over there	...	Didnæ.
They ...	...	Dælakanaree.
These here ...	...	Dee'gnalla gnannæ.
Those ...	...	Noolakanambee.

SENTENCES ILLUSTRATIVE OF PRONOUNS.

They two stole my shield.

| Puuliitcha | kattang | mananda | malkar | gnan. |
| Two | of them | took they | shield | mine. |

They all are bad.

| Gnummæ | gulleen | deen. |
| Not | good | this. |

Their children are bad.

| Gnummæ kuutnan | deednan | tukuæ tukuæ. |
| Not good | these | children. |

I will not speak to them.

| Pang'iitch | deen | kueewakk. |
| Will not | to them | speak. |

That man will kill them.

| Purtiicheen | nuulambee. |
| Will kill | that one. |

This man will take their spears from them.

| Kuuroænæchin | tiiyæra. |
| Will be taken | spears. |

Is this spear his own?

| Gnarnatta | deen | tiiyærong. |
| Who owns | this | spear? |

Are these spears their own ?

    Kiiyong geetch   tiiyæra   gnu gnallan gnatbee.
    Many   spears   their own.

She is a good mother.

    Gnuuteung   kneerang   neung.
    Good   mother   it.

Her son loves her.

    Muutæ   wanuung   kneerang   neung.
    Loves   he   mother   his.

This is her son.

    Deen   kuupri   neung.
    This   son   hers.

Is this her own son?

    Nuubee   tukuæ   gnu.
    This   son   yours?

That woman killed her own son.

    Partanuung   tukuæyuung   teelang   tunnumbuura.
    Killed   her son   this   woman.

I kill an opossum.

    Burtanno   kuuramuuk.
    Kill I   opossum.

My waddy killed the opossum.

    Waarwharang   gnan   burtanong   kuuramuuk.
    Waddy   mine   kill   opossum.

The opossum bit me.

    Buundang   gnan   kuuramuuka.
    Bit   me   opossum.

We two—you and I—will go away.

    Yannang'all.
    Go will we.

We two—he and I—will go away.

    Yannang'along.
    Go will we.

We will all go away.

    Wakuumba   wan.
    Go   all of us.

It is gone away.
> Wakuutanong.
> It is gone.

They will look for us.
> Weetka   kuurtnayæ.
> Look   for us.

They will not find us.
> Bang   ayæ   tambuurtakoot.
> Not   us   find.

They will find our dwelling.
> Tambuuratakoort   wuurn   gnatnæn.
> They find   dwelling   ours.

This shield is my own.
> Deen   mallhnan   gnatonghatt.
> This   shield   mine.

This dwelling-place is our own.
> Deen   wuurn   gniiyæ.
> This   dwelling   our own.

You are good.
> Gnuuteung   gnin.
> Good   you.

Thy name is Louisa.
> Nobee   gnuuk   leegno   Louisa.
> There it is   name   Louisa.

He will kill thee.
> Parta   hno.
> Kill   you.

You two are going away to-day.
> Puularneeapuula   gninduuk   puulang   teenbee.
> Two of us   you   go away   to-day.

You all go away.
> Nu   deen   wakuumbaawhaar.
> You   these   all go.

They were looking for you.
> Wueetchkan   hnuun   gnuutka.
> Looking   they   for you.

They will find you.

> Tumbuurtan   kuunhnuutin.
> Find you   they you.

They will burn down your dwelling.

> Pappakuut   wuurn   gnuutææn.
> Burn   wuurn   yours.

Some blackfellows will burn your dwelling.

> Marra   papakuut   wuurn   gno.
> Blackfellows some   burn will   wuurn   yours.

Is this waddy thine own ?

> Nuutook hnat   deen   warwhaar.
> Yours   this   waddy.

This dwelling is mine.

> Deen   wuurn   gnan.
> This   dwelling   mine.

This is his dog.

> Deen   kaal   ong.
> This   dog   his.

The dog bit him.

> Puundan deen   kaal a.
> Bit   dog

Give the spear to him.

> Wuukakee   tiiyeera.
> Give   spear

Take the shield from him.

> Karoin   kartakæ   malka.
> Take   from him   shield.

VERBS.

There are three Moods, Indicative, Imperative, and Potential; and two Participles, the Present and the Past. The Passive Voice is formed by the Past Participle with the Pronoun. The Indicative Mood has two Tenses, Past and Future. The Present Tense is the same as the Past. The only difference between an interrogative and an assertive sentence is in the inflexion of the voice.

ILLUSTRATIVE VERB 'TO GO,' ' YAN.'

To go, yan.
Going, yannak.
Gone, yannan.

Indicative Mood.

I am going to Terang to-morrow.

Yannako	mullæbaa	Terang o.
Go will I	to-morrow	Terang to.

Thou art going.

Yannak	gnin.
Going	you.

He is going.

Yannak	ditnanæ.
Going	this.

We two are going.

Puularneea	gnatook	hnaayæ	yannak.
Two	we	us	going.

You two are going.

Puularneeapuul	yannak.
You two	going.

We all are going.

Paaruung kuurneawan	yannak.
All of us	going.

You all are going.

Wakuumbawar	nuunanbewar	yannak.
Away	them	going.

They two are going.

Deen	gnulla'gnin puularneakk	yannak.
These	two of us	going.

They all are going.

Wakuumbakot	yannak.
All	going.

I went away yesterday.

Gnaakat	gniitch	yinnan.
Yesterday	self	gone.

Thou didst go to Geelong.

> Nuu   gnuurabee   gnok   Geelong   nguura.
> You   about   there   Geelong   at.

He went to Geelong.

> Puura   Geelong   kutta.
> Away   Geelong   at.

She went to Geelong.

> Puura   Geelong   kutta.
> Away   Geelong   at.

We two went away.

> Puularneea   yunna   gnuluung.
> We two   went   away.

We all went away.

> Wakuumbaawanuung.
> All gone.

You two went away.

> Gninduuk   puulang   yunna puulang.
> You   two   went away.

You all went away.

> Nuunumbeewarr   wakuumban.

They two went away.

> Poreena.

They all went away.

> Wakuurneeanuut.

I shall go away to-morrow.

> Mullæbaa   mirtakk.
> To-morrow   I go.

Thou wilt go away.

> Yanna'gnin   gnuutuuk.
> Go will   you.

He will go away.

> Yanna'gnin   gnuutuuk.
> Go will   he.

We two will go away.

> Gnatook   hniyæ yuung   yanna   gnulluun.
> We   both   go   away.

We all will go away.
> Waakoobawhaan   yannak.
> All   go.

It is all gone.
> Wakuumbanoot.
> It all gone.

You two will go away.
> Puularneearpuul   yannak.
> You two   go.

You all will go away.
> Wakuurneea katto.
> Will depart.

They two will go away.
> Puularneeapuul   yannak.
> They two   go.

They all will go away
> Wakuurneeawan.
> They will go.

You tell me that you go away to-morrow.
> Kuetka mahneenann   mullæbaa   yannahninuung.
> Tell me   to-morrow   you go.

Tell me if you are going to-morrow.
> Kuetka maakin nubee'gna   yanna gnin   mullæbaa
> Tell me there   you going   to-morrow.

I may go next week.
> Yanna kueeya   gnaakii   mullænuung.
> Go will I   I think   day or two.

ILLUSTRATIVE VERB 'TO KILL,' 'BURTEEN.'

Indicative Mood.

I killed the dog.
> Burtano   kaal.
> Killed   dog.

You killed the dog.
> Gnuutooka   burtang'in   kaal.
> You   killed   dog.

He killed the dog.

    Burtanong'ook   kaal.
    Killed he   dog.

We killed the dog.

    Burtang'along   kaal.
    Killed we   dog.

You killed the dog.

    Burtakakæ   gnuutooka   kaal.
    Killed   you   dog.

They killed the dog.

    Burtanoot   dæælakanaræ   kaal.
    Killed   the   dog.

I will kill the dog.

    Burtako   noobæ   kaal.
    Kill I   that   dog.

You will kill the dog.

    Gnootoka   burtakæ   kaal.
    You   kill   dog.

He will kill the dog.

    Deelaræ   gnoom   burta   kaal.
    He   kill   dog.

We will kill the dog.

    Gnatoong   haayæ   burtang'al   kaal.
    We   will   kill   dog.

You will kill the dog.

    Gnuutooka   gnuutæn   burtakato   kaal.
    You   will   kill   dog.

They will kill the dog.

    Noolakanabæ   burtapuul   kaal.
    They themselves kill   dog.

Imperative Mood.

Kill the dog.

    Burtakæ   gnuutooka   kaal.
    Kill   you   dog.

Participles.

Killing the dog.

Burtano	kaal.
Kill	dog.

The dog is killed.

Burtatanoot	kaal.
Killed	dog.

Potential Mood.

I might kill the dog.

Burtakuuyang	an	kaal.
Kill	might	dog.

You might kill the dog.

Gnuutoka	burtaka	kaal.
You	kill	dog.

He might kill the dog.

Burtakang	ong'aan	deelaræ	kaal.
Kill	might	he	dog.

We might kill the dog.

Burtakueaa	watna	kaal.
Kill	might	dog.

You might kill the dog.

Gnuutoka	burtaka	kaal.
You	kill	dog.

They might kill the dog.

Burtakuuta	watna	didnanæ	kaal.
Kill	might	this	dog.

NUMERALS.

I.—CARDINAL NUMBERS.

THE aborigines represent cardinal numbers from one to one hundred by a combination of words and signs.

In the Chaap wuurong language the names for units are :—

One ...	...	Kæp yang gnuurak.
Two ...	...	Puuliit whummin.
Three ...	...	Kartorr.
Four ...	...	Puuliit baa puuliit—two and two.
Five ...	...	Kæp mun'ya—one hand (outspread).
Six ...	...	Kæp tulliyær mun'ya—one finger, hand.
Seven ...	...	Kæp mun'ya baa puuliit—one hand and two.
Eight ...	...	Kæp mun'ya baa kartor—one hand and three.
Nine ...	...	Kæp mun'ya puuliit baa puuliit—one hand, two and two.
Ten ...	...	Puuliit mun'ya—two hands (outspread).

Between ten, twenty, thirty, and on to one hundred, units are not named, but are indicated by holding out the fingers and thumbs.

Eleven commences the combination of words and signs, and as there is no name for it, or any number up to and inclusive of nineteen, the word for ten is named and one finger is held out; for twelve, the same word and two fingers; for thirteen, the same word and three fingers; and so on by words and signs to one hundred.

Twenty is called kæp mam—one twenty.

Thirty ...	...	Kæp mam, ba puuliit mun'ya—twenty and two hands.
Forty ...	...	Puuliit mam—two twenties.
Fifty ...	...	Puuliit mam, baa puuliit mun'ya—two twenties and two hands.
Sixty ...	...	Kartorr mam—three twenties.
Seventy ...	...	Kartorr mam, baa puuliit mun'ya—three twenties and two hands.

Eighty	...	Puuliit mam, baa puuliit mam—two twenties and two twenties.
Ninety...	...	Puuliit mam, baa puuliit mam, baa puuliit munya—two twenties, two twenties, and two hands.
One hundred*...		Larbargirrar, which concludes expressed numbers; anything beyond one hundred is larbargirrar larbargirrar, signifying a crowd beyond counting, and is always accompanied by repeated opening and shutting the hands.

In the Kuurn kopan noot language the cardinal numbers are :—

One	...	...	Kiiappa.
Two	...	...	Puuliitcha.
Three	...	...	Baaleen meea.
Four	...	...	Puuliitcha baa puuliitcha—two and two.
Five	...	...	Kiiapp marrang—one hand (outspread).
Six	...	...	Kiiapp marrang baa kiiappa—one hand and one.
Seven	...	...	Puuliit tulliyerr marrang—two fingers, hand.
Eight	...	...	Kiiapp marrang baa baalen meea—one hand and three.
Nine	...	...	Kiiapp marrang puuliitcha baa puuliitcha—one hand, two and two.
Ten	...	...	Puuliit marrang—two hands (outspread).
Twenty	...	Kiiapp peep.
Thirty...	...	Kiiapp peep baa puuliit marrang—twenty, and two hands.
Forty...	...	Puuliit peep—two twenties.
Fifty...	...	Puuliit peep baa puuliit marrang—two twenties and two hands.
Sixty...	...	Baaleen meea peep—three twenties.

* I need scarcely point out that this is wholly at variance with the statement made by Mr. E. B. Tyler in his 'Primitive Culture,' that 'Among the lowest living men—the savages of the South American forests and the deserts of Australia—five is actually found to be a number which the languages of some tribes do not know by a special word. Not only have travellers failed to get from them names for numbers above two, three, or four, but the opinion that these are the real limits of their numeral series is strengthened by their use of their highest known number as an indefinite term for a great many.'—Vol. i., p. 220.

Seventy   ...   Baaleen meea peep baa puuliit marrang—three twenties and two hands.

Eighty...   ...   Puuliit peep baa puuliit peep—two twenties and two twenties.

Ninety...   ...   Puuliit peep baa puuliit peep baa puuliit marrang—two twenties and two twenties and two hands.

Intermediate units between the tens are not named, but are indicated as in the Chaap wuurong language.

One hundred ... Barbaanuung.

Any farther number is wuurt baa dærang wuurt baa dærang, which means a great many beyond count, and is accompanied by holding out the hands, repeatedly closing and opening the fingers, and saying, ' Kæ, kæ, kæ.'

II.—ORDINAL NUMBERS.

Ordinal numbers are used by the aborigines only in numbering the days of a month in making appointments ; and, as their months are marked by the re-appearance of the moon, their ordinal numbers do not go beyond twenty-eight. They are indicated both by signs and words. The signs are made by touching with the index finger certain parts of the hand, arm, neck, ear, and head ; commencing with the space between the thumb and first finger of the left hand, going up the arm, over the head, down the right arm to the right hand, and then to the thumb and fingers of both hands. 'First,' is represented by touching the space on the back of the left hand between the thumb and fore-finger ; 'second,' the left wrist ; 'third,' between the left wrist and the elbow ; 'fourth,' the elbow ; 'fifth,' space between the left elbow and the shoulder ; 'sixth,' the left shoulder ; 'seventh,' the left side of the neck ; 'eighth,' the left ear ; 'ninth,' the left side of the head above the ear ; 'tenth,' the right side of the head above the ear ; 'eleventh,' the right ear ; and so on to eighteenth, the space between the right thumb and forefinger ; then, 'nineteenth,' the little finger of the left hand ; and so on to 'twenty-eight,' the little finger of the right hand. The names of these numbers are the same with those of the different parts which are used as signs. Thus, in the Chaap wuurong language, 'first,' is paapee munnya, 'father of hand ;' 'second,' tartkuurt, 'wrist ;' 'third,' peepuulæ gnarram, 'fat of arm ;' 'fourth,' kukukutt chukk, 'elbow ;' 'fifth,' kallgneeang gnuurakk; 'sixth,' karrup karrup palk; 'seventh,' chaarkum; 'eighth,' wart-whirngbuul; 'ninth,' towillup; 'tenth,' titit. The remaining numbers down to the eighteenth are the same as those representing the opposite side. 'Twenty-eighth' is kiiapp warteep tannyuuk, 'one moon.'

In the Kuurn kopan noot language the numbers are—'first,' gnærang marrang; 'second,' kaanang kuurt; 'third,' muurtmeetch; 'fourth,' puulkuyeetch; 'fifth,' millæwuurk; 'sixth,' warratpeenyakk; 'seventh,' tarkuurn; 'eighth,' waawing; 'ninth,' mirngmirnitt; 'twenty-eighth,' kiiappa kuurn-taruung, 'one moon.'

In making appointments, the day is indicated by both name and sign, by touching the part and mentioning the word which represents both the part and the number. When an appointment is made through a messenger, the number is sometimes distinguished by affixing some mark to the part representing it on his body, in order to obviate any mistake on the part of a stupid or forgetful messenger.

NOTES.

(Translation by Professor Strong.)

———◆———

A.—NOTE TO CHAPTER XI.

Quum violata est pudicitia, si in mulierem sit vis illata, penes maritum est jus mortem in violatorem inferendi. Sin autem violata sit innupta, testimonio ejus a primoribus tribuum, quibus intersit ipsa cognito, si quidem pro probato teneantur quæ objecta sint, violator ille prope ad mortem a necessariis mulieris fustigatur atque ducere ilam cogitur. Quod si violatorem vel amici vel necessarii ejus defendere conantur in eos pari modo animadvertitur. Inde non raro pugna universa oritur cujus neque feminæ expertes sunt.

Femina quæ levitate quadam morum famosam se praebet, vocatur 'Karkor neegh heear' atque a necessariis ejus culpatur et poenâ afficitur. Post hoc nisi se melius gerit inter se consilium habent necessarii ejus, atque si probata sit culpa, avunculus ejus, vel quidam e consanguineis (excepto patre vel fratre), arreptâ occasione ex improviso plagam illi in posteram colli partem sublato ramo infert. Tum corpus uritur, sparguntur cineres neque cuiquam illam lugere licet.

B.—NOTE TO CHAPTER XI.

In quibusdam tropicæ Australiæ partibus circumciduntur pueri qui in pubertatem initiantur: hic autem mos indigenis in hoc libro descriptis ignotus est.

C.—NOTE TO CHAPTER XII.

Quæ nupta est per menstruandi tempus, sola per se e parte adversa foci domesticid dormire cogitur, neque vel cibum vel potum aliuscujusque capere permittitur. Neque quisquam est qui vel cibum vel potum ab illâ tactum consumere velit, ut qui illos invalidos reddat. Innupta autem vel vidua quæ idem patiatur in eandam legem quoad cibum et potum cogitur; eadem caput pingere atque corpus usque ad medium rubro limo cogitur; neque junioribus innuptis domum menstruantis inire licet. Eadem si cui in semitâ occurat, exire debet. Ambulare quidem atque interesse amicorum colloquiis licet neque moleste turbari, neque tamen saltare aut cymbalum agitare in corroboreis licet. Itaque natura ipsa videtur easdem leges indigenis nostris docuisse quæ Moses ille divino spiritu afflatus tulit ad sanitatem Israelitarum conservandam.

D.—NOTE TO CHAPTER XII.

MULIER quæ se parturire sentiat dormire cogitur adversa e parte ignis domestici a marito separata, neque illi licet tangere ut edere anguillas kangarosve vel aves. Cibus ejus ea oposso constare debet, animalibus minoribus atque radicibus. Post natum infantem liberata est ab hisce legibus. Sed tamen lex illa de cibo non semper observatur. Atque maritus sæpe numero inducitur ad satisfaciendam uxoris appetentiam certi cibi, imprimis anguillarum quæ in deliciarum numero habentur. Laqueos ad anguillas carpiendas a vicinis paratos violare hanc in rem creditur bonam sortem auferre. Si igitur quis suspicionem habeat quod laqueus suus anguillis destitutus sit culpam facti ejusin nuptum virum injicit cujus mulier in ea conditione sit ut suspicionem illam confirmet. Atque non aliam ob causam sæpe numero ultio fit.

E.—NOTE TO CHAPTER XIII.

QUUM mulier in ipso partu sit, in humo resupina sedet inter nutricis brachia, tanquam in sellâ quâdem motoriâ esset. Si secundæ tardius se a corpore separaverint, tum corpori in pronum flexo lapides calidi adponuntur, quorum calor plerumque separationem efficere solet. Secundas semper sepelire mos est. Funis umbilicarius nervo halmaturi (kangaroo) ligatur, atque conchâ muricis exacuti secatur. Deinde vulnus unguento quodam ungitur, facto e carbone pulverato, cum adipe commixto, in quod deinde limus adustus, in tenuem pulverem contritus, conspergitur. Funis in tenues partes secatur, pars quæque in fragmento parvo pellis didelphidis contegitur. Hæ suspenduntur per collum illius a quo infans nomen accepturus est atque per colla fratrum infantis si puer sit; sin autem puella in sororum colla. Post paullum temporis aut incenduntur aut sepeliuntur.

F. — NOTE TO CHAPTER XIV.

THE CIRCULATION OF THE BLOOD.

THERE is no doubt that the aborigines had a knowledge of the circulation of the blood from the heart through the arteries, and of its return by the veins. To these blood-vessels they give distinctive names. An artery is called 'gnullman;' a vein is called 'karkuuran kuureek,' 'running blood.' Very careful inquiries have been made into this subject from the most intelligent of the aborigines; and it is evident that they recognize the connection between the heart and the pulse, and the fact that, while the arteries carry the blood from the heart, the veins return it to the heart again. On its being hinted to them that they may have got this information from the white man, they said that they knew all about it long before the white man came. It need scarcely be said that they have no idea of the circulation of the blood through the lungs, or of the functions of the different parts of the heart, as brought to light by the researches of Servetus, Le Vasseur, and William Harvey.

G.—NOTE.

REPORTS OF GOVERNMENT INSPECTORS OF ABORIGINAL SCHOOLS.

As a fitting conclusion to this work, and in corroboration of the very high estimate which the author has formed of the intelligence of the aborigines, he has the greatest pleasure in giving the following summary of a number of reports of the Government inspectors of the Victorian State schools, and of remarks which have been kindly written by them for his use.

At each of the aboriginal stations there is a State-school, which is periodically examined, along with other schools, and on the same footing with them, by the Government inspectors of schools. The experience of these gentlemen is that, up to a certain age, the aboriginal children are quite equal to those of European parentage in their capacity for learning the ordinary branches of an English education. Indeed, the former excel the latter in those studies which depend on memory and power of imitation; but, on the other hand, those branches of knowledge which require abstraction, and in which a greater demand is made on the reasoning faculties, are learned by them with difficulty. In reading, writing, spelling, singing, and geography, they distance white children in rapidity of attainment, their penmanship especially being of unusual neatness and excellence, and the accuracy with which verses are repeated being very remarkable ; but grammar and the higher branches of arithmetic are very puzzling to them. In respect of discipline their conduct is excellent ; good order and steady application to books is secured with ease, and for class or military drill they show great liking and aptitude.

The inspection of the aboriginal school at Ramahyuck, in Gippsland, during the last eleven years, gives a percentage of results higher than the other State schools in Victoria ; and while, no doubt, this excellence is largely due to the regularity with which the children attended school, and to the skill and zeal of the gentlemen who taught them, it fairly shows that aboriginal children are at least equal to others in power of learning those branches of education which are taught in the State schools of Victoria.

The reader will be interested to learn, that, on several occasions of examination by a Government inspector, the percentage of the Ramahyuck school was a hundred—*a result unparalleled by any other school in the colony.*

THE END.

Walker, May, & Co., Printers, 9 Mackillop-street, Melbourne.